RICHARD CROSSMAN
AND THE
WELFARE STATE

Stephen Thornton is Lecturer in Comparative Politics in the School of European Studies at Cardiff University. He has written widely about the British Labour Party and social security policy, including work published in *Contemporary British History and Public Policy and Administration*.

RICHARD CROSSMAN AND THE WELFARE STATE

PIONEER OF WELFARE PROVISION AND LABOUR POLITICS IN POST-WAR BRITAIN

STEPHEN THORNTON

Tauris Academic Studies
LONDON • NEW YORK

Published in 2009 by
Tauris Academic Studies,
an imprint of I.B.Tauris & Co Ltd
6 Salem Road, London W2 4BU
175 Fifth Avenue, New York NY 10010
www.ibtauris.com

In the United States of America and in Canada distributed by
St. Martins Press, 175 Fifth Avenue, New York, NY 10010

International Library of Political Studies 27

ISBN: 978 1 84511 848 8

A full CIP record for this book is available from the British Library

A full CIP record for this book is available from the Library of Congress

Printed and bound in India by Replika Press Pvt. Ltd.
copy edited and supplied by Swales & Willis Ltd, Exeter, Devon

This book is dedicated to Ruth, Sam and to my grandparents: Nancy and Conrad Thornton, Lillian and Bob Lydiate. Thank you.

CONTENTS

Acknowledgements

Peter Dorey, Andrew Connell, Neil Wood, Mark Donovan, Barry Jones, Hugh Compston, David Broughton, Rosanne Palmer, Steve Marsh, Alistair Cole, Karen Owen, Peter Sutch, Peri Roberts, Joanne Sayner, Adam Sharr, Mark Lang, Sara Knight, Sean Knight, Jenny Thomas, Mike Thomas, Heather Moyes, Carwyn Fowler, Kathryn Jones, Janet Morrison, Pam Morrison, Rodney Lowe, Paul Bridgen, Helen Fawcett, Peter Townsend, Glen O'Hara, Helen Parr, Hugh Pemberton, the late Baroness Castle, Rasna Dillon, Elizabeth Munns, Lester Crook, Fiona Wade, Richard Willis, the custodians of the various archives consulted, the soothing sounds of Kate Rusby, George Winston, and Sigur Rós, Susan North and the rest of my family, particularly Michael Thornton for the rescue mission, and Ruth Thornton for most everything.

All the above provided help along the way, consciously or otherwise, in the production of this book. A number of those above have some connection with the School of European Studies at Cardiff University, which is a fine place of which to be a part. Pete Dorey deserves a second mention as he was there at the start, middle, and end of this project, providing friendly advice when necessary (often). The mistakes are, of course, mine, but they will be made available on eBay presently.

Stephen Thornton
Cardiff

INTRODUCTION

15 December 2007 marked the centenary of one Richard Howard Stafford Crossman: Cabinet Minister; parliamentarian; academic; journalist; diarist; socialist (of a sort); iconoclast. Few noticed. Indeed, though his name does still make the odd appearance in recent work,[1] Richard Crossman seems to be fading into the footnotes of Labour Party history. As Kevin Hickson notes, with surprise, Crossman did not make it into a recent major collection of biographical essays of leading figures in the history of the Labour Party,[2] despite 'his contribution to the party in opposition, and as a minister, diarist and academic commentator'.[3] This is unfortunate. As Crossman's biographer, Anthony Howard, suggests, though never gaining one of the great offices of state, Crossman was one 'of those meteors that occasionally lighten the British political firmament',[4] and the primary goal of this book is to attempt to halt this gathering amnesia, and return some of the spotlight back on one of the more dazzling figures of the twentieth-century British labour movement.

When remembered at all these days, Crossman tends to be regarded more as a political voyeur rather than as a major political actor. Certainly his groundbreaking *Diaries* – three from his time as a minister[5] and one covering his long period as a backbencher[6]– did much to prise open some of the secrecy that traditionally surrounds the workings of the British political system, and, for all their faults, it is indeed, in Howard's words, 'these bulky volumes that contain his monument'.[7] However, there was more to Crossman than this. In this book an attempt will be made to shed light on a different aspect of Crossman's political career: his largely forgotten role in the development of post-war British social policy.

There is one obvious reason why Crossman has not traditionally been granted a position as a leading protagonist in the tale of the welfare state. Despite all his Cabinet posts including an element of social policy – not least his final position as Secretary of State for Social Services – he failed to leave 'any lasting legislative memorial behind him'.[8] Of particular regret to Crossman himself was the failure, during his period at the Department of Health and Social Security (DHSS), to implement Labour's National Superannuation Plan, a scheme with which he was closely associated for over fifteen years. However, despite the failure of this particular scheme to reach the Statute Book – it was dislodged from the procedural conveyer-belt through Parliament by Harold Wilson's unwise election call in 1970 – the automatic conclusion should not be that Crossman made little impression on the development of social policy in the UK. As will be explored, the policy process works in subtle and strange ways, and profound changes can occur without traditional legislative outputs.

In essence, this book will be an elaboration of the Eleanor Rathbone Memorial Lecture – entitled 'The Politics of Pensions' – that Crossman delivered in May 1971 at the University of Sheffield, during the sadly brief period between the ending of his ministerial career and his death in April 1974. In this lecture about the rise and fall of the National Superannuation Plan, Crossman introduced his topic by saying:

> I thought that the thing I could most usefully do . . . was to retell the story with which I am most closely associated. It describes the attempt of a handful of people . . . to launch what I still think is a revolutionary idea which one day must be achieved. I will try to show you how the idea was launched, how it was brought into party politics in opposition, how it became part of an election campaign, how a government came in which was due to implement it, and how it failed to implement it.[9]

This, to a great extent, is also the plan of this book, to explain the conception of an idea, this idea's rapid rise up the political agenda, and its eventual demise, noting all the while the impact of this idea on the wider world of welfare politics. Crossman recognised that though 'this curious little tale . . . ends with a whimper, rather than a bang', the story of 'how an idea is realised in action is the essential study to make politics intelligible'.[10] Moreover, he regarded it as 'a story rich in lessons'.[11] The claim that this episode vividly illustrates the unpredictability of politics, and, in particular, the social policy process, over thirty years after Crossman delivered his lecture, still holds true. Indeed, increased access to archive material, and developments in the study of public policy, potentially allow even more lessons to be learned. Moreover, besides any lessons learned, the story of Crossman's crusade to change the social security system is, in its own terms, a gripping historical narrative involving naked political rivalry, combative interest groups, a tragic suicide, and actuaries.

Ultimately, the primary purpose of this book is to provide a link between the past and present. Regarding the teaching of social policy, Martin Powell and John Stewart have noted that:

> In the past many of the leading figures in social policy writing had interests in history – for example Richard Tawney, T.H. Marshall, and Richard Titmuss. However, social policy has lost its 'historical imagination', with many students – Thatcher's children, and in a few years Major's children – not being exposed to social policy history, and with many publishers believing that anything before 1997 or even 2001 belongs to 'history' rather than social policy.[12]

This book is an attempt to restore a small amount of this 'historical imagination'. And this lack of appreciation of the past extends to politicians. As Glen O'Hara and Helen Parr have argued, there is an attitude amongst certain New Labour types 'that sees 1997 as "year zero"'.[13] They cite, as 'exhibit A', a speech by former New Labour Prime Minister, Tony Blair, in which he referred to the 1960s as a 'sad episode' when Labour ministers 'were not ready . . . to see change was coming, accept it and then shape it to progressive ends'.[14] This gives the impression that innovation was foreign to what might be dubbed Old Labour. This is unfair. Indeed, as will be illustrated, it was not during the 1990s and 2000s that Labour politicians began to explore concepts such as developing public–private partnership, utilising the

Inland Revenue to deliver benefits, and planning a national savings scheme for pensions. Rather, it was during the 1950s and 1960s.

GUIDE TO THE BOOK

Apart from Chapter 1, the structure of this book will be largely chronological, and will loosely follow the political career of Richard Crossman. Chapter 1 will introduce some biographical details about the colourful individual around which this book revolves. It will continue by supporting the argument that an individual can make an impression on the policy process, but will stress the importance of not exaggerating the impact that can be achieved by any one factor. To this end, Anthony Seldon's model for explaining change – one that highlights the interplay between a number of factors – will be introduced.[15]

Chapter 2 will begin the substantive story. It will examine the earliest days of Crossman's interest in social policy when he was merely a backbench Opposition MP with a sideline in journalism. It will demonstrate that, from as early as 1954, Crossman was calling for the end of the existing system of Beveridge Report-inspired universal, flat-rate welfare provision. This so-called Beveridge system itself will be examined, as will some of the earliest critical responses – from left and right – to this generally popular, if flawed, welfare regime.

The story of Crossman's involvement in the planning of social reform will continue into Chapter 3, which will explain how Crossman was given the task of leading a committee to restructure the Labour Party's approach to welfare, and how, with particular guidance of some academics from the London School of Economics, this group constructed the Labour Party's policy document *National Superannuation: Labour's Policy for Security in Old Age*. This text, which was published in 1957, was the first mainstream pronouncement from a major British political party to advocate the introduction of an earnings-related pension scheme – famously offering 'half pay' on retirement[16] – and, as such, it proved to be one of the most significant documents in the post-war development of British social security policy. However, as will be demonstrated, the creation of *National Superannuation* was the result of tension and compromise, as not all sections of the Labour Party were keen on the approach Crossman was advocating. In addition, this chapter will discuss the Conservative government's response to Labour's scheme.

Chapter 4 will focus on the period between 1959 and 1964, the Labour Party's final period in Opposition before the Labour government of Harold Wilson was elected. One issue to be highlighted will be a partial re-prioritising of the Labour Party's social policy goals during this period, with some in the Party's main social security policy community calling for a more targeted approach. As will be explained, this development was prompted by, amongst other things, perceived weaknesses in the original superannuation scheme, and also by, what was called at the time, the 're-discovery of poverty'. As will be explained, it was also a period where Crossman found himself competing against a major political rival for control of the Labour Party's social security policy process.

In Chapter 5 it will be explained that, for a few years, Crossman was reduced to the role of unhappy spectator, as Wilson − Labour Prime Minister, 1964–70 and 1974–6 − initially decided to give the social security portfolio to other colleagues. These first difficult few years of the Wilson administrations will be assessed, and, of particular contemporary interest, the fate of the 'income guarantee', a forerunner to Gordon Brown's attempts to rope the tax system into providing welfare benefits, will be examined. One aspect to be highlighted will be the astonishingly incoherent organisational structure which Wilson initially forced upon the departments desperately trying to administer social policy.

Chapter 6 will focus on the period when Crossman began to re-assert his presence in the social security policy process, including his period as Secretary of State for Social Services between 1968 and 1970. At this point it will be necessary to investigate 'the most puzzling aspect of his tenure at the DHSS',[17] the hesitancy to implement, and resultant failure of, the national superannuation scheme. Examination will also be made into the late changes made to the scheme, one of which prefigured New Labour's attraction to the concept of public-private partnership. The role played by the private pension industry in forcing changes to Crossman's scheme will be studied in detail, as will the part played by a series of inter-departmental committees of officials set up the review the Labour Party's plans for welfare reform. The book will conclude by assessing Crossman's role in the development of welfare policy in post-war

Britain. It will be argued that Crossman should be remembered as an important figure, not so much for what he achieved as a minister, but more because of his role as advocate for certain ideas – ideas that accelerated a process which, eventually, transformed the British system of welfare.

1

IDEAS,
INDIVIDUALS,
CIRCUMSTANCES
AND INTERESTS

INTRODUCTION

The purpose of this chapter is to provide background information. To gain some early insight into the unusual character of this book's eponymous hero, the first section will examine, in brief, the life of Richard Crossman. The final sections will put forward the case that accounts such as this one, which emphasise the importance of individuals and the ideas they advocate, are valuable. However, it will also be suggested that as, amongst others, Anthony Seldon has argued, it is vital to put these individuals and ideas into context.[1]

CROSSMAN: A SKETCH

One of Crossman's friends from his days at Oxford, the poet W.H. Auden, once mused that, 'A shilling life will give you all the facts'.[2] It seems only fitting, then, to continue this chapter by providing some brief biographical details: they will not provide all the facts, but they will give clues to Crossman's complicated personality. This is only intended as a 'sketch' of Crossman. Those interested in discovering a more detailed picture of the life and times of one of the most quixotic figures in the labour movement should consult, and enjoy, Anthony Howard's vivid *Crossman: The Pursuit of Power*[3] – from which much of the following section is taken. Some further insights can be gained through perusal of the entertaining, if not always reliable, *Dick*

Crossman: A Portrait by Crossman's former parliamentary private secretary – and lodger – Tam Dalyell.[4] Though Crossman himself is dead by the second page of the first chapter, the late Hugo Young's *The Crossman Affair* is worth reading as a gripping account of the struggle to publish the infamous *Diaries*.[5] The *Diaries* themselves provide the most direct and intimate form of communication between Crossman and the reader and, notwithstanding their numerous flaws,[6] remain fascinating and illuminating reading.

Richard – Dick to his friends, and enemies – Crossman was born in 1907, the second son in an upper-middle class family that eventually numbered six. The family home was on the edge of Epping Forest in what was then rural Essex. Crossman's 'strong-minded, energetic' mother, Helen, came from a family of pharmaceutical chemists; his father, Charles Stafford, was a respected – and very respectable – lawyer, who eventually rose to become a High Court judge.[7] Crossman's 'bump of irreverence'[8]– the term he used himself to describe his relentless urge to challenge certain aspects of orthodoxy – was, according to Dalyell, 'inherited from his mother'.[9] It was, however, 'his father's style of life that nurtured the conditions for rebellion'.[10] For Crossman, memories of enforced rituals, such as morning prayers at precisely 7.55 and changing into evening dress for dinner, lingered long after his father's death in 1941.

Britain's rarefied public school system has, over the years, educated a large number of important figures in the Labour Party. This list includes party leaders such as Clement Attlee, Hugh Gaitskell and, more recently, Tony Blair. It also includes Crossman, who attended his father's *alma mater*, Winchester College, from 1919 to 1926. Indeed, Crossman did more than merely attend that venerable institution, he, in that peculiar decade that followed the Great War, came to 'embod[y] the spirit of Winchester in a way no one else could'.[11] Though clearly very intelligent, it appears to have been Crossman's energetic personality that most attracted the attention of the school authorities – particularly that of headmaster, Monty Rendall – and the admiration, occasionally verging on devotion, of many fellow students.

Howard is adamant that it was Crossman's school, rather than his family, that 'shaped his character'.[12] One aspect of this was that, as much as Crossman enjoyed his 'bump of irreverence', it was contained within an overall respect for the establishment. According to Dalyell, that Crossman began as life as a Wykehamist 'fagging' for Anthony 'Puffin' Asquith, son of the former Prime Minister, 'gave Crossman a sense of his own position in the élite of the nation that never left him'.[13] A piece Crossman himself wrote in a review of a book about his old headmaster does support the view that his school, more than any other influence, moulded his character. He remarked:

> the secret of Winchester – and, indeed, of the classical tradition in our leading public schools – is that it imposes on a boy's mind a complex structure of rules, a rigid hierarchy of values and a system of taboos, privileges and obligations utterly remote from his home life or from the world outside.[14]

Even more revealing, Crossman later suggested that there are three types of Wykehamists. One such grouping appears entirely auto-biographical:

> A few – their minds sharpened by six years of mental struggle with the tradition but in lifelong reaction to it – remain grateful to Winchester for teaching them that all institutions, laws and persons in authority may turn out to be as bizarre a mixture of the good and the fraudulent as their old Headmaster. They are the radical throw-outs of the Public School system; and some even become "traitors to their class".[15]

It was certainly at Winchester that Crossman cultivated the 'intellectual arrogance' that he himself later believed to be an unpopular by-product of the public school system.[16] This most obviously manifested itself in his development of a brutal debating technique. This talent he brought home during holidays and regularly deployed to humiliate his mother – much to his father's displeasure. Another person the brash young Crossman used to annoy with this tormenting of his mother was a neighbour who regularly came round, with his wife Violet, to play tennis on summery Saturday afternoons. This neighbour was a diffident but promising Labour junior minister: his name, Clement Attlee.

From Winchester, Crossman took the well-worn path to New College, Oxford. Eschewing political activity – he did not, for instance, join the University Labour Club – Crossman concentrated, bar the occasional homoerotic distraction, on scholarly attainment. As testament to Crossman's scholastic ability, before his first-class degree in classics had even been awarded, he was offered a fellowship at New College. Prior to his commencing this post, Crossman took an experience-broadening year in Germany, starting in October 1930. Crossman gained much from his travels: a clear-sighted impression of the potential threat of Nazism; some salutary lessons learned through close association with a major communist publicist; and a future wife.[17] Regarding that last acquisition, the twice-married, morphine-addicted Erika Gluck was not the obvious woman for Crossman to marry – but then, Crossman rarely opted for the obvious. Married life began in July 1932 and did not last the year; the first Mrs Crossman left, reputedly for a new man, at Christmas.

Crossman's brief marital misadventure did not hinder his academic career, and he quickly developed a reputation as an inspiring lecturer. This opened other avenues. The BBC became interested, and, in 1934, Crossman began a series of short radio broadcasts on Germany. His work was generally well received, and he gained more exposure with his 'If Plato Lived Again' series in 1936. In addition, Crossman began his association with the Workers Educational Association, proving a very popular public speaker. Remarkably, in 1935, he also had time to stand for, and win, a seat on Oxford City Council, becoming the leader of the small group of Labour Party members. He also, in April 1937, fought a by-election in West Birmingham, performing creditably without winning. Thus Crossman, still just in his late twenties was making an impression in many arenas.

1937 was a turning point for Crossman. Though this year saw the publication of his most important academic work, the still useful *Plato Today*, Crossman's academic career was cut short through his entanglement with Inezita (Zita) Baker, the wife of an Oxford zoologist. For Crossman, the results of this affair included involvement in a very messy divorce, a second marriage in December 1937, and resignation from New College. In contrast, his journalistic and political careers flourished, and these, rather than academia, were to be the avenues down which Crossman was to travel. In July 1938, Crossman was appointed assistant editor of the influential weekly magazine *New Statesman and Nation*, and earlier, at the end of 1937 – on the strength of his impressive showing at the West Birmingham by-election – he had gained nomination as prospective Labour candidate for Coventry. In the end, however, it was not until 1945 that Crossman eventually stood for election in the redrawn Coventry East constituency.

It was the Second World War that intervened, and Crossman spent much of it working for the War Office as a propagandist, including a period as Deputy Director of Psychological Warfare at the Allied headquarters in Algiers.[18] At the close of the war he was awarded an OBE for his service. To his superiors he proved, on occasion, troublesome and disobedient, but – in words of Sir Robert Bruce Lockhart, the Director of Political Warfare Executive – this was more than compensated for by 'his agile mind, his almost daemonic energy, his considerable skill in broadcasting and in leaflet-writing'.[19]The war changed Crossman, he became, in Howard's words, 'no longer merely the carping journalistic critic, still less the ivory tower academic. He had become, in effect, a man of the administrative world – if one of independent, and sometimes inconvenient convictions'.[20]

These 'inconvenient convictions' surfaced soon after Crossman easily won his Coventry East seat during the Labour landslide election of July 1945. Foreign Secretary Ernest Bevin – in a decision he must have come to regret sorely – gave Crossman his first important job as a member of the Anglo-American Commission to investigate the future of Palestine. After becoming persuaded to support the Zionist cause, Crossman played a decisive role in cajoling the Commission to recommend, unanimously, the immediate admission into Palestine of 100,000 Jewish survivors of the Nazi regime.[21] Crossman's stance, which eventually came to include support for a Jewish homeland, put him at odds with the Labour government and, in particular, with the redoubtable Bevin. Crossman widened his criticism of Bevin's foreign policy, most notably through his speaking on behalf of an amendment to the King's Speech in late 1946. Here he called for the government to 'provide a democratic and constructive Socialist alternative to an otherwise inevitable conflict between American capitalism and Soviet Communism'.[22] Despite Crossman's obvious ability, this rebellious streak – combined with Attlee's memories of Crossman as a brash, mother-tormenting schoolboy – grievously limited his chances of gaining a position in government.

Crossman's position on the left of the Labour Party was confirmed with the publication, in early 1947, of the famous pamphlet with the almost self-explanatory title, *Keep Left*, which Crossman had co-authored with Michael Foot and Ian Mikardo. The pamphlet advocated, *inter alia*, an extension of the government's programme of nationalisation, and – with this being Crossman's main contribution – the creation of a regional European security system to act as a 'Third Force' between the USA and the Soviet Union.[23] *Keep Left* gained some momentum, spawning a sequel three years later, *Keeping Left*, and even giving its name to a Keep Left Group, which officially formed in July 1949, with thirteen members – including Crossman and his future Cabinet colleague and friend, Barbara Castle – turning up for the first meeting.[24] At the 1950 election Crossman maintained a healthy, if reduced, majority in Coventry East, but the Labour government's overall majority was slashed to six. Between this election and the next, the following year, Crossman 'kept a surprisingly low political profile'.[25]

After the strange 1951 election – which the Labour Party lost despite gaining more votes than the victorious Winston Churchill-led Conservatives – the Keep Left Group became inextricably linked with the loose assemblage that coalesced around the charismatic figure of Aneurin Bevan, of National Health Service renown. Bevan had become a figure-head for left-wing dissenters after he famously resigned his Cabinet post in April 1951 – with two others, one being future Labour leader Harold Wilson – in response to the proposed imposition of charges for dental treatment and spectacles; a move designed to help finance a massive rearmament programme for the war in Korea. It was inevitable that Crossman was to become, in the parlance of the time, associated with the Bevanites.

Outside politics, the event that most deeply affected Crossman at this time was the sudden death – on 6 July 1952, the result of a brain haemorrhage – of his second wife, Zita. Following his wife's death, Crossman briefly became disillusioned with politics. He seriously considered becoming Principal of the University College of North Staffordshire – what was to become the University of Keele – and was devoting considerable time to his journalistic career.[26] However, Crossman's election, by the mass Labour Party, to the National Executive Committee (NEC) at the end of September 1952 did re-ignite his political spark, and his subsequent fifteen-year stint on the NEC was to become an important influence on his political attitudes. Indeed, Dalyell goes as far as to say that 'the NEC was to be the centre of his life'.[27] That said, his first speech to the Labour Party Conference, the day after his election to the NEC, was an utter disaster, when, with a misjudged joke, Crossman managed to alienate his own supporters – an event that elicited a rare smile from the usually sphinx-like Attlee.[28]

After the shock of Zita's death in 1952, Crossman's personal life began to improve, and two years later he married his third wife, Anne McDougall. Moreover, following their marriage, the couple were given ownership of Prescote Manor in Oxfordshire, where Anne had grown up. The marriage was a success: it lasted happily until the end of Crossman's life in 1974; there were two children, Patrick and Virginia; and Prescote became Crossman's rural sanctuary.[29]

1955 was an interesting year for Crossman. His political relationship with Bevan, which was never rock-solid, virtually ended in March of that year following a dispute over defence policy.[30] Crossman then saw his majority in Coventry East halved at the general election in May, one which saw the Prime Minister, Anthony Eden – who had recently succeeded the ageing Churchill – increase the Conservative majority in the Commons to sixty. Crossman also lost his job at the *New Statesman*, but gained a new one as a twice-weekly columnist for the rather more popular *Daily Mirror*. In addition, the end of the year also saw Crossman roundly condemned by Bevanite colleagues for not publicly supporting Bevan in the Labour leadership contest that followed Attlee's resignation in December. This absence of support was, in Bevanite eyes, bad enough; that Crossman pledged allegiance to Bevan's arch-rival, Hugh Gaitskell, was damn near a hanging offence. The 'Double Crossman' tag was not invented at this time, it was a schoolboy nickname, but it was a charge that did achieve particular resonance during this period.[31] However, of most significance – in terms of this book at least – was a speech Crossman made to the Labour Party Conference in October. Here, rather by accident, Crossman put in a successful performance, not on foreign affairs, but on a subject in which he had only relatively recently taken interest, pension policy. This speech lit a fuse that changed the Labour Party's, and Britain's, social security policy forever: background to, and fallout from, Crossman's pension speech will be the stuff of later chapters.

Crossman's career was on the up for most of the rest of the 1950s. He did, at this stage, get on well with new Labour leader Hugh Gaitskell – someone he had known since school days at Winchester.

Moreover, Gaitskell was adept at keeping Crossman productively occupied, not least by giving him the task of chairing the committee responsible for formulating Labour's new superannuation scheme. The only major blot on his copy-book occurred in July 1957, when, in one of his newspaper columns, Crossman suggested that Labour's trade-union sponsored MPs were, with only very few named exceptions, of poor quality. Crossman's lack of tact was, at times, extraordinary. Nevertheless, Crossman managed, just, to gain re-election to the NEC at that year's Party Conference. Moreover, at the Conference, when explaining the document his committee had drawn up for the Labour Party – *National Superannuation*: *Labour's Policy for Security in Old Age* – Crossman:

> delivered one of those bravura displays of sheer expository power that no figure in the Labour Party has ever been able to match. He spoke with barely a note for nearly an hour and did not lose the rapt attention of his audience for a moment.[32]

The closing year of the decade saw Crossman using his old propaganda skills to considerable effect at the heart of Labour's general election campaign. Despite what was regarded as a good campaign, Labour lost: the Conservatives, now under the leadership of Harold Macmillan, increased their majority to 102. Nevertheless, in November 1959 – a month after the election – Gaitskell rewarded Crossman by appointing him to the Opposition Front Bench. Crossman was now formally responsible for pension policy. However, not long after, Crossman's career began to stall.

It was during those final months of 1959 that tensions began to grow between Crossman and Gaitskell. These strains erupted in early 1960 when Crossman openly called for Gaitskell to reconsider his proposal to abandon Clause 4 of the Labour Party constitution – the symbolic socialist commitment to the public ownership of the means of production – which the Labour leader had strongly advocated at the 1959 Party Conference. As early as March 1960, Crossman was forced to resign his Front Bench position, and he then used his freedom to become a leading critic of revisionism, the ideological position favoured by Gaitskell which actively sought alternatives to public ownership as a method of attaining social justice and equality. This revisionist position was strongly associated with Anthony

Crosland, whose relationship with the Party leader had grown closer as the Crossman/Gaitskell association foundered. Later in 1960, Crossman encouraged one of his closest political colleagues, Harold Wilson, to stand – as a representative of the left – against Gaitskell for the Party leadership. It was a contest Gaitskell won comfortably. Crossman also became heavily involved in the dispute over Labour's defence policy, again falling on the opposite side to Gaitskell. Understandably, Gaitskell was in no rush to return Crossman to the Front Bench – though it is claimed that Gaitskell would have appointed Crossman to his Cabinet had he become Prime Minister.[33]

As it was, Crossman – despite the odd highlight, such as another effective speech on pensions at the 1962 Party Conference – spent the first years of the new decade wondering whether he would ever leave the political backwaters. At the start of 1963, Gaitskell's sudden, fatal illness changed the situation; 'while there is death there is hope',[34] as Crossman himself later remarked dryly. In the aftermath Crossman became a member of Wilson's successful leadership campaign, which subsequently heralded Crossman's release from the backbenches, as Wilson gave him a Front Bench role as Labour spokesperson on science. Science was not a subject about which Crossman had much experience, but he performed ably, and he did play some role in prompting Wilson's famous 'white heat of the technological revolution' speech at the 1963 Party Conference.[35] As time went on Crossman's responsibilities came to include aspects of education policy, and he developed a reputation as a formidable Front Bench figure. Indeed, Crossman appeared, at long last, to be becoming a responsible senior politician. He even gave up his parallel career as a journalist at the end of 1963.

The four-seat majority gained by Labour at the general election of October 1964 allowed Wilson to furnish Crossman with his first ministerial job. To his surprise, the now fifty-six year old Crossman was not handed the education portfolio, nor was he given the chance to oversee the implementation of the pension scheme with which he remained associated. Instead, Crossman was made Minister of Housing and Local Government, with a seat in the Cabinet. It was a job about which Crossman later confessed he 'knew virtually nothing'.[36] Indeed, that Crossman had 'no preconceived ideas' about the department was the very reason – according to Crossman's new ministerial colleague at Housing, Bob Mellish – that

Wilson gave Crossman the job.[37] Despite this, Crossman was very active during his near two-year stint at Housing, during which time he piloted through a number of important pieces of legislation, including the 1965 Rent Act.[38] However, his time at Housing is probably best remembered because of later accounts of the battles he conducted with the civil service, and, in particular, with the formidable Dame Evelyn Sharp, the department's long-standing Permanent Secretary. Sharp provided this vivid – if biased – picture of Crossman's attitude to his officials:

> He would *not* listen. He distrusted us from the start and made that clear. He was a bully. He was a bull in a china shop and he felt like a bull in a china shop. I think he wanted to be a bull in a china shop, he wanted to hear the china smashing.[39]

Having weathered – albeit temporarily – a difficult economic situation, Wilson called another general election for the end of March 1966. The result was an increased Labour majority of ninety-seven. A few months later, in August, Crossman was given what appeared a promotion, becoming Lord President of the Council and Leader of the House of Commons. Grand though his new title appeared, it meant that Crossman was left without a department – he had 'exchange[d] power for status'.[40]

Despite his early discontentment with his new position, Crossman became as active as ever in his new position: active, if not terribly successful. A proposal he supported to televise the House of Commons failed – on a free vote – by just one vote. His attempt to introduce an extensive system of cross-party select committees to scrutinise departments also led to frustration as only two such bodies were created during his time in office. Finally, and most famously, Crossman began a fresh attempt to reform the House of Lords. The process Crossman initiated was eventually pulled off the rails by an amazing coalition of right-wing Conservative backbenchers, led by Enoch Powell, and left-wing Labour MPs, led by Michael Foot, who felt that the reforms were, respectively, too radical and not radical enough. Though unsuccessful, it should be highlighted that, in the few decades following Crossman's efforts, Parliament did welcome television cameras, an extensive – if still under-powered – select committee system was established, and the House of Lords was reformed. Crossman was ahead of his time.

By the time the Lords' reform was in the process of being mugged, Crossman had already left for pastures new. A reshuffle created by the resignation, in March 1968, of Foreign Secretary, George Brown, led indirectly to an opportunity for Crossman to co-ordinate, initially as a non-departmental 'overlord', the separate ministries of Health and Social Security. Crossman was disappointed again – he had always hankered after the Foreign Office – but, with a chance to implement 'his' pension scheme, Crossman was persuaded by Wilson to accept this rather awkward job. Crossman, therefore, gave up his Leadership of the House, but remained Lord President until Health and Social Security were merged later in November 1968. At that point Crossman became the first Secretary of State at the newly formed Department of Health and Social Security.

Despite his new job, at least on the social security side, incorporating areas in which Crossman was something of an expert, his time at the DHSS was, again, one largely marked by disappointment and frustration. In particular, regarding specific policies, Crossman was appointed, in Wilson's words, to take 'special responsibility for supervising the preparation of the new superannuation scheme'.[41] Unfortunately, that scheme was not prepared quickly, and, as mentioned earlier, it failed to make it onto the Statute Book. In contrast, on the health side – which appears to have interested a jaded Crossman rather more than social security[42] – he did much to force improvements in mental hospitals after bravely publishing, in full, a damning report of criminal neglect at the Ely Mental Hospital in Cardiff. Nevertheless, Crossman utterly failed to achieve what he claimed Wilson hoped his old ally would accomplish in his final position in government. This was, ambitiously, to prove 'as memorable as Beveridge'.[43]

Wilson called a general election for 18 June 1970, but Crossman already knew – whatever the result – he would be leaving the Cabinet. In October 1969, he had secretly agreed to become the next editor of the *New Statesman*, once that particular session of Parliament had come to an end. And, following the surprise Conservative victory in 1970, Crossman did indeed pick up his journalistic career at his old employer – though he continued to combine this with his job as Member of Parliament for Coventry East. For a number of reasons, Crossman's time as editor at the *New Statesman* was not a happy one, and it lasted less than two years. In his final two years Crossman wrote a column for *The Times*, attempted to write some books, and even became a television presenter – of *Crosstalk*, a BBC1 programme of conversations with figures as diverse as Harold Wilson, Enoch Powell, and, remarkably, his old sparring partner at Housing, Evelyn Sharp. He also enjoyed being on hand to see much more of his family. He was diagnosed with cancer of the liver in September 1973, and informed he had about six months to live. Having been able to celebrate his old ally Harold Wilson's return to Number 10 in February 1974, Crossman died, at Prescote, on Friday 5 April, at the age of sixty-six.

Despite a reputation for proving terminal, death did not close Crossman's political career. Crossman's priority, on hearing of his unfavourable prognosis, 'was to ensure the future of his diaries',[44] and he did indeed get them into publishable form by the time of his passing. Then the battle began: Crossman's ghost – ably supported on earth by his widow, Anne – versus the establishment. This reached a peak when the Wilson government – in the form of the Attorney-General, Sam Silkin – applied for an injunction to stop the *Diaries* being published. To considerable surprise, the Lord Chief Justice, Lord Widgery, decided that publication of the first volume could proceed unhindered.[45] It was an important posthumous victory, and a fitting climax to Crossman's career. Crossman was susceptible to charges of fickleness, but about certain issues he was consistent, and attempting to open up the machinery of power to closer public inspection was one of them. However, as suggested earlier, there is a sense that the *Diaries* have overshadowed other important elements of Crossman's political career. This book will bring some of these aspects into the light.

Before this process of illumination can proceed in earnest, to add colour to this initial sketch of the life of Richard Crossman, some comments by colleagues, and others, about this multi-faceted man will be noted. To begin, Denis Healey – a Cabinet colleague of . Crossman, though never a friend – is characteristically forthright, remembering Crossman as:

a large man with spectacles, mousy hair falling lank on each side of his forehead, and a mouth which turned down at the corners with an expression of Burglar Bill in the dock. I was impressed by his brilliance until Hector McNeil reminded me: 'It's easy to be brilliant if you are not bothered being right.' Crossman had a heavyweight intellect with lightweight judgement. He was an exciting teacher, and would have made a magnificent successor to Laski at the London School of Economics. As a politician, and even more as a minister, he left much to be desired.[46]

This portrait of intellectual capability and poor judgement is a common theme, with another former colleague – but, again, not exactly a friend – Douglas Jay suggesting that 'Dick was a powerful engine without a steering-wheel'.[47] The former leader of the Transport and General Workers' Union, Jack Jones, put it another way, remarking that Crossman 'typified for me the academic who, in working class parlance, "didn't know his arse from his elbow"'.[48]

One further aspect Healey highlighted was that, 'Like a Greek sophist, Dick was always more interested in the process of argument rather than its conclusion'.[49] This quirk of Crossman's personality was cheerily exposed in an anecdote told by Ray Gunter, Wilson's first Minister of Labour, to the journalist, and later broadcaster, John Cole: the scene was a meeting of a sub-committee of the NEC; the matter for discussion, an issue about staffing. As the meeting began, Crossman was a lone voice on one side of the debate; four trade unionists, including Gunter, opposed him:

'But one by one . . . Dick won us over by the sheer brilliance of his argument, until the last of my colleagues said: 'All right, Dick boy, you've convinced me – I'll go along with the rest.' At that moment Dick suddenly struck his forehead with his palm, and said: 'One moment, comrades! I've forgotten about Factor X, which undermines the whole of my argument. I'm now of the mind that you all were originally.'[50]

Unsurprisingly, the trade unionists were unimpressed by this volte-face, and voted Crossman down, despite originally agreeing with the position Crossman finally supported.

Crossman's editor, Janet Morgan, makes a similar point. Having noted that Crossman, like Lord Melbourne, was, 'that rare phenomenon, a genuinely independent personality',[51] Morgan relates that most of Crossman's opinions:

were the product of dispute, deliberation (often instantaneous) and a mischievous habit of taking an opposite view. Precedent and consistency were not, unless it suited him, intrinsically good. Such an attitude was bound to be unpopular with devout members of the Party.[52]

Alongside – and related to – Crossman's joy in argument was a further element of his character that has caught the eye of some commentators. This feature was Crossman's often distant relationship with socialism, a feature odd in one generally regarded as being on the left-wing of the Labour Party. As Kevin Theakston remarks:

> The *Diaries* paint a picture of an elitist, wealthy, manor-house-living, upper-middle-class socialist intellectual feeling remote from ordinary people (e.g. in his local constituency party in 'depressing' Coventry) and whose 'socialism' is becoming more and more attenuated. He is increasingly doubtful about 'clumsy, academic interventions in the economy' and thinks that taxation is too high.[53]

There is a certainly a strong sense that Crossman moved to the left during his school days merely because, with his particular background, it was the ideological position that would most prompt occasions for heated debate – and tickle his famous 'bump of irreverence'. Crossman himself admitted that his radicalism had 'never been based on a moral or egalitarian philosophy'.[54] However, as will be illustrated throughout this book, Crossman did have a mostly coherent vision of what might be called 'M&S' socialism. To explain, throughout his career Crossman believed that socialism should not be about redistribution as such, but rather, that socialism should be directed towards enabling the mass of the population to enjoy 'something really good' which, at that time, only a privileged few were able to appreciate.[55] Crossman alluded to this philosophy when explaining to an audience 'the "M&S" revolution',[56] an idea prompted by a lunch Crossman spent with Sir Simon Marks – then chairman of the famous British retailing institution Marks & Spencer – in the late 1940s. Crossman explained:

> Having been presented with a particularly delicious and exotic fruit salad, I couldn't resist remarking on it to the Chairman of

Marks and Spencer. He looked at me with those huge gentle eyes and observed with great seriousness, 'That fruit salad you ate was not only good but extremely expensive. It is the aim of this organisation, my dear Dick, within ten years to make it possible for the average citizen to eat that fruit salad at Marks and Spencer. Life for me consists of noticing what is really worth having among the pleasures of the rich and enabling everyone to get them.'[57]

Thus, it might be said, Crossman was not just a socialist, he was an 'M&S' socialist. However, in true Crossman fashion, he was not always consistent on the matter of breaking down the walls of privilege, particularly when he witnessed the results. For example, in the very same lecture in which he mentioned the 'M&S revolution', Crossman made a snobbish remark implying that 'student disorder and unrest' had been prompted by the policy to expand access to higher education to the masses.[58]

Combining the character assessments of many, Theakston has produced a vivid and largely accurate picture of Crossman the politician:

> He was not a 'smooth' or 'safe pair of hands' type of politician. His reputation was that of an intellectually arrogant bully or steam-roller (but himself was thin-skinned and insecure); someone who could and would not listen to others; who was inconsistent and unreliable in his views and judgements ('Double-Crossman'); who approached politics in a machiavellian and conspiratorial way but at the same time was his own worst enemy and amazingly gaffe-prone.[59]

This is a compelling picture, and any attempt to restore some of Crossman's reputation cannot ignore the obvious flaws that Theakston, and many others, have highlighted. It would certainly be difficult to shake off completely Edward Pearce's image of Crossman as 'a silly clever politician'.[60] Furthermore, it would be pointless to suggest that Crossman's ministerial career was anything other than a disappointment. However, there is one largely positive aspect of Crossman's political life that tends to be lost in some of these portraits, and it is something that Crossman himself thought was his most serviceable political attribute. On Gaitskell's election as Labour Party leader in 1955, Crossman wrote a letter of congratulation which included the line: 'My value to the Party, so far as I have one, is as an awkward, independent ideas man who can be relied upon to chase an idea further than it is convenient'.[61]

It is around this concept of 'Crossman the idea-chaser', rather than 'Crossman the Minister', that a case can be made to rehabilitate, at least partially, his political reputation. Indeed the late Ben Pimlott has already suggested that one of Crossman's considerable strengths was that he proved 'a fertile source of ideas', though he did add that this attribute was rather undermined by insufficient single-mindedness.[62] This latter qualification is perhaps fair, but only up to a point. As noted already, Crossman would pursue certain ideas with relentlessness. His ambition to remove the secrecy surrounding the workings of government was evident from early in his career and continued after his death. And, though he was unable to achieve much toward that end in terms of legislation, he did nudge the British political climate towards one of greater openness, not least through the publication of his *Diaries*. A less celebrated idea to which Crossman cleaved for twenty years – and the main topic of this book – was the plan to break the UK welfare system free from the restriction of flat-rate provision. And, again, though his ministerial activities did not result in immediate radical change, the idea he propagated did prompt subtle shifts in UK social policy – shifts that continue, after a fashion, to prove significant.

FACTORS IN SOCIAL POLICY

As suggested in the previous section, this study rests on the notion that ideas, and their advocates, ought to be regarded as significant players in the UK social policy process. This requires some justification, as not all would agree. For example, taking a neo-Marxist approach to the issue of pension policy, Eric Shragge suggests that socio-economic determinants completely overshadow all other possible factors.[63] Nevertheless, as will be illustrated, there is widespread support for the claim that ideas and individuals do, in the end, matter.

In his seminal study of British social policy in the 1960s, *Poverty, Politics and Policy*, Keith Banting is keen to stress the central roles played by ideas and their advocates. He argues:

The individual who analyses problems in a new way, or who recombines existing elements so as to introduce a novel pattern, takes the first indispensable step towards innovation. Those who contribute to such conceptual shifts are major agents of innovation, however insignificant they may otherwise appear in politics.[64]

This is an important statement of support for the notion that ideas did play an important role in the UK social policy process, not least during the period covered in this particular study. However, it must be added that, for Banting, policy making is more than just an intellectual activity. Policy making, he suggests, is also an institutional process. No matter how brilliant an idea, unless it reaches those who possess authority 'by virtue of their positions in political institutions', and is accepted by them, then implementation of that idea is impossible.[65] Equally, as much as providing opportunities, institutions – such as political parties, the civil service, and interest groups – can, if they do not welcome particular ideas, seriously constrain the activities of policy-makers. Thus, for Banting, ideas and individuals are important, but, equally, the institutional context in which they operate cannot be ignored.

Hugh Heclo shares a similar approach to Banting in emphasising the significance of certain individuals and their ideas; though, again, other institutional factors, such as the role of national bureaucracies, are also regarded as highly significant.[66] One dusty area in particular that Heclo helps to illuminate is that inhabited by particular individuals, who, from the nether-regions of the political arena, push ideas forward. Regarding the period in question, Heclo identified individuals such as Richard Titmuss, Brian Abel-Smith, and Peter Townsend, names that will re-appear many times during the course of this narrative. Though often unheralded, these figures, he suggests, have played a highly significant role in the UK social policy processes. To elaborate, Heclo argues that, 'Typically, social policies have been most directly influenced by middlemen at the interfaces of various groups'.[67] He adds:

these agents of change have usually had access to information, ideas and positions outside the run of organisational actors. Their formal party allegiances have differed greatly but all have used their various positions to bring pensions, unemployment insurance or superannuation questions onto political agendas.[68]

Richard Crossman himself was, in his spare time, a scholar impressed by the role played by ideas. As Howard notes, 'Dick believed in the power of ideas in Politics – and this was bound to put him frequently at loggerheads with a Party leadership (for whom ideas all too often seemed dangerous things, best kept under control)'.[69] In supporting the notion that ideas, and their advocates, are important, Crossman also rectified, in advance, Heclo's failure to recognise the role of 'middlewomen' as well as 'middlemen' in advancing those 'dangerous' ideas. He did this by drawing attention to the pioneering work done by Eleanor Rathbone to promote the idea of family allowances in the UK. Rathbone, despite eventually becoming an MP, was regarded more as 'a person who got things done from outside politics'.[70] In so doing, Crossman argued that Rathbone, and others like her, performed a prominent and often neglected role in the political process. As Crossman explained:

> The great changes in British society have not been thought up either in the House of Commons or in the political parties. They have all been brought into politics from outside by individuals or by pressure groups running their own crusades outside politics and impinging on politicians who are the hucksters, the mediators. Politicians make good by borrowing ideas.[71]

Like Banting and Heclo, Crossman was not suggesting that ideas alone explained the policy process. Indeed, his lecture on *The Politics of Pensions* was as much a tart account of the institutional constraints that thwarted the original superannuation idea as it was a description of the origins and progress of the idea itself. Yet, ideas, Crossman believed, had an important tale to tell.

More recently, Anthony Seldon has also suggested that ideas can play a significant role in the political process. Examining the general development of Britain in the second half of the twentieth century, Seldon argues that 'ideas clearly are crucial to an understanding of post-war British history'.[72] However, to continue the theme started earlier in this section, Seldon suggests that the impact ideas have made is, in reality, heavily circumscribed. Thus, despite Maynard

Keynes's famous dictum about the world being largely ruled by ideas, these ideas, Seldon suggests, 'need to be seen in the context of the interplay of interests, individuals and circumstances'.[73] Seldon's approach has proved influential in public policy[74] and, in the next section, each of Seldon's 'four factors in producing change: ideas, individuals, interests and circumstances'[75] will be discussed in greater detail.

IDEAS

With some reservations, Seldon uses Ralf Dahrendorf's definition of an idea – that is, 'a notion of where we go from where we are . . . a vision of the future state of affairs, which may or may not be desirable'[76] – to begin his discussion about the impact of ideas. Following this, Seldon boldly, and very usefully, states that, 'Ideas exist on two levels'.[77] Seldon calls one of these levels the plane of 'overarching ideas'.[78] These are ideas that exist at the 'macro' level, and, as Seldon argues, they 'condition the entire way that a generation understands, models and interprets events'. In this sense they constitute, as Peter Dorey notes, 'a dominant or *hegemonic* set of ideas and values concerning the purpose and objectives of government and public policy'.[79] One of these hegemonic sets of ideas and values was found during the first few decades after the Second World War when Keynesian ideas of economic management formed the 'dominant mentality'.[80] Another such example is identified from the late 1970s onwards when ideas of neo-liberalism and individualism gained advantage over those more *dirigiste* values commonly articulated during the years of the Keynesian settlement.

Seldon's second, or rather lower, level of ideas consists of those ideas that are 'essentially facilitating rather than agenda-setting'.[81] These micro- or meso-level ideas, Seldon argues, can only proceed if they are in sympathy with the dominant idea of the time. To use two of Seldon's own examples, during the 1980s the idea of constitutional reform was regarded as hostile to the neo-liberal spirit of the time, and was thus thwarted, whereas the idea of nuclear deterrence did not challenge the prevailing macro-level idea, and was taken up with gusto. This can be linked to Roger Cobb and Charles Elder's useful contribution to the concept of the policy agenda. They distinguish between the 'systemic' agenda, which 'consists of all the issues that are commonly perceived by members of political community as meriting public attention'[82] and the more select and formal 'institutional' agenda, said to comprise 'those problems to which public officials give serious and active attention'.[83] Returning to Seldon's two examples, it could be argued that, during the 1980s, nuclear deterrence was part of the institutional agenda, whereas constitutional reform never progressed from the systemic to the institutional agenda because it did not fit comfortably with the dominant set of ideas and values of that period.

At this point in the discussion about the nature of ideas it is helpful to link it to specific ideas that lie at the heart of this study. To expand, two meso-level ideas will be examined in detail in this book, both linked, to some extent, with Crossman: national superannuation and the income guarantee. National superannuation will be the first – and most complicated – idea to be sketched out here. Indeed, national superannuation was more than one idea; rather it was a bundle of ideas that burst forth on to the UK political agenda in the mid-1950s. Furthermore, it was not a static concept: it mutated many times following its original genesis in an obscure Fabian Society pamphlet published in 1953. Many more details about this concept, and the background to its arrival, will be described in the next few chapters, but, at this stage, only key elements need be mentioned. The national superannuation to be loosely defined here will be of the 1957 'vintage', probably the most famous version of the scheme, and one outlined in the earlier mentioned policy document *National Superannuation: Labour's Policy for Security in Old Age.*

The most celebrated aspect of national superannuation was the notion of providing a state pension scheme whereby an earnings-related system would replace the existing national insurance model of flat-rate contributions and benefits. In short, under national superannuation, if you were, say, to earn more than average, you were to contribute more than average to the state whilst in work, and would receive above-average levels of benefit from the state on retirement. It was a simple idea, and hardly original. Even Crossman admitted that much of national superannuation was 'borrowed from Sweden or Germany',[84] and the US had operated a similar scheme since the 1930s. As will be illustrated later, Switzerland was another source of inspiration. However, though simple in theory, as will be seen, the details were rather less straightforward. Another feature of national superannuation was the ambition to include nearly everyone within the state system; thus forcing the existing, and expanding, UK private pension industry into terminal decline. The third significant element of national superannuation was the bold aspiration to finance future benefits through the establishment of a fund stocked by contributions invested by government-appointed trustees into equities and gilt-edged securities. This, as will be explored, was the almost incidental proposal that, had it been implemented, would probably have created the greatest splash in British politics. However, as noted earlier, national superannuation was not implemented, and, as will be explored, to some extent this was because, using Seldon's terminology, this meso-level concept increasingly failed to chime with the period's overarching ideas.

The second of the meso-level ideas to be examined is that of the income guarantee. Again this particular idea enjoyed a number of different guises; furthermore, like national superannuation, it expanded from a concept designed solely for pensioners to one that covered a variety of disadvantaged social groups. The version to be introduced here is the one the Labour Party offered to the public at the 1964 general election. Designed to supplement national superannuation, the income guarantee was a scheme targeted at existing pensioners in poverty. The central idea was to fix a minimum level income, with those below this level having supplementary benefit paid to them in order to make up the shortfall. Significantly, where this system differed from the traditional means test was in the proposed utilisation of the existing taxation system to make the necessary calculations. This, it was hoped, would reduce some of the stigma attached to the existing means-tested national assistance scheme – a feeling of shame that prompted many to refuse benefits to which they were entitled. This particular version of the scheme was most strongly associated – not this time with Crossman, though he played a role in its development – but with Douglas Houghton, the minister with responsibility for the social services in Wilson's first Cabinet. Houghton's position, however, was not sufficient to save the income guarantee from being abandoned in 1965. Despite this rejection, elements of this scheme have been since hauled back from time to time, most obviously with the various tax-based credit systems with which New Labour's first Chancellor of the Exchequer, and current Prime Minister, Gordon Brown, has been associated. Thus, to return to Seldon's model, it might be argued that this old meso-level idea has, thirty years later, found sympathy with the New Labour *zeitgeist* and, like a seed long dormant under frozen soil, has revived and sprouted vigorously.

INDIVIDUALS

As with ideas, Seldon suggests a number of different levels at which individuals might exert influence on the policy process. These are: 'persons operating within the governmental process, those in an intermediate position, and those external to government'.[85] With a certain Crossman-like contrariness, attention here will focus primarily on the latter level; the level that consists, Seldon suggests, of people who 'have made arguably little impact on policy since 1945',[86] namely academics, journalists, and writers.

Despite Seldon's sweeping claim that 'those working in universities, commentators and writers, whole disciplines indeed, have been largely ignored by government',[87] he does note some exceptions, amongst them certain sociologists such as T.H. Marshall and the aforementioned Brian Abel-Smith and Peter Townsend. These individuals, Seldon suggests, did indeed possess some influence on governments – particularly of the Labour variety – from the 1940s to the 1960s. And, as suggested earlier, Seldon is far from alone in recognising this particular source of influence, with many also including the name of the very influential and long-serving head of social administration at the LSE, Richard Titmuss.[88]

Having mentioned Titmuss, Abel-Smith and Townsend a few times already, it is worth providing a little biographical background to these three individuals who, as will be illustrated at length, play a prominent role in this story. To begin with the senior member of this trio, Richard Titmuss was born on 16 October 1907, the son of a Bedfordshire farmer.[89] His formal education ended at the age of fifteen, and he subsequently went to work for an insurance company. Whilst working, from the late 1930s onwards, he began to write articles and books on many social policy issues, a development not unconnected to his marriage, in 1937, to Kay Miller. In 1942 Titmuss was invited to join a team of historians who were writing the civil history of the Second World War, the end result being his influential *Problems of Social Policy*, published in 1950. In this study of the development of social services during the war Titmuss emphasised the positive role of collective action and the resolve of ordinary people in the face of adversity. On the strength of *Problems of Social Policy*, Titmuss was appointed – despite his lack of formal qualifications – to the new Chair of Social Administration at the London School of Economics. He held this position, with considerable success, from 1950 until his death on 6 April 1973, aged 65, having only recently published his other great masterpiece, *The Gift Relationship*, a book that celebrated the potential of collective altruistic action to prove more effective than market forces, through the example of blood donation.[90] Though he probably would have modestly disagreed, Titmuss has rightly been called 'the leading figure in post-war British social administration'.[91]

As influential as he was at the LSE, it is important to note that, in David Reisman's words, 'Titmuss was more than just an academic'.[92] For example, he was a member of many government committees, on a wide range of subjects. These included the National Insurance Advisory Committee, the Royal Commission on Medical Education, and the Community Relations Commission. And – despite his hearty opposition to means-testing – Titmuss also served as Deputy Chairman of the Supplementary Benefits Commission from 1968 to 1973. Of more relevance to this study, in the 1950s Titmuss became an adviser to the Labour Party on issues of social policy. Indeed – as will be examined – he was co-opted onto the Labour Party's influential Study Group on Security and Old Age in 1956. Regarding his influence in this role, Crossman suggested that the advice Titmuss gave to the Labour Party 'laid the foundations of their social security programme and their attempt to achieve an integrated social policy'.[93]

Brian Abel-Smith was born in London on 6 November 1926 into a family with royal connections. He was educated at Haileybury College, and – after post-war army service – Cambridge. Health policy was Abel-Smith's main area of research, and he made an early impression by, in 1953, contributing an influential memorandum to the Guillebaud inquiry into the costs of the National Health Service. This memorandum – which demonstrated that the infant NHS was rather more cost-effective than some supposed – was co-written by Richard Titmuss, and Abel-Smith joined Titmuss at the LSE in 1955, becoming Professor of Social Administration there a decade later. He retired from this position in 1991. He died, aged sixty-nine, on

4 April 1996. In Abel-Smith's obituary, Peter Townsend described his old colleague as 'the neglected creative genius of post-war social policy in Britain'.[94]

Though health policy was Abel-Smith's primary research interest, he probably made a greater impression politically with his work on poverty. In 1953 he published *The Reform of Social Security*, the pamphlet Crossman acknowledged as the genesis of national superannuation, and – like Titmuss – Abel-Smith was later invited to serve on Labour's Study Group on Security and Old Age. However, his most immediately influential work was *The Poor and The Poorest*, a book co-written with Peter Townsend and published in 1965. This book was at the heart of the so-called 'rediscovery of poverty' in British society, a development that prompted, *inter alia*, the formation of the influential pressure group, the Child Poverty Action Group. Like Titmuss, Abel-Smith was not merely an academic commentator; he was fully engaged in the political world. Abel-Smith was a senior adviser in the 1964–70 and 1974–79 Labour governments. He was also Treasurer and, later, Vice-President of the Fabian Society. Townsend suggests that Abel-Smith might have pursued a political career of greater profile had it not been for the risk of public humiliation should his homosexuality become more widely known.[95] Nevertheless, despite his limited political profile, Julian Le Grand has observed that, 'There are few academics who have changed the world – and even fewer who have changed it for the better. Brian Abel-Smith was one of that select group.'[96]

The youngest – and only surviving – member of this group is Peter Townsend. He was born in 1928 in Middlesborough, though much of his childhood was spent in London. He was brought up in difficult circumstances by his mother, a singer, and – more dependably – by his grandmother.[97] Townsend went on to study at Cambridge. He followed this by becoming a researcher at Political and Economic Planning (PEP) – what is now the Policy Studies Institute – in 1952, before moving to the new Institute of Community Studies in 1954. In 1955 he co-wrote, with Abel-Smith, *New Pensions for the Old*, another important stepping-stone in the development of national superannuation, and – inevitably – he later became a member of the Study Group on Security and Old Age. In 1957 Townsend wrote the influential *The Family Life of Old People*, and joined Titmuss and Abel-Smith at the LSE. *The Poor and The Poorest* came out in 1965, by which time Townsend had been appointed Professor of Sociology at the new University of Essex. In 1979 Townsend published perhaps his most famous work, the influential national analytical survey *Poverty in the United Kingdom*. He moved to Bristol in 1982 to become Professor of Social Policy, and since 1999, has been Professor of International Social Policy at, rather fittingly, the LSE.

Townsend, like Titmuss and Abel-Smith, has been willing to extend his activities beyond the traditional groves of academe. The list of committees on which Townsend has participated, and often chaired, is very long one. It includes the Child Action Poverty Group, the Psychiatric Rehabilitation Association, the Disability Alliance, the Government Working Group on Inequalities and Health, and, more recently, the Standing Committee on Allocation of NHS Resources for the National Assembly of Wales. For good measure, Townsend has been consultant to a diverse range of institutions, from Islington Borough Council to the United Nations, and is also Vice-President of the Fabian Society. Townsend is an exceptional figure in social policy, and one of the few British academics who, like Titmuss and Abel-Smith, can rightly claim to have made a significant, and positive, difference to the lives of many people.

It follows that the role played by these particular sociologists in prompting changes to existing policy will be a subject examined closely in this book. Moreover, particular attention will fall on the contribution Titmuss, Abel-Smith and Townsend – a trio sometimes known, in the vernacular of the late 1950s, as the LSE 'skiffle group' – made to the construction of the Labour Party's policy to introduce national superannuation. Though it will be suggested that these individuals were highly influential, it will also be argued that the impact they made sometimes provoked unanticipated results. In particular, it will be claimed that one outcome of Abel-Smith and Townsend's successful attempt to change policy-makers' perceptions about poverty in the 1960s was a diminution in the likelihood that national superannuation would ever be implemented.

Obviously, in this particular book, a case will be made that Crossman, as an individual, also made an important impression on the social policy process. Much attention has focused on Crossman as an individual who, in Seldon's typology, operated 'within the governmental process' and, in particular, his fairly miserable record at transforming radical proposals into legislation whilst a minister.

However, relatively little has been said about his earlier role in the 1950s when, external to government as a mere Opposition back-bencher, Crossman enthusiastically advocated the nascent national superannuation concept, and almost single-handedly pitched it into the mainstream of political discussion in the UK.

Later, when examining Crossman's role as an advocate for a particular idea, the work of John Kingdon will be drawn upon. As background to this, it is worth briefly introducing some of Kingdon's theories. In his most famous work, *Agendas, Alternatives and Public Policies*, Kingdon argues that policy formation is the result of the flow of three sets of processes, or 'streams'. These 'largely independent' streams are identified as 'problems, policies, and politics'.[98] Problems are issues that are deemed as requiring attention, policies are pro-posals for change, and events such as election results and swings in the popular mood are the important aspects of the political stream. Kingdon further argues that success in the policy process is 'much more likely if problems, policy proposals, and politics are all coupled into a package'.[99] Linking this to Crossman's role, Kingdon draws attention to what he calls 'policy entrepreneurs'. These are, in Kingdon's eyes, individuals willing to invest their resources to push particular proposals or problems to the fore, with the aim of prompting important players in the policy process to take notice. In addition, Kingdon highlights the particular function of policy entrepreneurs 'for coupling solutions to problems and for coupling both problems and solutions to politics'; the goal being to improve their pet scheme's chance of success once the attention of the political elite has been grabbed.[100]

In this study it will be argued that Crossman was the chief policy entrepreneur for national superannuation, and that Douglas Houghton performed a similar function for the income guarantee. It will also be suggested that, though neither idea was transformed directly into policy, the agenda-setting efforts of both Crossman and Houghton were sufficient to propel both ideas on to the policy process. That the policies eventually implemented as a result of these entrepreneurial actions bore little resemblance to the original ideas advocated does not mean that these initial activities lacked significance, merely that the policy process was – and is – more chaotic than many people realise.

CIRCUMSTANCES

Having focused thus far on individuals and ideas, it is time now to draw attention to the context in which they operate. Thus, turning once more to Seldon, an important, if sometimes neglected, member of his 'four factors for producing change' will be considered. Seldon defines 'circumstances' as 'events which constrain policy options and in many cases dictate a certain course of action'.[101] He continues by suggesting yet another typology, this time consisting of two varieties of circumstances, 'external and internal' both of which, he insists, 'provide opportunities, and in some cases the necessity, to recast policy'.[102]

War is a classic example of an external circumstance, whether a world war or a smaller-scale conflict such as Korea or the Falklands or, by extension, those that have followed the terrorist attacks of 11 September 2001. Also included in this category are economic shocks, including the one faced by British policy-makers in the 1960s when it became clear the UK economy was losing ground to many competitors, not least to members of the recently assembled European Economic Community.[103] Though links have been made between the radical welfare reforms of the Attlee government and the world war that preceded it,[104] this particular story – focused, as it is, on the period between the mid-1950s and 1970 – covers a relatively quiet period in Britain's martial history. That Harold Wilson was unwilling to bend to President Lyndon Johnson's request to send British troops to Vietnam played its part in maintaining this peace. Thus, in this study, more attention will be paid to economic circumstances, and it will be suggested that economic difficulties faced by the Wilson governments of the 1960s did indeed play a role in constraining new policy options, not least the income guarantee.

Internal constraints, Seldon suggests, are those that 'originate primarily within Britain'.[105] Demographic change and the perception of governmental failure are amongst the examples Seldon uses to illustrate this particular category. Clearly, regarding the first of these examples, much social policy has been influenced by changes to the demographic character of the UK. Rising life expectancy has been one such phenomenon: one that pension policy-makers have noted, and have responded to in similar ways, for many years. For example, in 1954, the Conservative government-appointed Committee on the Economic and Financial Problems of Old Age – the Phillips

Committee – reported that, 'The number of old people is increasing, and will continue to increase for some years to come, both absolutely and relatively to the size of the working population'.[106] In 2005, the New Labour government-appointed Pensions Commission – the Turner Commission – reported that, 'Long-term pension policy needs to be robust in the face of rising life expectancy'.[107] Both Committee and Commission, separated by over half a century, suggested, as one response to this demographic pressure, that the age at which pensions could be claimed ought to rise.

Though ever-increasing life-expectancy has been an obvious constant pressure on social security policy, there is another slightly more obscure and unpredictable 'internal circumstance' that a number of scholars have identified as a powerful structural constraint on policy-makers, one indirectly linked to that notion of governmental failure which Seldon highlighted. This constraint is the past. For example, when referring generally to the UK policy process, Rose and Davies argue that, 'Policymakers spend far more time living with the consequences of inherited commitments than with making choices that reflect their own initiatives'.[108] They note that change becomes difficult as relevant groups and bureaucrats become associated with particular existing policies, with the result that attempts to repeal those policies provoke electoral and institutional opposition.

In a similar vein, a number of scholars have been impressed with the notion of 'path dependency', an idea used to explain the phenomenon that 'once an historical choice is made, it both precludes and facilitates others. Once a particular fork is chosen, it is very difficult to get back on the rejected path'.[109] Constraints from the past are a particular concern for historical institutionalists, and one of the foremost scholars from that tradition is Paul Pierson. Pierson has done much to link social policy with notions of path dependency. For example, referring to contrasting developments in welfare reform between the UK and USA during the 1980s, Pierson has argued that the constraining inheritance of particular established past policies in the USA – ones absent in the UK – help to explain how US policymakers failed to take a more radical journey towards welfare retrenchment.[110] Moreover, he has suggested that an analysis of policy feedback – which he defines as 'the ways in which previous policy choices influence present political processes' – should now be 'an integral part of any investigation of social-policy change'.[111]

In extending the idea that decisions made in the past constrain the actions of future policy-makers, Pierson has argued that 'policy feedback not only affects the resources of organized interests and the mind-sets of political elites; it also creates incentives and provides information for individual members of the electorate'.[112] Pierson introduced a new concept to policy feedback theory to address this point, one he calls 'policy lock-in'. As he explains:

> policies may encourage individuals to adapt in ways that lock in a particular path of policy development. By 'lock in' I mean that they bring about the policy-induced emergence of elaborate social and economic networks that greatly increase the cost of adopting once-possible alternatives and inhibit exit from a current policy path.[113]

Helen Fawcett is the scholar who has done most to utilise Pierson's idea of policy lock-in to the study of the post-war development of UK social security policy. Returning to Krasner's metaphor of an important decision later proving a 'fork' in the road, Fawcett has suggested that one such 'fork' occurred with the implementation of the Beveridge-inspired post-war social reforms associated with the creation of the welfare state. She has argued that, once in place, this particular system 'proved extremely hard to either abandon, ameliorate or reform'.[114] Regarding pension reform in particular, Fawcett suggests that the Beveridge system,

> by creating short-term pressures for increases in the basic retirement pension and causing, through the very inadequacy of that pension, the growth of a powerful private sector, policy lock-in effects developed, and it became progressively more difficult to reform the system.[115]

Interestingly, pension policy in particular appears susceptible to the claim that the past decisions constrain the availability of later choices, with Pierson – and John Myles – influentially suggesting that, internationally, 'pension policy is a *locus classicus* for the study of path-dependent change'.[116] It follows that the importance of the past as a constraining 'circumstance' will be an important element in this particular tale.

INTERESTS

Seldon identifies 'interests' as the final influence on the policy process. Following a pattern, Seldon distinguishes between particular types of interest. 'External interests' comprise the first category, with pressure groups providing the prime example.[117] Of these groups, Seldon highlights in particular the trade unions, suggesting that – until the late 1970s at least – they were 'arguably the most consistently powerful of all pressure groups in post-war Britain'.[118] Moreover, with Seldon, Hugh Heclo is just one of a number of scholars who have suggested that trade unions have played a significant role in the development of social policy during the period in focus.[119] However, as will be explained in due course, though the unions did indeed wield great influence, often the pressure they were trying to bring was reduced because not all the unions involved were pushing in the same direction at the same time.

In addition to the trade unions, other important groups appear in this story. Indeed it would be very difficult to ignore the often very vocal role played by the insurance industry – an industry that developed at a very rapid rate in the UK in comparison to elsewhere in Europe. As, in particular, Leslie Hannah has reported, the industries responsible for providing Britain's private pension schemes have often united to vent anger at some decisions proposed by policy-makers. For example, following the publication of Labour's superannuation scheme in 1957, the insurance industry unleashed a 'barrage of opposition to the plan'.[120] It has certainly been the case that, throughout the post-war history of state pension system in the UK, there has existed acute awareness that changes to public schemes can dramatically impair or, for that matter, improve the prospects of private pension scheme providers. This concern has often been translated into pressure on policy-makers – often noisily, but also sometimes more softly – and this needs to be examined.

Seldon also regards political parties as 'external interests', highlighting, in particular, the importance of the Conservative Party as the party in power for much the greater proportion of the second half of the twentieth century.[121] Indeed, particularly over the development and post-war reform of pensions policy, it is the role of the Conservative Party that has caught the eye of a number of scholars, not least because of its generally consistent ideological commitment to encouraging private pension provision. For example, Hiroshi Araki has argued that the Conservative Party has trumped Labour by trans-forming the pension system into one which reflects Conservative 'core principles of freedom and personal responsibility'.[122] Central to Araki's thesis is the suggestion that these Conservative principles have been distinct and consistent since the early 1950s, in contrast to a rather more vague commitment from Labour towards a more state-centred welfare policy, with this putting the latter party at a dis-advantage.[123]

Though 'external interests' are important, Seldon suggests that the 'more important vested interests by far . . . are those internal to government'.[124] The senior civil service provides Seldon with his primary example and, indeed, there have been a number of sugges-tions that a particular bureaucratic mindset has led the social policy process down certain paths, while excluding others. Interestingly, Crossman himself was one of those who, at times, voiced concern about the power of the civil service. After his stint at Housing, Crossman declared that, 'The higher Civil Service was a coherent and cohesive oligarchy presenting Ministers with narrow alternatives of choice'.[125] Crossman also, in typically contrary fashion, later argued that, 'We have a Civil Service which will carry out the programmes of politicians',[126] though he did add a caveat – one that brings us neatly back to the first of Seldon's factors – that officials would only do this 'provided the politicians are willing to fight night and day for their ideas'.[127] The ambiguous role of the civil service is the last of the various agents to be assessed in the telling of this multifaceted story.

SUMMARY

The point of this chapter was to introduce the individual around whom this study revolves, namely the 'silly clever' Richard Crossman. It was suggested that, as important as his eye-opening *Diaries* were, there was more to Crossman than these books. Though not suggesting that Crossman's ministerial career was anything other than satis-factory – in the OFSTED inspection sense of that word – it will be argued that Crossman bequeathed an important legacy through his self-imposed role as an 'awkward, independent ideas man'.

Besides his concern to expose the workings of government to a wider audience, it has been submitted that the most significant idea Crossman chased was national superannuation. As will be examined in detail in future chapters, in his near two-decade pursuit of this idea – one that was predominantly concerned with improved provision for future generations of state pensioners – Crossman made an impression on the welfare policy process far deeper than could have been expected when he made that career-making speech to the Labour Party Conference in 1955. However, rather like the events in Gabriel Chavallier's delightful *Clochemerle*,[128] once a fateful idea has surfaced – in the fictional adventure, to construct a public latrine – events tend to take unexpected turns, and the final outcomes which follow from initial decisions often have little to do with original intentions. In *Clochemerle*, the end result was the fall of the French government. As will be illustrated, in Crossman's case, the outcome was less dramatic, but equally unanticipated.

As important as introducing the study's main protagonist, the additional job of this chapter was to put into context the limited role in the policy process that can be played by any one individual. To achieve this, Anthony Seldon's four-fold approach to explaining policy change was introduced, one in which explanatory weight is granted to individuals but also to ideas, circumstances, and interests. As Seldon stresses, any account that fails to account for all these possible causes for change 'provides but a partial reading of events'.[129] To avoid this fate, every attempt will be made to incorporate each factor fully into this tale. To that end, this study – in addition to following Crossman's unusual career – will include an examination of two particular meso-level ideas with which he was associated, national superannuation and, to a lesser extent, the income guarantee. An analysis will also be made of the roles played by other significant, if less recognised, individuals such as Brian Abel-Smith. Furthermore, the impact of particular circumstances will be examined, in particular the constraints on policy-makers resulting from past decisions. In addition, the pressure that emanated from the trade unions, business groups, and political parties will be assessed, and the role of the civil service appraised. And links to contemporary social policy will be made. That should be enough.

2   CHALLENGING BEVERIDGE

At the Labour Party Conference of 1955, during a routine debate on the topic of national insurance, Richard Crossman – with uncharacteristic nervousness – rose to reply on behalf of the NEC. The next fifteen minutes was to change the general perception of Crossman within his own party and elsewhere, surprising the many that believed him to be little more than a troublesome meddler. He made this record of the event:

> When I got up to reply, there was not a single clap, mainly, I think, because they couldn't see who was replying but also because they weren't interested and wondered why on earth I was doing it. Apparently I cannot have looked at my notes because I was congratulated warmly on speaking without them and asked how I could deal with such a complex subject without preparation! By the time we got back to the Grand Hotel, I knew that we had had a real political success, having been congratulated by Hugh Gaitskell, Sam Watson, Clem Attlee, Maggie Stewart and, not least, by Sydney Jacobson and Bill Connor, who were absolutely astounded at what had happened and didn't trouble to disguise it. Strange what a difference a quarter of an hour can make in one's life! After that I was a potential minister! It only shows on what flimsy evidence people base their estimates of one's capacity.[1]

Certainly Crossman's performance is interesting as an example of the way a single speech can transform a political career – and still can, negatively as well as positively, as disappointed Tory leadership hopeful David Davies discovered at the Conservative Party Conference in 2005. However, the real significance of Crossman's little speech was that it prompted the mass ranks of the Labour Party to look critically at the national insurance system the Attlee government had introduced less than a decade earlier. He was suggesting that this generally popular scheme, which the succeeding Conservative governments had not really altered, was fatally flawed – particularly in relation to pension provision – and required reconstructing. Crossman, understandably, had no expectation that this message of Labour policy failure would be received so rapturously. That it was requires explanation. A description of the system about which Crossman was so critical can start this process.

THE BEVERIDGE MODEL OF NATIONAL INSURANCE

The system which Crossman took to task in 1955 was one associated with the name Sir William (from 1946, Lord) Beveridge; though, as will be made clear, despite this system bearing his name, it was, in reality, only a partial reflection of Beveridge's original concept. To provide some background, Beveridge had been a key civil servant during the social reforms undertaken by Liberal governments during the earliest decades of the twentieth century and later was an important figure in the academic world. He had been keen to offer his assistance to the government during the Second World War. This offer of help was not one accepted with overwhelming alacrity, and, in 1941, Beveridge found himself very unhappily nudged into the seemingly innocuous position of chairing the interdepartmental Committee on Social Insurance and Allied Services.[2] Surprisingly, Beveridge transformed what appeared to be a worthy but rather dull exercise examining the state's rather muddled system of social security into something much more adventurous. Indeed, by his efforts, Beveridge eventually became regarded by many 'as the "Father of the Welfare State" and as the presiding genius of modern social security'.[3]

At the start of this process few would have anticipated Beveridge's later near-deification. His job was to tidy things up, not create a revolution. And, in 1941, there was much sorting out to do. As

Beveridge's biographer, Jose Harris, notes, in that year, 'no less than seven government departments were directly or indirectly concerned with administering cash benefits for different kinds of need'.[4] The provision of old age pensions was particularly messy. Some pensioners, seventy and older, received a non-contributory pension (that is, one paid for out of general taxation), based on legislation from 1908. Some, aged between sixty-five and seventy, received a contributory pension (that is, one based on a system of insurance) by virtue of legislation introduced in 1925. And others, seventy and over, received an non-contributory pension by virtue of the 1908 Act, but did so through contribution rights laid out in the 1925 legislation. To confuse matters still further, in 1940 the government reduced the pensionable age for insured women and wives of contributors to sixty, and introduced a means-tested supplementary pension for the poorest claimants.[5]

Understandably, Beveridge was keen to simplify this confusing state of affairs. The primary vehicle proposed for this clarification was the establishment of a universal system of national insurance to vanquish 'Want', one of Beveridge's famous 'five giants' – the others being 'Disease, Ignorance, Squalor and Idleness'.[6] To that end, Beveridge introduced the idea of a 'national minimum' with the aim that nobody should live below a particular level of subsistence. Mass means-tested provision was to become a relic of the past. The idea was that, in return for a weekly contribution, the state would secure sufficient income for those whose earnings had been interrupted by unemployment, sickness or an accident. Furthermore, the state would provide for retirement, for those who had lost a spouse, and would help 'to meet exceptional expenditures, such as those connected with birth, death and marriage'.[7] In the popular phrase of the time, Beveridge envisaged the state providing support 'from cradle to the grave'.

Beveridge was adamant that, with only rare exceptions, 'All insured persons, rich or poor, will pay the same contributions for the same security'.[8] He considered an alternative system in which contributions were related to income to be a form of income tax by another name, and this, in his eyes, went against the notion of national insurance. Similarly, all benefits were to be set at a flat rate, and at the same rate regardless of reasons for the claim. In addition, Beveridge suggested that all contributions – from individuals, employers, and the state – should be paid into a single, distinct, actuarially sound 'Social Insurance Fund'.[9] Beveridge foresaw the continuation of means-tested provision, but not, as before, as a central pillar of the social security scheme, but rather as a safety net to meet abnormal subsistence needs.[10] More widely, to take on some of those other 'giants', Beveridge suggested that the state should provide comprehensive and universal health care and that it should attempt to maintain full employment, a measure that was of crucial importance to the financial viability of the whole scheme.[11] In short, Beveridge was advocating what became known as the welfare state – a term which, ironically, Sir William himself disliked.

The *Report on Social Insurance and Allied Services* – or, as it quickly became known, the Beveridge Report – was published in December 1942, and became hugely popular with the public. Indeed, as Nicholas Timmins notes, it took the salacious charms of Lord Denning's report on the Profumo scandal for an official paper finally to beat the sales – some 635,000 copies – accomplished by Beveridge's effort.[12] The expectations many people attached to this report – mingled with the feeling of optimism resulting from the recent Allied victory at El Alamein – was considerable, and, as Pat Thane argues, the Beveridge Report itself 'came to symbolize the widespread hopes for a different, more just world'.[13] Certainly, as Harris suggests, the Beveridge Report did become 'the most popular blueprint for social reform ever produced in Britain'.[14]

However, despite the popular response to the Beveridge Report, the wartime coalition government proceeded very cautiously. Progress accelerated following the general election of July 1945, after which Clement Attlee was able to form a Labour government that enjoyed, for the first time in its history, a clear parliamentary majority. The National Insurance Act was passed the following year, establishing the universal system of flat-rate benefits that Beveridge had advocated. The companion National Assistance Act, which supported the insurance-based scheme with a means-tested 'safety-net', was passed in 1948.

However, not all of Beveridge's recommendations were acted upon, and this was to cause some problems for the future. One significant break from Beveridge's original proposals was the abandonment of the financially prudent suggestion that full pensions would not be available until recipients had contributed for twenty years to the Social

Fund. Instead, full pensions were paid immediately to those insured since 1925, and after only ten years for those who joined later. This breach of actuarial propriety was considered a political inevitability. As the first Minister of National Insurance, James Griffiths, explained, those who had retired – or were about to retire – had faced two world wars and the depression, and thus 'deserved well of the nation and should not wait for twenty years'.[15] However, this action did seriously weaken the financial foundation of the whole scheme, and guaranteed that the Social Insurance Fund, as such, remained a 'fiction'.[16]

A second departure from Beveridge's original proposals was the rejection of the goal of attaching flat-rate cash benefits to subsistence levels. There were a number of impediments to implementing this proposal. One was a lack of agreement regarding what actually determined a reasonable level of subsistence. Another was a realisation that the flat-rate system would make it difficult to maintain anything other than a below-subsistence level of benefits, as contributions could only be as expensive as the lowest-paid workers could afford. Many civil servants felt that the system, as proposed, was 'both illogical and impractical'.[17] One result of the subsequent desertion from this fundamental – if confused – aspect of Beveridge's vision was that means-tested national assistance came to play a much greater role in future welfare provision than many had hoped. It also helped lead to the situation where governments were henceforth under constant pressure from, in particular, pensioners to increase their inadequate level of standard benefit.[18] This situation was not helped by Treasury insistence that the state subsidy to the national insurance system be set at a level lower than Beveridge had recommended.

One further outcome of Beveridge's flat-rate system was the fillip it gave to the private pension industry. To explain, during the first half of the twentieth century the number of pensions provided outside the state system had increased gently, having been given the odd prod of encouragement by the state itself – notably through the Finance Act of 1921 which provided some tax relief on pension fund contribution.[19] By the time of the Beveridge Report, it was noted that this sector was 'substantial in itself though small in proportion to the total numbers of persons of pensionable age'.[20] The flat-rate nature of the pension suggested that what the state could offer would never be generous, and this meant that many wealthier individuals continued to seek out additional income on retirement. Indeed,

Beveridge suggested that the system bearing his name 'should leave room and encouragement for voluntary action' so that individuals could augment what the state was willing to provide.[21] Many took heed, with the percentage of the work force covered by occupational pension schemes rising from 13 per cent in 1936 to 33 per cent by 1956.[22] As will be noted later, for later left-wing commentators such as Richard Titmuss, this was to become a serious issue of concern.

Thus some difficulties for the future were prompted by breaches to Beveridge's original proposal, such as the failure to establish an actuarially sound national insurance fund, and others were born of the Beveridge Report itself, such as the faith shown in the efficacy of the flat-rate system. A further problem associated with Beveridge himself was his insistence that the insurance principle was to remain at the heart of the British system of welfare. The insurance principle had been a crucial element in the British system of state welfare ever since Herbert Asquith's Liberal government had introduced the National Insurance Act in 1911 – a piece of legislation which Beveridge, as a civil servant, contributed to creating. This Act compelled many employees, including all manual workers, to pay a contribution – supplemented by employer and state, the famous '9d. for 4d.' – in return for health and unemployment insurance. In 1925, the Widows', Orphans' and Old Age Contributory Pensions Act expanded this insurance scheme to include old age pensions. Therefore, by advocating his universal National Insurance scheme, Beveridge was, in some ways, only suggesting an expansion of the existing system. Unfortunately, this existing system contained a significant flaw. Like all insurance-based social security schemes, they tend to work satisfactorily for those in regular employment, but much less satisfactorily for those who are not. Women, in particular, tend to be put at a considerable disadvantage.

In short, for all its strengths and obvious popularity, the model of social security inspired by the Beveridge Report had its faults; these weaknesses resulted both from the original design and from the changes made to it by the Attlee government. In particular, one widely held concern was that the combination of below-subsistence, flat-rate benefits and a very inflexible flat-rate contributory system had created an unstable situation, not least by encouraging an expansion of means-tested provision. Beveridge himself looked on aghast at this development. In 1953, from his position on the Liberal benches of the House of Lords, Beveridge was moved to remark that 'National Assistance, which the experts and I thought would have to continue on a small scale but would gradually diminish, so far from diminishing is increasing year by year'.[23] He added that social security was still, in many cases, not being provided 'as a right in virtue of contributions of insurance' but, rather, was still a matter of 'poor relief'.[24] In consequence, only a few years after the implementation of the National Insurance Act, proposals came in thick and fast to knock the Beveridge system down.

SUGGESTIONS FOR REFORM

Two particular issues in particular grabbed the attention of those interested in reforming the UK social security system of the early 1950s. One, as Beveridge lamented, was the continuing inadequacy of standard benefits. The other problem, perceived most acutely in the Treasury, was cost. Pensions were a particular concern as the failure to establish a fully funded system, combined with increasing longevity, suggested that the Exchequer would have to carry an ever-expanding financial burden. A number of individuals, from across the political spectrum, responded to these problems.

One particularly influential response came from two rising stars of the political right, Iain Macleod and Enoch Powell, both then working in the Conservative Central Office. Their paramount concern was rising cost, which, they argued, amounted to a 'crisis in the social services'.[25] Rather against the spirit of the time, even amongst mainstream Conservatives, Macleod and Powell suggested that one possible solution to the financial problem was to move away from the universalistic regime that Beveridge had initiated, and head instead toward a more targeted approach to social security. As they expressed it: 'The question which therefore poses itself is not should a means test be applied to a social service, but why should any service be provided without a test of means'.[26]

Unsurprisingly the work of Macleod and Powell sparked a response from the left. One of the most imaginative of these ripostes came in the form of a Fabian pamphlet entitled *The Reform of Social Security*, published in September 1953. Its author was a then twenty-six years old researcher with the National Institute of Economic and Social Research, and his name was Brian Abel-Smith. Though largely ignored at the time, Abel-Smith's publication became significant because it was later acknowledged, by Crossman, as the genesis of the rather more conspicuous national superannuation scheme.[27]

In *The Reform of Social Security*, Abel-Smith provided a stark critique of the existing system. He wrote, 'In spite of all the plans, hopes and dreams of the past ten years we have failed to abolish all want, to meet all need. This bleak truth is a challenge to every Socialist'.[28] Abel-Smith's proposed solution to this – at this stage – largely ignored problem was, unsurprisingly, not the means-tested one favoured by Macleod and Powell. Abel-Smith regarded the means test as a device that perpetuated the class divide, was unfair on savers, was expensive in terms of manpower, and engendered a sense of injustice. He dubbed it 'a hangover from the old Poor Law',[29] and warned, with his eye on Macleod and Powell, that 'the Labour Party must be on its guard against reactionary plans for "reform"'.[30] However, very significantly, Abel-Smith did not regard only the reforms suggested by these two Conservatives as unsuitable. He also criticised existing Labour plans, which, at that time, tended to be restricted to calls for greater generosity of benefits within the confines of the existing system. He realised that to achieve any significant increase in the level of benefits would, necessarily, involve a significant rise in the rate of contribution, and that this would, inevitably in a flat-rate system, place 'a heavy burden on the lower paid worker'.[31] Instead, in the most significant of his many proposals, Abel-Smith suggested retaining national insurance but, rather than stick with the problematic flat-rate system, it should be altered to one that included 'variable contributions and variable benefits connected to them'.[32]

Abel-Smith acknowledged the Swiss Old Age and Survivors' Scheme as the inspiration for this idea of an earnings-related social insurance system. The particular advantage of the Swiss model for a socialist such as Abel-Smith was that it lessened the usual problem of such systems when it comes to the issue of pensions: the continuation, or even exacerbation, of the often stark income differentials found in work into retirement. The Swiss model achieved mitigation, though not elimination, of inequality by including a minimum pension, to be paid almost irrespective of contribution record, and a maximum pension, worth only twice the amount of the minimum.[33]

That an earnings-related system – at least one based on the Swiss model – could, ironically, lessen inequality in old age was a crucial factor in attracting some on the left, eventually, to appreciate the concept. Growing concern that the current flat-rate system was itself causing considerable inequality helped here. It was Abel-Smith's future colleague at the LSE, Richard Titmuss, who successfully alerted the public to the growing problem of what he termed 'two nations in old age'.[34] He was concerned that the existing flat-rate system in the UK was, contrary to original hopes, creating 'greater inequalities in living standards after work than in work'.[35] As noted earlier, it was the growth in private pensions that accounted for this paradox, with Titmuss contrasting the 'generous provision which society is earmarking for the future benefit of the professional, executive, and salaried classes', largely through tax breaks for certain private pension schemes, with the 'relatively meagre National Insurance pension, fast becoming the new Poor Law'.[36]

Abel-Smith was certainly aware of this concern when writing *The Reform of Social Security*. Indeed, echoing Disraeli and pre-empting Titmuss, Abel-Smith remarked that 'Britain in adversity is still two nations'.[37] Furthermore, when focusing particularly on provision for retirement, he noted that:

> Private superannuation schemes for the salaried and the upper crust of workers are growing so fast that the provision for old age through the state system is gradually becoming a sump for those excluded from other superannuation arrangements, be it by grade or occupation.[38]

Thus some form of Swiss-style earnings-relation – which allowed for a more flexible system than the UK's flat-rate model without too glaringly transferring the inequities of income into retirement – was regarded by Abel-Smith, and, a little later, by Titmuss himself as a possible solution to this problem.

The issue of inequality manifested itself in another influential aspect of Abel-Smith's proposal: the goal to create a scheme that incorporated virtually everybody, without the need for supplementation, either through a means test or from the private sector. 'Social security as understood by the left', Abel-Smith argued, 'must provide benefits which are adequate and bear some reasonable and consistent rela-tionship to the cost of living; and it must provide benefits which are shared by all classes'.[39] To highlight this latter solidaristic goal still further, Abel-Smith cited Barbara Wootton when she suggested that:

> The strongest argument for showering gifts upon rich and poor alike is that nobody need then know who is poor, and who is not. That, however, is an argument from egalitarian premises; and as such it has an academic ring if the rich prefer to continue to look after themselves, and are also left free to do so. Real equality is only achieved when all classes not only can, but do, use the same services.[40]

Thus, for Abel-Smith, a fair system of social security was not so much one primarily concerned about redistribution, but, rather, a regime that would be used by all classes, not just the poor, in a manner similar to the National Health Service.

The next stage in the development of Abel-Smith's scheme came in March 1955 with the publication of another Fabian pamphlet, *New Pensions for the Old*,[41] written by Abel-Smith and Peter Townsend. *New Pensions for the Old* was both a refinement of Abel-Smith's earlier work and a critical response to some official reports reviewing the existing National Insurance system, in particular *The Report of the Committee on the Economic and Financial Problems of the Provision of Old Age*, published a year earlier. To give some background, the Committee on the Economic and Financial Problems of the Provision of Old Age – the Phillips Committee, as it was usually known – was established by the Conservative government with the ambition of creating solutions to some of the perceived failings of the current system. Restraining rising costs was considered a priority. Contradicting Beveridge, the Phillips Committee boldly announced that:

> A contributory scheme cannot, in our view, be expected to provide a rate of benefit which would enable everybody, whatever their circumstances, to live without other resources, either by their own providing or by way of national assistance'.[42]

The solutions offered included wholeheartedly embracing means-tested supplementation, the expansion of private pension schemes, and – as noted in the previous chapter – raising the age levels at which state pensions were paid.

Abel-Smith and Townsend were less than impressed by the efforts of the Phillips Committee, and were keen to provide a coherent alternative to the vision of the future outlined by it. This was largely achieved by *New Pensions for the Old*, a pamphlet demonstrating a continuation of Abel-Smith's earlier hostility towards the idea of increased means-testing. Indeed, Townsend added to the list of criticisms of national assistance by highlighting the problem of stigma, having 'witnessed the reluctance, and refusal of a substantial minority, of older people in the East End of London to apply for assistance although they would appear to qualify for it under the regulations'.[43] Indeed, he added that no measure of tinkering with the means test would prevent, from many of those most in need, 'the still persistent refrain of not wanting "to plead poverty"'.[44]

For Abel-Smith and Townsend, the paramount problem remained that of 'two nations in old age': namely the 'aged rich' who could draw on occupational pensions, and the 'aged poor' who had no other pension on which to draw other than the basic state version.[45] They argued that, 'In any general scheme for social security, citizens should stand together without regard to difference of status, function or wealth'.[46] Thus the 1955 pamphlet took Abel-Smith's original solution, and expanded it to its logical conclusion by explicitly suggesting a future state insurance system based on earnings-related contributions and benefits. Furthermore, it was here that the term 'National Superannuation' was first used, with the explanation that the state will 'make the principles of private superannuation fulfil the needs of a national social service'.[47] Though the authors admitted that 'much thought needs to be given to details',[48] they did suggest two ways in which future schemes could be designed to incorporate, at least in part, earnings-relation. One such model would be based on a two-tier system in which the basic flat-rate pension was maintained but bolstered by an earnings-related supplement. The other possible scheme would include a wholly earnings-related pension, though one supported by a basic minimum.[49] Interestingly, as will be developed in later chapters, both these alternatives were taken up by future pension policy-makers when designing pension schemes.

Though the concept of national superannuation was put forward with a little less hesitancy in 1955 than it was in 1953, there remained some wariness. Certainly much thought was given to justifying a scheme that, on the face of it, perpetuated inequalities into old age. Abel-Smith and Townsend's case was that, though their proposed scheme did indeed include some inequalities, these were less than those fostered by the existing arrangements, despite the presence of the flat-rate principle. As the two authors put it:

when we take a broad view of the economic provision of old age, including occupational pension schemes, it is seen at once that this flat-rate principle has never been applied. And indeed, it is illogical that it should be applied as long as there are differentials in earnings. If earnings in working life were absolutely equal, only then would flat-rate provision for old age be a sacrosanct corollary. The least we can do is ensure that there are not more inequalities in old age than in working life.[50]

Despite the lingering diffidence, by 1955 national superannuation was, if still far from concrete in terms of detail, then at least a fairly coherent concept – a state pension scheme with some element of earnings-relation designed to include almost everyone without the necessity of public or private supplementation. However, national superannuation was just one of a number of ideas bobbing about in what John Kingdon would call the 'policy primeval soup'.[51] The fate of many such schemes is to remain largely ignored, perhaps only attracting the interest of a few policy specialists. For national super-annuation, the future was more eventful. Indeed, for a little while at least, national superannuation was a matter of national debate. That this was so was largely down to the efforts of one idiosyncratic Opposition backbencher, Richard Crossman.

CROSSMAN AND 'THE END OF BEVERIDGE'

According to Crossman's own account, his association with the policy that was to make his political name began rather by chance. He claimed that the then Chair of the Labour Party, Dame Edith Summerskill, inveigled him into replying, on behalf of the NEC, to a series of awkward resolutions at the 1955 Party Conference. They were awkward because all these resolutions demanded a large increase in the flat-rate pension and, in Crossman's own words, 'We all knew that we could not commit the next Labour Government to this because it was too expensive'.[52] Thus Crossman expected that his 'first experience of speaking for the Executive at the Conference was going to result in a defeat of the platform by the floor'.[53] At this low ebb, the night before the debate, he met Peter Shore, then head of Labour's research department, who mentioned the work of Abel-Smith and Townsend. So, again in Crossman's own words:

I took it [*New Pensions for the Old*] to bed. Now there come times in the life of an intellectual when illumination happens. I read that pamphlet. I understood it. I'm not very good usually at economics but I understood it. With a blinding flash I understood national superannuation.[54]

The following day Crossman turned potential embarrassment into the resounding and surprising success noted earlier in this chapter. He achieved this by persuading the Conference that the existing social security system was flawed, and that it should postpone committing itself to the flat-rate increase until it had had a chance to examine 'this new marvellous idea'.[55] And, as such votes then compelled the NEC to submit a fleshed-out proposal on the lines agreed to a future Conference, '[b]efore the day was over the National Executive were saddled with national superannuation'.[56] Crossman, with characteristic candour, went on to report that there was considerable ignorance about national superannuation itself: 'Nobody had heard of it. They said, "What is it?" I said, "I'm not sure myself, I've got a pamphlet on it. I've just read it. It's marvellous"'.[57]

It is possible that Crossman did indeed only seriously examine the work of Abel-Smith and Townsend on the eve of his famous Conference speech – though his *Diaries* suggest rather more preparedness than his later comments would imply.[58] It is certainly the case – despite the naive tone used in his recollection of the events of 1955 – that Crossman had been familiar with the key social security debates for some time. Moreover, he had already engaged in some striking public criticism of the Beveridge system.

As early as 1952 Crossman had had words to say about social policy, when he edited the *New Fabian Essays*, a work still regarded by some as the seminal exposition of the welfare state through the perspective of Fabian theory[59] – though, as will become clear, Crossman himself was critical of particular aspects of Fabianism. To give a little background about this very influential – if vague – perspective, the original Fabian Society was established in the 1880s, and came to include such middle-class intellectuals as Beatrice and Sidney Webb and George Bernard Shaw. Though regarded as a broadly socialist theory – it was indeed Sidney Webb who drafted, in 1918, the famous Clause 4, which formally committed the Labour Party to the public ownership of industry – Fabianism did accept the continued existence of the market, and that of political institutions such as Parliament. Fabians believed the state to be a neutral vehicle, which, in the right hands, could be used to regulate capitalism and gradually reduce inequality.[60]

The heyday of Fabian influence was immediately after the 1945 election, and Crossman noted two principles from within the Fabian tradition that guided the Attlee government:

> The first states that it is the responsibility of the democratic state to provide for every citizen, as of right, security against unemployment, sickness and old age. The second runs that it is the function of the state to plan the use of our natural resources so as to maintain work for all and ensure fair shares of the national income between different sections of the community.[61]

Crossman also argued, in a familiarly Fabian fashion, that 'The true aim of the Labour Movement has always been not the dramatic capture of power by the working class, but the conversion of the nation to the socialist pattern of rights and values'.[62]

Significantly though, Crossman felt there were important problems with the system established by Attlee. He believed the most pressing of these flaws to be the failure to encourage popular participation within the new institutions, not least the welfare state. Breaking away from the traditional faith displayed by Fabians towards the status of the 'expert administrator',[63] Crossman declared that, 'The main task of socialism today is to prevent the concentration of power in the hands of *either* industrial management *or* state bureaucracy'.[64] Again drawing away from the classic Fabian approach, Crossman also suggested that Britain was a disagreeably elitist state; a situation he thought not improved by the impression given by the Attlee government that:

> socialism was an affair for the Cabinet, acting through the existing Civil Service. The rest of the nation was to carry on as before, while benefits were bestowed from above upon some, and taken from others.[65]

As was typical of Crossman throughout his career, he believed a solution could be found by having as many people as possible participating in the control of institutions, 'even at the cost of "efficiency"'.[66]

Though very little in Crossman's contribution to the *New Fabian Essays* was directly relevant to the social security debate with which he became involved a few years later, his chapter did demonstrate his engagement with the general area of social policy, and his willingness to censure the existing welfare regime. His criticism of 'a nation deeply imbued with a sense of social status and inhibited by an oligarchic tradition'[67] also suggests why, later, he was immediately attracted to national superannuation. As noted earlier, this scheme – created by two fellow members of the Fabian Society – was expressly designed with the intention of lessening the type of social segregation that so displeased Crossman. Indeed, as Crossman much later elaborated, the philosophy behind national superannuation fitted his own ideological perspective so comfortably that he declared that it was with this scheme that 'I found my ideal of socialism'.[68] That ideal was, in his words, 'the transformation of economic privileges into citizens' rights';[69] that is, as mentioned in the previous chapter in the discussion of 'M&S' socialism, Crossman was not so much interested in the goal of redistribution, but rather, in taking something that a small group of citizens found desirable – in this case, a good company pension – and developing it in a way so that everyone in society could profit by it.

Though the *New Fabian Essays* displayed that Crossman's attention had spread well beyond his earlier preoccupation with foreign affairs, it was not, according to his long-term editor Janet Morgan, until late 1954 that Crossman became 'deeply interested' in the debate on national insurance[70] – though, interestingly, Crossman had, since December 1953, been a member of the National Executive's Social Services Sub-Committee.[71] Whenever it was that Crossman's new passion was kindled, it gained its most vivid illustration in a piece Crossman wrote for the *New Statesman and Nation* in December 1954, one that bore the startling title, 'The End of Beveridge'.[72] And just to emphasise the point raised by this provocative title, Crossman concluded the first paragraph of the article with an unambiguous declaration that 'the Beveridge method has run into a dead-end'.[73]

In this piece for the *New Statesman*, Crossman covered much of the ground already laid out by Titmuss, Abel-Smith, and Townsend. He noted the failure of reformers to create a 'real' insurance scheme; that is, one based on coherent actuarial principles. He added that recent reforms proposed by the Conservatives would only have the effect of 'destroying the last pretence that the level of contributions is in any way related to the level of benefits'.[74] He was also very critical of the acceptance by the government that national insurance benefits would not, without other resources, provide a full rate of subsistence. He noted witheringly that, 'About 1.2 million people have had to have their Insurance benefits supplemented, and nearly one million of these have been retirement pensioners'.[75] In addition, Crossman – very clearly echoing Titmuss – suggested that Britain was quickly moving towards a position where there would be 'greater inequalities in old age than in working life, between those whose income rests ultimately on a means-test and the salary earners whose retirement income is related to the income of their final working years'.[76] He continued this point by posing a question that enjoys considerable resonance over fifty years later: 'Is the task of providing real security for old age to be turned over to private insurance companies?'.[77]

Crossman's eagerness to prompt the Labour Party into launching the wrecking ball into the existing system of social security was made clear in the article's rallying call: 'Now that the Beveridge Plan, whose ideas were obsolete when it was written, has been amended out of all recognition, the time has come for the Labour Party to make a fresh start'.[78] It is noticeable that Crossman did not mention, by name, the possibility of this 'fresh start' being based on the concept of earnings-relation, nevertheless, it is clear from his conclusion that he was thinking along these lines. After a suggestion that provision for old age in particular needed serious reassessment, Crossman argued that, 'We shall have to examine the social implications of the present expansion of private schemes, and ask whether the principle of flat-rate benefits and contributions is the right one'.[79] So, maybe, on the eve of his career-making speech Crossman was fresh to *New Pensions for the Old*, but the arguments and ideas enunciated in that pamphlet were, to a considerable extent, already very familiar.

THE 1955 LABOUR PARTY CONFERENCE

Thus it was at the Labour Party Conference of October 1955 that Crossman – with rather more preparation than he later suggested – first sprung the ideas of Abel-Smith and Townsend on a wider audience. As suggested earlier, these ideas went down surprisingly well – surprising because the central idea of earnings-related benefits was, as Crossman himself noted, 'an unpopular concept'.[80] Moreover, Crossman did not try to hide this idea in his speech. The audience was told bluntly that the existing system included a number of flaws – the most grievous being its reliance on 'a flat rate poll tax'[81] – and that it needed replacing, ideally with a system based on 'the principle of superannuation'.[82] He also went on to explain carefully what this principle amounted to: 'each person being allowed to contribute year by year while he is working to a scheme which assures him that he will be able to have – let us put it this way, because most salaried people expect this – at least half pay'.[83] There was every reason for Crossman to expect a rough ride, yet he had the Conference lapping up his words.

Clearly – on a good day – Crossman was a dazzling performer, with a style honed by years in the lecture hall, but his success at the 1955 Conference can also be attributed to another factor. The message Crossman was delivering appeared to get the Labour Party out of a big hole. As has been made clear, it had been obvious for a number of years that the Beveridge system was floundering, and some form of coherent party policy on this issue was necessary. However, for some time before the Conference, the most striking element of Labour's policy on national insurance, particularly the crucial issue of pensions, was its singular lack of coherence. Indeed, as Heclo notes, 'so divided was the labo[u]r movement that it fought the May 1955 election without any agreed pension policy'.[84] So it was, until Crossman's intervention, that division rather than unity marked Labour's policy towards national insurance.

As Crossman candidly pointed out in his speech, within the labour movement at that time – indeed, just within the National Executive itself – there were, in fact, three opposing points of view regarding the fate of national insurance, and all three were on show at the Conference.[85] One faction was represented by the totemic figure of Aneurin Bevan. Bevan had, for a number of years, been critical of the national insurance system, picking at a particular paradox of this supposedly universal regime with the question, 'Why should all have contributions cards if *all* are assumed to be insured?'.[86] His radical recommendation was to abolish the insurance principle altogether, suggesting instead that 'the finances should be found by the general

Exchequer'.[87] Another point of view – in vigorous opposition to that of Bevan – was that represented by Sir Alfred Roberts, Chairman of the Trade Union Congress Social Insurance Committee. The TUC tended to remain very faithful to the Beveridge model, and, as Roberts made very plain, there was strong support from this quarter for the idea that workers' contributions to the national insurance scheme provided a safeguard against future governments reducing pension provision.[88] Simply increasing flat-rate contributions – and gaining a greater proportion of support from the Exchequer – was the TUC's answer to the problems facing the national insurance system. The third point of view was that which envisaged an earnings-related scheme of some sort, and Crossman managed to pull off the tricky task of making this, his preferred option, appear both a compromise between the other two alternatives, and attractively radical.

Thus, along with Crossman's rhetorical skill, the fact that factions in the Labour Party were in open hostility over the issue of national insurance was clearly one of the factors that explained the 1955 Conference's surprisingly enthusiastic response to the scheme Crossman advocated. It was regarded as a means of potentially uniting the Party on the issue of social security reform.[89] However, this fraternal fighting also illustrated the fact that the labour movement included many who supported schemes very different to national superannuation, and they were not about to allow this donnish upstart to reconstruct Labour Party policy without some form of fight. Indeed, a rueful Crossman later admitted that much of the social policy planning that occurred after the success of the Conference was taken up by attempting to transform Abel-Smith and Townsend's concept into a form 'which was assimilable both by the great trade union leaders and by the militant left wing'.[90]

The next chapter will focus on the process by which the ideas of Abel-Smith and Townsend were made more palatable to various tastes in the labour movement, and were moulded into a relatively practical political scheme, one which, with Crossman's dynamic championing, came to shape Labour Party social policy for many years. As will also be examined, this scheme – published in 1957 under the title *National Superannuation: Labour's Policy for Security in Old Age* – also provoked a spiky response from the Conservative government.

3   THE CUNNING PLAN

From a public policy perspective, Crossman's speech to the 1955 Labour Party Conference was significant in that it started the process by which the academic ideas articulated by Abel-Smith and Townsend moved from, to use Cobb and Elder's terminology, the 'systemic' agenda to the more formal 'institutional' agenda.[1] In other words, because of the push given by Crossman, national superannuation moved from being a topic chatted about by a few experts to one given serious attention by senior civil servants and ministers. Obviously this process needed more propulsion than just one speech, no matter how barnstorming, to force the still inchoate national superannuation concept into the British political mainstream. The shove necessary to maintain the momentum gained through Crossman's speech was provided by the working body expressly established to come up with a fleshed-out superannuation proposal for a future Labour Party conference. This working body was a sub-committee of the Home Policy Committee of the National Executive, and was formally known as the Study Group on Security and Old Age. The activities of this Study Group, Crossman suggested, violently accelerated the development of the national superannuation concept.[2]

The Study Group held its first meeting on 16 April 1956.[3] Hilary Marquand, a former Minister of Pensions initially chaired it, but, by November of that year, Crossman had taken over this particular responsibility.[4] Among the other politicians to claim membership of the Study Group was the new party leader, Hugh Gaitskell. However, though Gaitskell did play a role in the construction of the plan,[5] he only attended one meeting of the Study Group itself, and that was merely the initial gathering in April. More long-term contributions to the Study Group were made by James Griffiths, Douglas Jay, Margaret Herbison, Edith Summerskill and, from November 1956, the Shadow Chancellor – and future Labour Prime Minister – Harold Wilson. The TUC had representation on the Study Group from the start, and, crucially, academic ballast was provided by Richard Titmuss, who was co-opted onto the Study Group at the first meeting, and Abel-Smith and Townsend, who were to join later. Within a few short months members of the Study Group had constructed a largely coherent policy document in time for the 1957 Labour Party Conference. This pamphlet – largely written by Crossman[6] – was called *National Superannuation: Labour's Policy for Security in Old Age*; and it was a striking document. As Fawcett points out, it proved a rarity amongst Opposition party policy papers 'in being a fully worked out blueprint rather than a statement of general principles and desirable objectives'.[7]

The first edition of *National Superannuation* was published in May 1957, and it arrived in two parts. The first of these was a general statement of policy to be submitted to that year's Labour Party Conference, for which the National Executive took full responsibility. The second part consisted of a largely technical illustration of the way in which principles outlined in the earlier section might work in practice, and this was the sole responsibility of the Study Group's 'technical sub-committee'.[8] This sub-committee consisted of Titmuss, Abel-Smith, and Townsend. According to Crossman, this two-part division was one of Wilson's crafty ideas, designed so that 'We [the Labour Party] shall get all the kudos for their research and they [Titmuss et al.] will be responsible for all the detailed figures'.[9] Despite this division of responsibility, the three academics were the driving force behind the entire document – in Crossman's words, 'They have provided all the dynamic'[10] – a matter not lost on the Conservatives who were quick to dub them 'the skiffle group of professors who had got their sums wrong'.[11]

The most eye-catching proposal in *National Superannuation* was the pledge to provide the average worker a pension worth 50 per cent of their wage, at a time when the existing system only replaced 18 per cent of average male earnings.[12] This followed Crossman's 'half pay' suggestion at the 1955 Conference, and it represented the public birth of Labour's once famous promise to provide 'half-pay on retirement'. More generally, it marked a hugely significant episode in Labour's quirky relationship with the principle of linking social contributions and benefits to the size of an individual's pay packet. As will be illustrated, getting this commitment to establish an earnings-related scheme in print was not straightforward, as many members of the Study Group were initially far from convinced about the merits of the earnings-relation principle itself. Crossman was a key figure in selling the principle to the wary; as he put it himself, 'This was my work; to make the Titmuss academic idea palatable to the Labour politicians and the trade unions'.[13]

THE BIRTH OF 'HALF-PAY ON RETIREMENT'

Minutes from two of the earliest meetings of the Study Group – which display the contributions of individuals before the less transparent practice of merely recording general summations was introduced – demonstrate the difficulties faced by Crossman in his job of sweetening opinion towards national superannuation. At one meeting, in July 1956, Titmuss announced that 'we must either expect occupational pensions and national assistance to become the dominant systems of provision for old age in the future or envisage an entirely new, comprehensive compulsory superannuation scheme'.[14] The response to this challenge from some sections of the Study Group was distinctly hostile.

Objections to the idea of a national superannuation scheme reflected, to an extent, divisions that had surfaced at the 1955 Labour Party Conference. One of these dissenting views – one associated strongly with the trade unions – rejected the claim Titmuss made that preserving the national insurance system would inevitably lead Britain down a regrettable path towards two worlds in retirement. This opinion was expressed by the TUC representative on the Study Group – one C.R. (Dick) Dale – who reminded other members 'that the TUC General Council could not accept the view that the original basis of the [Beveridge] scheme, namely a flat-rate benefit at an adequate subsistence level, could be abandoned'.[15] The other major voice of dissent came from the left of the Labour Party. Following the line taken by Aneurin Bevan at the 1955 Conference, W.H. Clough attacked the contributory nature of the scheme Crossman was proposing. Brandishing a big ideological stick, Clough also argued 'that the graded benefits are not in accordance with best socialist principles', and added that, in his view, 'socialism fought for equality of incomes, and also, therefore, in old age'.[16]

However, despite this chorus of disapproval, within a few months the Study Group had agreed that earnings-relation should form a central tenet of any future Labour government's social policy reform programme. Indeed, as early as September 1956, the specific idea of 'half pay on retirement' had been accepted, with the Study Group recommending that 'a compulsory national superannuation scheme' be established, with the aim that 'benefits under the National Superannuation scheme would increase the National Insurance retirement pension to a level approximating to 50 per cent of earnings'.[17] Clearly Crossman – and others, notably Titmuss – had been very persuasive.

The primary tactic Crossman used to warm the unions towards the idea of national superannuation was compromise. This, however, was not always obvious. At that meeting in July 1956, Crossman was unambiguous in his rejection of the TUC's general position. He quickly responded to Dale's expression of support for the existing system by arguing that the notion that a flat-rate scheme was capable of setting an adequate level of benefit had, in reality, 'long since been abandoned'.[18] Yet, despite this flat dismissal of a flat-rate solution, Crossman did signal some willingness to give some ground to the unions. He announced that 'he was quite prepared to allow the TUC to retain their theories if they permitted some reality in practice'.[19] He had also stated, at an earlier meeting, that, 'It would be ludicrous to scrap the whole present scheme. The Movement seems divided on the issue'.[20]

Thus, from the earliest meetings of the Study Group, Crossman was suggesting the possible survival of the national insurance system of which the unions were so fond, even after the proposed introduction of a national superannuation scheme. Just as significantly, the unions, for their part, also displayed early flexibility. For example, Hilary Marquand noted that some TUC members had privately informed him that they 'did not necessarily object' to the idea of graded contributions for graded benefits.[21] The key result of this mutual accommodation came in September 1956, when the Study Group collectively recommended the establishment of a national super-annuation scheme 'as a supplement to the present National Insurance scheme'.[22]

The recommendation to run an earnings-related scheme in conjunction with the existing flat-rate one was publicly repeated in the following May's *National Superannuation*. The document explained that a two-tier pension scheme was being proposed, one in which the earnings-related element would rest on the existing flat-rate pension scheme; indeed, the authors of *National Superannuation* boldly promised to increase the flat-rate pension by 50 per cent of its existing value. It was also proposed that the entire pension be made 'inflation-proof', by annually adjusting rates 'for changes in prices in accordance with a special pensioners' price index'.[23] This latter proposal Crossman regarded as one of the more laudable and significant parts of the scheme. Despite reservations from Gaitskell, worried by the financial implications of the proposal, Crossman considered it crucial that, as the economy grew, pensioners should be provided with an automatic rise, in order that, in future, they were 'not merely jerked up out of the slough by political pressure every now and then'.[24] Though benefits were to be a combination of flat-rate and earnings-related, the contributory system was to be predominantly earnings-related. Employees, up to a set limit, were to pay contributions worth three per cent of their earnings, employers were to pay a contribution worth five per cent of those earnings, and the Exchequer was to pitch in with a contribution worth two per cent. Indeed, the proposed earnings-related contributions were essential in order to provide the wherewithal with which to fund the proposed 50 per cent increase in the flat-rate pension, as it provided the opportunity to raise contributions immediately without drastically increasing the contribution rate of the less affluent.

Thus radical measures were being proposed, but the decision to maintain the existing national insurance scheme – albeit in conjunction with national superannuation scheme – did strike a discordant note of conservatism. Clearly, in many ways, it would have been easier to scrap the existing system and replace it with a completely earnings-related regime, something that was freely admitted in *National Superannuation*.[25] Moreover, in the document, Titmuss and the other authors did not hide the fact that the opinion of trade unionists – who, they claimed, 'hold tenaciously to the "insurance principle" in their thinking about old age pensions'[26] – was a significant factor in the decision not to abolish national insurance.[27]

However, it should be noted that pressure from the unions was not the only reason for this proposed difficult process of 'welding' together of national insurance and national superannuation. There was also, as Titmuss himself identified, a potentially serious 'transition' problem.[28] It was recognised that starting a new scheme completely afresh would have created, in time, a new generation of pensioners entitled under the superannuation scheme to benefits that were conspicuously better than those still being offered to the older generation of national insurance pensioners. This was considered 'socially unjust'.[29] By attaching superannuation to national insurance, it was argued, such an obvious division between generations of pensioners would be avoided.[30] There was also the point, highlighted by Fawcett, that creating a link between superannuation and the principle of national insurance had the advantage of putting into the margins Bevan's suggestion for funding pensions through direct taxation.[31] Bevan's proposal had never really been considered practical for a reason Crossman mentioned in the 1955 Conference speech, when he remarked, 'I do not know what a Socialist Chancellor of the Exchequer would feel if the first thing he had to do was to raise income tax by 2s. or 3s. in the £ in order to pay for this, and thereby limit all the other jobs we have to do'.[32] Thus, because of a combination of factors, the 1957 proposal for an earnings-related scheme did retain some elements of the Beveridge model. Nevertheless, fundamentally, the scheme illustrated a radical break from traditional Labour policy, and powerfully reinforced the arrival of the principle of earnings-relation into the British social policy process.

Though the emphasis thus far has been on the compromise Crossman displayed in accepting the continuance of national insurance in the new proposals, perhaps the more significant story was that the unions accepted so much of the case for earnings-relation with relatively little dissent. Crossman was certainly expecting some sparring with the unions at an important meeting, held in February 1957, between the TUC Social Services Committee and a deputation from the Study Group. The purpose of this meeting was to discuss a paper on national superannuation. Crossman made a note that, at the given hour, 'sixteen-odd TUC filed solemnly in to do battle'.[33]

In the end, this 'battle' with representatives of the TUC was much less bloody than Crossman had been anticipating. The primary reason for this was the role played by a key individual, Sir Alfred Roberts, the influential head of the TUC Social Insurance Committee – and the primary spokesperson for union support of the insurance principle at the 1955 Conference, and elsewhere. Roberts's influence was such that, a day before the TUC–Study Group meeting, Crossman was told by George Woodcock – then Assistant General Secretary of the TUC – that 'once he [Roberts] accepted the principle of differential contributions, everything was in the bag'.[34] However, at this meeting, Woodcock did not know whether Roberts still retained the traditional TUC antipathy for all things earnings-related. As Crossman reported, with evident relief, it was clear at the following day's meeting that Roberts had indeed been converted. The meeting, Crossman wrote, 'went wonderfully because he [Roberts] started by saying the paper was extremely good, full of clever ideas, which would solve a lot of their problems'.[35] Crossman also went on to note that, 'There was no question on the differential principle, which seems to have been swallowed'.[36]

As will be explained later, Roberts and his union colleagues were not completely won over by all the aspects of the scheme Crossman and Titmuss advocated so strongly.[37] However, he appeared to have bought their arguments about the merits of earnings-relation. At the Labour Party Conference in 1957, Roberts declared, on behalf of the TUC – and, this time, in support of Crossman – that, 'We are prepared to depart from the flat-rate principle because of the hard facts which face us'.[38] At this point he mentioned his unsuccessful two-year negotiations with the Conservative government to try to increase the level of flat-rate pension, and emphasised that there was, henceforth, no guarantee that this pension would ever reach a level of minimum subsistence. He went on to state that, 'because of our examination [of the current pension system] and because of our conversations and discussions with the Labour Party Executive . . . we now endorse the principles of the National Superannuation Scheme'.[39] In short, experience had persuaded Roberts to agree with the conviction held by Titmuss and Crossman that the simple flat-rate system was, in a striking phrase from *National Superannuation*, 'a poll tax, which hurts the poorest most'.[40]

Thus, in the end, with a mix of compromise and convincing argument, the unions – or, at least, some influential figures within the TUC – were won over to Crossman's side of the debate. This was not, of course, the only battle to be fought. The other group that needed to be convinced that the principle of earnings-relation was not the spawn of some particularly devious capitalist devil was one drawn from the more stridently socialist wing of the Labour Party. To this end, Crossman and, in particular, his academic allies went out of their way to highlight the redistributive element of their scheme.

As noted in the previous chapter, from the very start, the fact that earnings-relation appeared to replicate differentials from the pay-packet to the pension was a sore point for many in the Labour Party. This opinion had not altered by 1956, with former Minister of National Insurance and Study Group member, James Griffiths, suggesting 'it would be very difficult to get our people to accept a pension based entirely on earnings'.[41] It was an issue about which the scheme's original creators were sensitive, and, as noted earlier, Abel-Smith and Townsend had already pointed out a partial way out with their recommendation of limiting the earnings-relation effect through the establishment of 'an appropriate minimum and maximum'. To re-cap, this suggestion would have allowed rather more than strict actuarial rules would normally countenance to be given to those who had not been able to contribute very much, and, equally, less to those – at the better-salaried end – who had. Thus, if not actually creating equality in old age, at least this version of earnings-relation appeared to promise less inequality in old age than existed in the Beveridge system. This was the point Titmuss was trying to make when attempting to win over sceptical socialists in the Study Group with the argument that, with an earnings-related scheme, 'although we must accept differentials in working life, we can narrow differentials in old age'.[42] Incidentally, Crossman took a more direct approach to heading off accusations that earnings-relation was not in accord with socialist principle, bluntly stating that, 'as the Movement did not believe in equality of wages . . . no principle was involved'.[43]

It was at the 4 July 1956 meeting of the Study Group that W.H. Clough – the committee member who had vigorously denounced earnings-relation for lacking socialist credentials – queried whether a 'top and bottom level' would be included in the scheme.[44] The minutes record that the Study Group 'generally agreed that this should be the case'.[45] It was then over to Titmuss and the rest of the 'skiffle group' to work out the details. In response, the academics suggested, firstly, the imposition into the scheme of what they dubbed 'a *ceiling*', a level beyond which contributions would not be payable and, thus, benefits would not be available, and 'a *floor*', a level below which no pension would be permitted to fall.[46] Regarding the ceiling, this was to be set at a rate of four times the average wage. Significantly, in the technical memorandum in the second part of *National Superannuation*, it was recommended that the maximum pension should only reach 'about 50 per cent above average industrial earnings'.[47] This difference between levels of contributions and benefits would have granted the potential for a very significant amount of redistribution. And it would have been necessary, as the minimum pension recommended – one of '£3 a week for a single person'[48] – represented, as noted earlier, a 50 per cent increase on the existing flat-rate pension. A possible result of this, according to Fawcett, was that 'a low-paid worker would receive a higher income on retirement than which s/he had earned during their working lives'.[49] In essence, the 'skiffle group' was demonstrating that a national superannuation scheme could be skewed into what might today be dubbed a 'stealth tax', a vehicle to redistribute wealth almost surreptitiously.

Despite the best efforts of the authors of *National Superannuation*, not everyone in the labour movement was convinced by their claim that the scheme was 'not only good economics; it is good socialist ethics too'.[50] At the 1957 Labour Party Conference, the one in which the scheme was presented for approval, one speaker – a certain C.N. Scott of East Renfrewshire – claimed that, 'It is not a socialist scheme; it contains not the merest nuance of Socialism', and asked the National Executive to take this 'clever actuarial distortion' away.[51] Crossman was having none of this. Indeed, at one point in his speech, Crossman suggested that, regarding benefits, 'the only anxiety I have is that when the better paid workers look at the amount of redistribution under the scheme they may jib and call it *too socialist*. . .'.[52] Sir Alfred Roberts, supporting Crossman's line, was more measured. Comparing the proposed scheme to existing provision, Roberts suggested that at least the earnings-relation on offer allowed 'a measure of some equality in the sense that you provide more for those people who are not able to pay more, and a little less for those people who have been able to save during their working lives'.[53] The combined efforts of Crossman and Roberts were enough for the Conference; national superannuation was carried.

With that decision of the Conference, earnings-relation – for the first time – formally became a central pillar of social policy reform for one of Britain's two main political parties. It was, it should be noted, a fairly idiosyncratic version of the concept; it certainly did not much resemble superannuation schemes sold by the private sector. In the Labour Party's scheme, contributions were to be genuinely earnings-related, but only up to the ceiling, and, in effect, benefits would only have been earnings-related for those – the more affluent – in receipt of the supplementary tier of pension provision. Furthermore, as regularly pointed out, the less affluent would have fared rather better under this version of superannuation than they would under a private earnings-related scheme, and the wealthy, rather less. This skewing of the principle was the result of maintaining a national insurance scheme within the overall system and of trying to incorporate within it a considerable element of redistribution. But, as Crossman accepted, to move the scheme forward, it had to be made acceptable to both 'the great trade union leaders and . . . the militant left wing',[54] and complicating the earnings-relation principle in this manner was a necessary part of this process.

THE ROLE OF THE PRIVATE SECTOR

Besides the issue of earnings-relation, probably the most significant issue that faced the Study Group was what to do about the pension schemes provided by the private sector. As noted earlier, the introduction of the Beveridge system had done nothing to halt the expansion in the numbers seeking to augment their state pensions with products from the private sector.[55] Of particular note were the increasing numbers of industrial and clerical workers, not least in the newly nationalised industries, able to claim some superannuation benefit come retirement time. It was this growth in occupational schemes – running parallel with the expansion in the numbers of those forced to seek means-tested benefit in addition to their state pension – which first turned the attention of Titmuss towards the problem of 'two nations in old age'. The proposals discussed earlier to introduce earnings-relation would have tackled some of the problems relating to the less fortunate 'nation'. In particular, the proposed 50 per cent increase in the minimum pension would have done much to lift many pensioners out of the need for means-tested support. However, these proposals, in isolation, would have done little to halt the expansion of the more privileged 'nation', particularly as the type of earnings-relation on offer was, as noted, a twisted version, one designed to allow for significant redistribution – not something any private scheme had to attempt. The wealthy, it would be supposed, would not join the state scheme if more lucrative versions existed outside the state, and yet, in order for the state scheme to work, the wealthy were needed for their contributions.[56] Thus, finding a method of keeping the more affluent in the proposed national scheme, without provoking a deeply unpopular reaction, became a critical issue.

In the Study Group, Crossman was the first to raise the issue of private pensions, with the simple query: 'how are we going to get over the problem of private superannuation schemes alongside a national scheme'.[57] It was Titmuss who replied to this question, but his response was rather vague. He merely suggested that the 'national scheme should be so satisfactory that the employers would have no incentive to run their own schemes in competition'.[58] Thus, discounting the option of abolishing private superannuation schemes, Titmuss simply hoped that the salaried classes would eventually join the state scheme through a rather nebulous process of 'attraction'.[59]

Titmuss's response, unsurprisingly, did not end the matter. At the following meeting of the Study Group, the issue of private schemes was raised once again, this time with Douglas Jay, a former minister at the Treasury, asking the crucial question. It was phrased with more precision than Crossman's earlier effort, with Jay arguing that 'we must decide whether to superimpose national superannuation schemes over the existing ones or whether the private ones should be abolished'.[60] Superimposition, rather than abolition, appeared to be Jay's preferred option. However, he also argued that to attract the wealthier into the scheme, a benefit rate of approximately two-thirds earnings would be necessary. And, as Jay himself pointed out, the problem with this suggestion was that, in order to make this level of benefit possible without raising the contribution rate too steeply, the Treasury would have to pitch in to a much greater extent than before. This, in turn, would have led to a significant increase in the rate of direct taxation, up to a level Jay doubted the country would accept.[61] The problem of private pension provision remained unresolved.

It is clear that the Study Group possessed little love for the private pension industry. Indeed Titmuss unambiguously declared 'the need to break the power of private insurance',[62] a strength of feeling possibly intensified by the bitter personal experience of losing sixteen years' worth of occupational pension rights when he left his job at the insurance company in 1942.[63] However, despite this hostility, nobody pursued Jay's alternative option, namely abolition. Sheer weight of numbers was a major factor here. The Study Group eventually estimated that, in 1957, around seven million were members of occupational schemes, a third of the national workforce.[64] There was a side-issue too. As noted earlier, amongst the increasing numbers of occupational scheme members were many trade unionists: the authors of *National Superannuation* went as far as to highlight the membership of such schemes by 'the higher grades of professional and white-collar workers, and . . . [some] industrial and clerical workers in large undertakings particularly the nationalised industries and public services'.[65] Moreover, some white-collar unions actually ran pension schemes. This meant that the TUC Social Insurance Committee was particularly concerned about the fate of existing schemes.[66] A further reason for the Study Group's caution is evident in the contribution to the debate of David Ginsburg, then Secretary of the Labour Party Research Department. Ginsburg noted 'that we must bear in mind the vested interests already in existence, and these would be much greater by the time we could introduce any scheme we had in mind'.[67] As will be illustrated later, the dramatic response of the private pension industry, the most vested of those interests involved, to the publication of *National Superannuation* – and later pension schemes proposals – will demonstrate the acuteness of Ginsburg's prophetic powers.

With abolition off the agenda, other suggestions included a further one from Jay – one hinting at his experience at the Treasury – to reduce the tax breaks available for private insurance schemes in order to make the proposed state scheme more desirable.

However, it was towards the end of the 4 July meeting of the Study Group that the most significant contribution was made to the debate about the future of private schemes. In reply to Jay's repeated point that 'those with high salaries would probably be disgruntled at this scheme unless they received say, two-thirds plus',[68] Gerald Reynolds – the Study Group's secretary and soon-to-be MP for Islington North – suggested that 'contracting-out of persons who are members of approved existing schemes might overcome this difficulty'.[69] And with those few words Reynolds pushed forward a process that has led subsequent Labour governments, not least those that operate under the New Labour tag, increasingly to utilise, and welcome, the private sector as the state's partner in providing social services. Not that this future was anticipated at the time. Had it been, it does seem most unlikely that the motley collection of trade unionists, socialists and left-wing academics that comprised the Study Group would have agreed that 'future discussions should proceed on the basis of a compulsory national superannuation scheme with power for persons already members of "approved" existing schemes, to contract out'.[70]

Before continuing the tale, it is worth providing some brief explanation of contracting-out. Generally speaking, contracting-out refers to a system whereby individuals are allowed to forego paying some, or indeed all, of their contributions towards a particular system of state welfare, provided that they are covered by an alternative scheme which provides benefits broadly equivalent to those that would have been provided by the state. In the UK, from 1926 until 1948, there did exist a rudimentary system of contracting-out for a limited number of individuals, such as those in the employment of the crown or working for local authorities. There was even – many decades before the 1980s – provision for individual contracting-out, in this case for those who had private income equivalent to the pension. However, there was, during this period, no general provision for ordinary occupational pension schemes to contract out of state provision. In other words, those able enough to afford a secondary pension had to contribute, in full, both to their private occupational scheme and to the state.[71] The introduction of national insurance in 1948 temporarily ended all forms of contracting-out in the UK. However, as indicated earlier, this development failed to prevent a significant increase in the number of occupational schemes. Moreover, by the end of the 1950s, both main political parties were looking again at the potential of contracting-out to solve some of their pension problems.

Turning to the Labour Party's efforts, as usual it was left to Titmuss, Abel-Smith, and Townsend to try, in a relatively short period of time, to make sensible proposals out of the Study Group's sometimes hazy conclusions. It was not an easy proposition. As Titmuss himself noted, once the Study Group had reached agreement on general principles, 'it would be desirable for another group of people to study the more technical aspects of the matter, for perhaps two or three years'.[72] The 'skiffle group' was given ten months.

The first aspect of note regarding the contracting-out proposals contained in *National Superannuation* is that the option of full contracting-out, as possible before 1948, was not seriously considered. The reason being that, as suggested earlier, allowing the possibility for people to exit completely from a state scheme that included redistributive features almost guaranteed that those doing the subsidising would, indeed, say goodbye, leaving a big hole where their contributions would have been. Thus what Titmuss, Abel-Smith, and Townsend suggested was a system of *partial* contracting-out. Everyone was to continue to contribute towards the basic flat-rate pension; it was only the supplementary earning-related pension that certain individuals would have been allowed to duck out from, with neither they nor their employers contributing towards it, nor receiving its due benefits. The presumption was that this limited form of contracting-out would have allowed the state scheme to remain viable.

The second, and probably most important, point to note about the 1957 contracting-out arrangements concerns the stringent conditions that were attached. Workers were only allowed to opt out of the national superannuation element of the proposed two-tier pension scheme provided their company operated an 'approved' occupational scheme.[73] This was a telling little detail because, to gain approval, the first condition was that 'its contributions and benefits should not compare unfavourably with those of the National Scheme'.[74] This loosely implied the provision of inflation-proofed occupational pensions, and this would have made it, in Fawcett's judgement, 'extremely difficult' for the private sector to meet the set requirements.[75] Had *National Superannuation* been implemented, there would have been yet more potential headaches ahead for the private sector. A second condition of approval was the provision of 'full transferability of pension rights'.[76] This would have guaranteed that when a worker changed occupational pension scheme on taking on a new job, his/her new scheme would have to include all the rights to benefits accrued from the old one – a practice very few pension schemes outside the public sector attempted. Even the Study Group's academic experts admitted that this condition 'may create technical difficulties'.[77] That was putting it mildly. A further condition was the outlawing of the custom whereby some employers made membership of a scheme a condition of employment. Another feature was the proposed granting of the right for an individual worker to leave an occupational scheme and 'contract into' the state scheme on an individual basis.[78] Taken together, had the 1957 proposals been implemented, the future existence of private occupational schemes would have been left seriously in doubt.[79] This would certainly have been the case if, as Titmuss and his colleagues anticipated, 'roughly three-quarters of the population' eventually joined the earnings-related element of the proposed state scheme.[80]

Thus, when examining the 1957 plan for the re-introduction of contracting-out, it is vital to concentrate on the conditions attached. It might be assumed that planning to bring back contracting-out displayed some warmth in the Labour Party towards the insurance industry. It did not, or at least, certainly not from Titmuss who, as noted earlier, had made it clear from the outset that nobbling this industry was actually one of the purposes of national superannuation. Indeed, Titmuss, at one stage, was keen to go further down the path to breaking the insurance industry than was eventually followed by suggesting that, once up and running, new entrants should only be allowed to join the state scheme.[81]

It should be concluded, then, that contracting-out was only regarded by the Study Group as a technical device to fend off some of the hostility the pension plans might have provoked amongst the insurance industry, some white-collar unions, and the millions due to collect an occupational pension. In particular, there was a concern that, without contracting-out, too many firms with good pension schemes, rather than pay both contributions towards their employees' occupational schemes and the increased contributions necessary for the national superannuation scheme, would immediately wind up their own schemes.[82] Contracting-out simply made it a bit cheaper to continue to run both. However, as will be illustrated, by re-introducing the concept of contracting-out to the UK social policy process, the Study Group unwittingly helped revive an idea that was transformed by future policy-makers into a very different beast.

OWNING THE COUNTRY

Before examining one attempt by a different set of policy-makers to mutate the ideas of contracting-out and earnings-relation into devices with very different ends to those envisaged by the Study Group, it is worth examining one more feature advocated in *National Super-annuation*: a rather daring method devised to finance, in part, the pension scheme. As noted earlier, one of the problems associated with the national insurance system was that, from the very beginning, it had never actually worked as a traditional insurance scheme – that is, one in which workers contribute into a fund, with this invested in stocks and shares, with this, in turn, providing the wherewithal to finance the workers' own benefits. Instead, national insurance came to be based on a pay-as-you-go system, one in which workers' contributions helped finance not their own future benefits, but those of existing pensioners and others in receipt of benefit. Crossman, and the other authors of *National Superannuation*, planned, to an extent, to rectify this perceived flaw.

In *National Superannuation* it was proposed that national social security contributions be split into two parts, one for unemployment and sickness benefit, and the other for old age and widows' pensions. Contributions to the latter would be put into a National Pensions Fund; one designed increasingly to support the financing of the national superannuation scheme.[83] This Pensions Fund was to be run in a similar fashion to commercial pension funds, by investing in equities and gilt-edged securities, with this activity to be controlled by trustees appointed by the Government. The stated aim here was to gain the confidence of the British people in this proposed new scheme by attempting to re-establish the insurance principle that had been at the heart of Beveridge's initial plan.[84]

Though the aim to re-establish the insurance principle was interesting, the really exciting part of this new policy was the potential it gave to invest all those juicy contributions. Crossman, in particular, was keen to use the proposed Pensions Fund as means by which the state could play a large role in the investment market. As it was expressed in the first part of *National Superannuation*, the trustees appointed 'will be able to ensure that the national savings piling up in the Pensions Fund will be used to help our national capital investment programme'.[85] Frank Redington, the Chief Actuary of Prudential Assurance, immediately saw the potential of this when Crossman told him of the plans in March 1957. Responding to Crossman's estimate that the Pensions Fund would gain between £180 million and £200 million of new savings every year, Redington exclaimed, 'Do you realize how much that is? . . . It's over three times as much as the Pru has to invest and the Pru has as much as all the rest put together. Why you'll own the country in ten years at that rate!'.[86] Unsurprisingly, Redington's outburst only managed to encourage Crossman's enthusiasm for this novel form of nationalisation.

Crossman had been interested in such an idea for some time. Indeed, in his celebrated speech at the 1955 Labour Party Conference, Crossman went as far as to say that,

> If there is an issue I could see the advantage of considering public ownership it is in terms of insurance – life insurance, pension insurance. We should not forget the enormous economic power that those who invest in these private insurance schemes exert on the community.[87]

While the terms of the Pensions Fund stopped short of full nationalisation, its operation would certainly have allowed the state to start exerting a sizeable proportion of that enormous economic power that Crossman had noticed was, in the mid-1950s, exclusively in the hands of the insurance industry.

The path from Crossman's rough idea to detailed policy was a not typical one. For once the Study Group appear to have had little to say about this crucial issue, other than two very general questions from Douglas Jay: namely 'How are we going to pay for it [the pension scheme]? Should it run within the existing scheme?'.[88] Moreover, as late as March 1957, Crossman's *Backbench Diary* suggests that adequate answers to Jay's questions had yet to materialise.[89] According to Crossman's account, much work towards a practical policy was achieved at an ad hoc meeting which he persuaded Hugh Gaitskell to call prior to a crucial meeting of the Home Policy Committee scheduled for 8 April 1957.[90] Gaitskell attended this meeting, as did, amongst others, Titmuss, Abel-Smith, and Jay. The Shadow Chancellor Harold Wilson was due to attend, but – to Crossman's considerable annoyance – he failed to show.

At this meeting, the idea of a trustee-run National Pensions Fund was debated. One of the individuals most enthusiastic about the idea was the party leader himself. Crossman suggested that the reason Gaitskell was interested in the Pensions Fund was due to 'the new policy statement on nationalisation'.[91] This policy statement, Crossman went on to explain, 'has accepted Hugh's [Gaitskell] philosophy that the road to further nationalisation lies through the buying up of equity shares through great public companies'.[92] The notion that Gaitskell's enthusiasm for the Pensions Fund was provoked by wider changes to Labour Party philosophy brings to mind Seldon's concept of lower-level ideas being taken up if they are in tune with the dominant over-arching idea of the time.[93] Now, it is clear that the Pensions Fund idea arrived independently of this re-conceptualisation of nationalisation, as the very next sentence Crossman wrote after mentioning Gaitskell's philosophy makes plain: 'What a delicious discovery – that, in the course of getting a decent pensions plan, we shall have evolved by far the most efficient and unobjectionable machine for buying up equities'.[94] Nevertheless, the Pension Fund's journey to the next stage of the policy process was dependent on gaining this acceptance from the party elite, and this required the idea being in sympathy with wider developments, as it was at the time. As will be illustrated later, this happy situation was but a temporary one.

Gaitskell's support for the Pension Fund was an important factor in its progress into Labour Party policy, as was the support of Wilson, who also displayed enthusiasm for the idea.[95] This support was important because others were clearly sceptical about the Pensions Fund. Jay, for one, pointed out – at that Gaitskell-called meeting – that the government would have to publish the Fund's accounts, the possible result being 'won't people see the hundreds of millions in the Fund and ask for increased old age pensions?'.[96] Those supporting the Pensions Fund replied that this pressure would, in the end, be relatively minor. Perhaps a more surprising source of criticism came from national superannuation's original architect, Abel-Smith. As Crossman reported, 'Brian Abel-Smith is a bit alarmed about this [the Pensions Fund]. Won't people be afraid, he says, of the charge that the Labour Government is gambling with the savings for their old age pensions? Won't our trustees have to be over-cautious and therefore unsuccessful in their investment policy?'.[97] Crossman did not note the response to Abel-Smith's concerns. Whatever that response was, it must have been a convincing one.

Only weeks later, Abel-Smith – with the other members of the 'skiffle group' – put his name to the published statement that, 'We are not ourselves disturbed by the prospect of the National Superannuation Fund playing a very large rôle in the investment market'.[98] Indeed, they reiterated that point from earlier in the pamphlet which suggested that one of the most significant aspects of the Fund was that any surplus would be 'invested in industry to create a larger national income'.[99]

The technical memorandum in *National Superannuation*, in which Abel-Smith and his academic colleagues declared their unruffled attitude to the idea of the state playing heavily in the investment market, also provided many details about the Pension Fund itself. Perhaps the most important of these details was that the Fund was never designed to provide all the finance necessary to run the national superannuation scheme, even by 2030, the year highlighted as the one in which the vast majority of pensioners would, at last, be entitled to the full earnings-related elements of their pension.[100] Contributions were to continue, as before, to provide the bulk of the cash, with the Fund only to be used as a contingency reserve.[101] One reason given for not attempting to introduce a fully funded scheme is one still wheeled out today when suggestions are made to transform any pay-as-you-go pension system into a fully funded one. This is the so-called double-payment problem, that is, one unfortunate generation has to foot the bill for both their own future pensions and those of existing pensioners, and that generation would be justly entitled to cry foul.[102]

The Pensions Fund was clearly the most exciting part of the plans to finance national superannuation. However, as noted, its significance was not that it signalled the end of the existing pay-as-you-go scheme – it was never intended to – but that it would have allowed the creation of a novel form of nationalisation. Moreover, this was spotted by the Conservatives, who, during the 1959 general election campaign, mounted a successful crusade against so-called 'nationalisation by stealth'.[103] Interestingly, despite these cat-calls, it is worth noting that it was a Conservative government, rather than a Labour one, that actually resuscitated the independent reserve fund idea, in the early 1970s. Moreover, as will be examined later, it was a New Labour government that re-revived the idea in the twenty-first century. 'Borrowing' ideas off other parties is a prominent theme of this story, as will be developed in the next section, one that briefly explores the Conservative government's reaction to Labour's national super-annuation scheme.

'STEALING CROSSMAN'S CLOTHES'

Approaching the 1959 general election, there were two plans for radical reform of the British pension system waiting in the wings. One, naturally, was Labour's national superannuation scheme, which Crossman hoped would prove a 'wonderful vote-winner'.[104] The other came from the Conservatives, who, just prior to the election, had guided legislation through Parliament to introduce their own new pension scheme, one that also included an element of earnings-relation. This requires a little explanation. Those in need of a more detailed account of this event than is about to be provided should be directed to Paul Bridgen and Rodney Lowe's highly informative *Welfare Policy Under the Conservatives 1951–1964*,[105] and to Bridgen's solo article on the subject in *Contemporary British History*.[106] Hugh Pemberton also provides a short, useful account in his chapter in the recent *Britain's Pensions Crisis*.[107] Bridgen, in particular, portrays the development of Conservative pension reform in the late 1950s as the product of a fierce debate within the party. This battle was between, on one side, representing the more progressive wing of the party, the 'One Nation' Conservatives, and, on the other, representing financial rectitude and tradition respectively, the Treasury and the Conservative right. The resignation of the Chancellor, Peter Thornycroft, and his ministerial team – including Enoch Powell – in 1958 was the most visible casualty of this war. In contrast, Pemberton, using the idea of path dependency, highlights that particular policy developments were largely forced on the policy-makers by the need to prop up the struggling National Insurance Fund.

Back in 1957, when *National Superannuation* was launched, the public response of the Conservative government was unsurprisingly hostile. One of the most memorable put-downs came from Oliver Poole, the Conservative Party chairman, who dismissed the scheme as 'half-pie in the sky rather than half-pay in retirement'.[108] Yet, in private, the Conservatives took Labour's pension scheme seriously, with, in particular, John Boyd-Carpenter, the Minister of Pensions and National Insurance, regarding it as a real threat.[109] It was certainly one of the prompts that pushed the government into working afresh to provide a new pension scheme of their own, if just, in Poole's private words to Crossman, 'to put something on the Statute Book that was irreversible and which would prevent us [the Labour Party] from going ahead with our plan'.[110]

It must be stressed, however, that the Conservatives had not been ignoring the pressures facing the social security system before the publication of *National Superannuation*. As noted earlier, many on the right were particularly anxious about the future financial implications of an ageing population, with the impending deficit in the National Insurance Fund provoking particular anguish. Prompting from the Treasury made certain this concern remained on the government's institutional agenda.[111] However, on top of this, the publication of *National Superannuation* clearly did increase the intensity of other more pressing calls for the government to do something. One of these insistent voices belonged to existing pensioners, keen to increase their inflation-ravaged benefits, and another, increasingly loud, outcry came from many workers – particularly those in the public sector – alarmed by the realisation of how far their incomes would plummet at retirement.[112]

Another important factor behind Conservative attempts to reform the Beveridge system was Harold Macmillan's appointment as Prime Minister – in succession to the ailing Anthony Eden – in January 1957. Macmillan was understandably keen to take the nation's attention away from the humiliation of Suez, and saw this reform process as one such opportunity.[113] Indeed, in response to Labour's scheme, Macmillan declared, 'Why should we not make a scheme of our own? It would not be put forward as an economic scheme to save the fund etc. . . . It would be put forward as an imaginative scheme of social reform'.[114] Macmillan therefore thought it possible to pull off the tricky feat of demonstrating to the electorate the more socially progressive side of Conservatism, and yet, at the same time, attempt to address the traditional Conservative concern regarding excessive public expenditure.

The route from Macmillan's suggestion to a coherent plan was a tortuous one. Moreover, it was a surprise that the pension system that was eventually to emerge from this process included a form of earnings-related provision, because, as Bridgen and Lowe note, that 'was not what most Ministers were contemplating at the start'.[115] To elaborate, one of the Conservative Party's chief reformers, Iain

Macleod – the Minister of Labour and leading figure of the 'One Nation' group – initially envisaged the continuation of the flat-rate national insurance scheme. His radical suggestion was supplementation of this basic pension through a system in which employers would be compelled to take out pension schemes for their employees, with the state merely providing an auxiliary scheme for those unable to obtain an occupational pension.[116] There was no element of earnings-relation at all in this proposal. The key players in broadening reform proposals to include the concept of an earnings-related pension were officials at the Treasury, and it was they, to a large extent, that shaped the resultant legislation.

Treasury officials were solidly against the proposed compulsory pension scheme. They distrusted the private sector, and any measure that would lose the Exchequer revenue, which was the potential result of proposed tax allowances on private pension contributions.[117] In line with their traditional concern regarding the impending deficit in the National Insurance Fund, officials looked first to a more targeted approach to social security to provide an alternative way forward. They were quickly told to look elsewhere by Macmillan and his senior ministers.[118] As Alan Deacon and Jonathan Bradshaw note, 'Macmillan's whole approach was based in part on the belief that any move towards means-testing would be an electoral gift to Labour, and in part upon a personal revulsion against anything which could be seen as marking a return to the 1930s'.[119] Instead, officials picked up the earnings-relation principle that Crossman had conveniently driven to the head of the policy agenda. They were, as Macleod noted to Macmillan, 'stealing Crossman's clothes'.[120]

In fact, the scheme the Treasury put forward suggested that they had pinched a shoddily manufactured imitation of Crossman's clothes. The officials' version of earnings-relation involved a far narrower band of earnings than had been proposed in *National Superannuation*, and the benefits were to be considerably less generous.[121] Unsurprisingly, the Treasury's plan also suggested a smaller supplement from the Exchequer. In addition, the scheme was to be made compulsory, and there was to be no contracting-out facility. Differences between the priorities attached to each reform account for the contrast between the two versions of the same principle. For Labour, closing the gap between the 'two nations in old age' was the primary goal, and one way in which earnings-relation assisted this was by providing the opportunity to raise higher contributions immediately, with the payback of higher returns only necessary sometime in the future. As highlighted earlier, the additional revenue could then be utilised to fund the proposed 50 per cent increase in the basic pension rate designed to lift many off means-tested support. Treasury officials saw their priority as balancing the books. Using the same logic as the Labour policy-makers, but for a different end, they worked out that the scheme would provide sufficient income during the first twenty-five years in operation to wipe out the future deficits in the National Insurance Fund. Furthermore, in the long-term, by not actually specifying the relationship between graduated benefits and contributions, even more savings could be made.[122]

After months of dispute, most Cabinet members favoured prudence over radical reform, and the Treasury's modified earnings-related scheme triumphed over Macleod's plan for compulsory occupational pensions. As Macleod lamented, 'What is left has nothing to do with social reform. It is a Treasury measure. It is financial slight of hand'.[123] However, Macleod, and John Boyd-Carpenter, had their own trick up their sleeves. For reasons to be discussed presently, they managed to convince enough Cabinet colleagues to at least tack on a limited contracting-out facility to the proposed scheme. The Treasury opposed this amendment, largely because, by failing to make the earnings-related pension compulsory, much of the financial attraction of the scheme was lost.[124] Incidentally, as with Labour's scheme, the system of contracting-out proposed by the Conservative ministers was one of *partial* contracting-out: it was only to be applied to the supplementary earning-related pension; all employees would have continued contributing towards the basic pension.

Despite the continuation of hostilities between the two sides within the government, public expression of the Conservative pension plans arrived in October 1958 with the publication of the White Paper, *Provision for Old Age*. The Treasury-led priorities were clear. The first listed objective was: 'To place the National Insurance scheme on a sound financial basis'.[125] This was the primary reason for the proposed introduction of earnings-related – or, as they were then more commonly called, 'graduated' – contributions and pensions. As was clearly explained in *Provision for Old Age*, 'Overall, the increased contribution revenue made possible by graduated contributions could secure that the large emerging deficits with which the scheme is at present faced would be eliminated'.[126]

Hinting at the balance of power behind the policy, the goal of encouraging occupational pension schemes was only listed as the government's third objective.[127] Nevertheless, this particular aspect of the Conservative plans was one that has had, perhaps, the most lasting impact. In contrast to members of Labour's Study Group, such as Titmuss, who wished to break the insurance industry, Conservative politicians, such as Boyd-Carpenter, were keen for the opposite to occur. 'I was anxious to encourage the private sector occupational pension schemes', recalled Boyd-Carpenter in his memoirs,[128] a sentiment within the Conservative tradition of supporting private sector solutions, where possible. Despite not being highlighted as the top priority, *Provision for Old Age* did not hide this goal of arousing a rather reluctant private pension industry. One striking sentence runs, 'The Government are convinced that changes in the field of National Insurance should be framed as not to prevent the *vigorous development* of independent provision for old age, whether through occupational schemes or otherwise'.[129] And, with the daring idea for a compulsory occupational scheme out the window, it was contracting-out that Boyd-Carpenter singled out as the suitable 'instrument' for stimulating the market.[130] Thus, in a fashion similar to the Treasury officials adopting the earnings-relation principle, Boyd-Carpenter and Macleod took an idea that Crossman had helped push to the centre of attention, in this case contracting-out, and twisted it to suit their own purposes.

As the Study Group had discovered earlier, one device that could be relatively easily manipulated to regulate the private sector was the stringency of conditions necessary for a scheme to pass in order to be accepted as part of the contracting-out arrangement. As Macleod and Boyd-Carpenter were seeking an expanded, not diminished, private sector, the conditions they proposed were far less severe than those envisaged by Labour's policy-makers.[131] In *Provision for Old Age*, the primary condition was for an approved insurance scheme to provide pension benefits which were 'on the whole as favourable as the maximum graduated rights of the new state scheme'.[132] At first glance, this looks very similar to the contracting-out condition in *National Superannuation* which states that 'contributions and benefits should not compare unfavourably with those of the National Scheme'.[133]

However, the devilish detail was that, whereas Labour's national scheme was to be 'inflation-proofed' – thus suggesting that occupational schemes would have to match this – the Conservative scheme was not.

Including relatively relaxed contracting-out conditions was only one aspect of the plan to drive the occupational pension market onwards and upwards. Contracting-out was only attractive if the alternative on offer was less appealing, and, as suggested earlier, the alternative supplementary earnings-related scheme the Conservatives were proposing was indeed suitably resistible. The plan was for employees earning between £9 and £15 a week – in a period when average male earnings were about £13 a week[134] – to pay additional contributions based on these earnings, with this securing for them so-called 'bricks' of extra pension on top of the existing basic state pension.[135] Each £1 of graduated earnings would constitute a 'unit', and fifteen such units would provide a male contributor an additional 1s. each week pension. Women had to accumulate eighteen 'units' to earn their 'brick'. Another particularly unappealing aspect of this scheme was that, for younger workers in particular, there was no guarantee that inflation would not render these 'bricks' virtually worthless by the time they could be claimed. Unsurprisingly, such terms, when they were translated into legislation, only encouraged millions to contract out. Indeed, as Heclo has pointed out, 'By April 1961 the number of contracted-out employees was 4.1 million rather than the 2.5 million originally estimated by the government'.[136]

As suggested, *Provision for Old Age* did form the basis of legislation, namely the National Insurance Act 1959, and this began to operate in 1961. The National Insurance Act 1959 did not win many plaudits. The insurance world was unimpressed, regarding the whole plan 'a political gimmick, not a pension scheme'.[137] For the Labour Party, the Boyd-Carpenter scheme – as it was quickly dubbed – was simply 'The Pensions Fraud'.[138] Even certain Conservative ministers lacked enthusiasm. Despite the scheme bearing his name, Boyd-Carpenter was unhappy about some of the compromises made,[139] and Macleod described the eventual plan as 'a little mouse of a scheme'.[140]

In terms of what the Act achieved, as a scheme to improve pension provision Nicholas Timmins unambiguously marks it down as 'an almost complete failure'.[141] Improving provision, though, had never been the aim. As Leslie Hannah – with more backhand than compliment – notes,

> The Conservative strategy had been to achieve as little for the state scheme as politically possible; and, if the primary measure of success is the consonance of objectives and achievements, their graduated pension scheme must rank as the most successful piece of pension legislation ever.[142]

Moreover, the Treasury-led goal of shrinking the National Insurance Fund deficit was achieved, as was the ambition of Boyd-Carpenter and Macleod to perk up the occupational pension industry.

There was also the unpublished goal, the one Poole mentioned to Crossman, to stymie future Labour plans. This, in its mouse-like way, the National Insurance Act of 1959 also achieved by nibbling away at the opportunities for future Labour policy-makers – such as Crossman – to implement national superannuation. This was largely accomplished by the encouragement it gave to workers to take out occupational pensions, which prompted a significant increase in the numbers covered by these pensions: from 8 million in 1956 to 11.1 million by 1963.[143] As illustrated earlier, the Study Group had been constrained by the fear of upsetting those with occupational pension rights back in 1956. This fear was only going to become more stifling as the numbers involved expanded. In addition, the increase in numbers emboldened the insurance industry, helping to transform it into a powerful interest group, one that would fight tenaciously to avoid the kind of diminution in its services that Titmuss, in particular, had in mind.[144] This story will be continued in future chapters.

ASSESSMENT OF CROSSMAN'S ROLE

So, returning to 1959, both main political parties went into election battle with social reform high on their agenda. More particularly, national superannuation became a topic for heated political debate, even if the exchanges between party spokespersons 'quickly became lost in actuarial technicalities'.[145] The electorate, perhaps unsurprisingly, failed to match the enthusiasm for the scheme of, say, Crossman who, later, rather ruefully agreed that his scheme was 'unintelligible to the ordinary public'.[146] This was something Tony Benn correctly prophesied back in 1957. Despite regarding national superannuation as being 'the most exciting thing that has happened since the Beveridge Report', Benn suggested that it was such a complicated idea that it 'will take months for the Party to understand it and years for the local Parties and the general public'.[147] The enlightenment envisaged by Benn had not occurred by 1959, and the Conservatives, making the most of a benign economy, trumped Labour's promise of radical social reform, and comfortably won their third election in succession. With this, the dramatic rise of national superannuation to the top of the political agenda came to an abrupt halt.

However, as the previous section illustrated, though the whole scheme was put in mothballs until a more sympathetic government was elected, ideas contained within the scheme that Crossman ably championed were to surface as policy shortly after the election – albeit in somewhat mutated versions of their original incarnation. This touches on John Kingdon's notion that policy ideas sometimes 'combine with one another, some survive, some die out, *and some survive in a form quite different from their origins*'.[148] Thus earnings-relation, for example, did reach the Statute Book, and, in part at least, this was because of Crossman's success in advocating the idea both to the Labour Party and to the wider public, encouraging the Conservatives to respond with their own scheme. The Conservative version of earnings-relation was indeed in a form quite different from the concept Crossman thought might vigorously shake British social policy free from the grip of Beveridge. Nevertheless, the introduction of even this rather vapid version of earnings-relation benefit was still a significant event in the development of post-war UK social policy, and, in particular, it proved an important step towards the wholesale rejection of Beveridge in Britain.[149] Thus Crossman – in his self-appointed role as 'an awkward, independent ideas man'[150] – did have some success at influencing the development of social policy, even if not quite in the manner in which he had hoped.

Equally significant were developments in the Labour Party. As noted, Crossman was the central figure that persuaded many in the party that the path forged by Beveridge and the Attlee government – only a decade earlier – was, in fact, leading towards a dead-end. This was no mean feat for a backbench MP with a tremendous talent for alienating people. Obviously, in 1959, the Labour Party was in no position to attempt reform based on this post-Beveridgian impulse, but it did mean that, when Labour was again returned to power, it was with a very different social policy agenda to the one pursued in the immediate post-war years. As later chapters will illustrate, much of this agenda was not implemented in the manner Crossman had hoped – despite his presence as a Cabinet minister – but the process was continued whereby the Beveridgian ideals of the 1940s were to be increasingly disregarded.

It is worth adding that, though Crossman was an important figure in the rather clunky process whereby British social policy moved away from the principles of Beveridge, the role of this one individual should not be overestimated. As Lowe makes clear, there were many factors at work in this particular development, not least the incoherence of Beveridge's original vision, which meant some sort of reform was inevitable.[151] Moreover, very similar processes were occurring elsewhere in Europe, most notably in Sweden. As in the UK, there was much discussion, during the 1950s, about the possibility of a national superannuation scheme being introduced to replace Sweden's existing, and faltering, flat-rate pension system. Unlike Britain, however, after a debate which proved 'prolonged, intense but ultimately conclusive',[152] such an earnings-related scheme was introduced, in 1960, and it went on to prove a catalyst for the development of the generally much lauded Swedish welfare system. Clearly, the successful foisting of the superannuation idea on to a national policy process did not depend on the existence of one Richard Crossman MP.

To gain a fuller picture of Crossman's role during the 1950s, it is perhaps helpful to re-examine briefly those four factors Seldon identified as prompting change: ideas, individuals, circumstances and interests. Regarding the first of these factors, as noted earlier, Seldon argued that 'Ideas exist on two levels', and that for the lower level ideas to succeed it is important that they chime harmoniously with the existing ideas at the macro-level.[153] Earlier in this chapter it was argued that national superannuation was able to travel rapidly along Labour's social policy process because, as a concept, it fitted snugly into Gaitskell's nascent revisionist agenda which involved the reconceptualisation of nationalisation. In addition, it could also be argued that national superannuation's early success in Labour circles was also assisted by the concept's chameleon-like ability to blend into yet another over-arching idea: this time, relative poverty.

To provide some background, by the early 1950s, poverty was starting to be regarded as yesterday's problem. For example, Seebohm Rowntree's third survey of poverty levels of York, in 1950, 'appeared to demonstrate that the post-war measures had all but eliminated poverty'.[154] Alongside a significant decline in unemployment, the key to this conclusion was Rowntree's definition of poverty, based, as it was, on a rather arbitrary notion of what constituted subsistence. In short, by 1950, it appeared, to Rowntree at least, that virtually everyone had enough to prevent starvation. The 1960s, though, saw the public backlash against this view that poverty had disappeared. Abel-Smith and Townsend led the charge with the publication, in 1965, of *The Poor and the Poorest*, with this culminating in the so-called 'rediscovery of poverty' in pockets throughout society, not least amongst children. This rediscovery largely came about through a major shift in how poverty was perceived and measured. As Abel-Smith and Townsend argued, 'poverty is essentially a relative concept and essentially one which refers to a variety of conditions and not simply a financial condition'.[155]

Though 1965 witnessed the idea of relative poverty flourish publicly, it was a concept that had, for some time, been growing in significance in academic and political circles. Indeed, as Abel-Smith and Townsend freely admitted, 'we are saying nothing new'.[156] Certainly such notions were evident in the following section from *National Superannuation*, published some eight years earlier:

> In Britain today old age, for the average worker, means a fall of nearly 75 per cent in the standard of life for which he has worked and to which he and his wife have become accustomed. This is poverty. No arbitrary and sophisticated attempts to draw lines of minimum subsistence could supply a better definition.
>
> We believe that an adequate pension can best be defined as a pension which prevents this catastrophic fall in living standards as a result of retirement or declining earning power. It means the right to go on living in the same neighbourhood, to enjoy the same hobbies and to be able to afford to mix with the same circle of friends.[157]

Awareness of this new approach to poverty also reached the political elite of the Labour Party. For example, Crossman noted an interesting quip from a future Labour Prime Minister: "'In ten years' time", Harold Wilson remarked at the NEC, "the National Assistance Board will be instructed to provide television sets to all applicants'".[158]

The idea of earnings-related benefits, and, in particular, the notion of 'half-pay in retirement', naturally fitted very comfortably into this gradual reconceptualisation of poverty. Indeed, by regarding the fall in standards of living at retirement as 'poverty', rather than simply as a matter of financial condition, earnings-related benefits could be regarded as a potential bonus of the system being advocated, rather than, as Abel-Smith and Townsend initially appeared to view the prospect, an unfortunate side-effect. Thus, at this stage, the idea which Crossman was hawking about – national superannuation – had the advantage of harmonising sweetly with wider ideas that were doing the rounds in the late 1950s, even if this cheery situation was not to last for long.

Thus Crossman was fortunate that he was advocating an important, but lower-level, idea that did not clash with the conceptual fashions of the time. He was also fortunate when it came to another of Seldon's factors, namely 'circumstances'. In particular, some of Crossman's success at launching national superannuation so swiftly into the heart of the Labour Party's social policy agenda can be attributed to the circumstances surrounding the famous 1955 speech at which he introduced this idea. Crucially, Crossman caught the Labour Party at a time when its social policy was in flux. The existing system was evidently struggling and the main two alternatives – to increase flat-rate benefits to the point where means-tested supplementation was unnecessary or to abolish national insurance altogether – were regarded as deeply problematic. To touch on public policy theory for a moment – using ideas taken from the 'punctuated equilibrium' model of Frank Baumgartner and Bryan Jones[159] – the Labour Party's social security agenda of the mid-1950s was far from stable, and this provided the opportunity for access to that agenda for an enthu-siastically backed new concept, such as national superannuation.

However, as Seldon argues, circumstances can constrain policy-makers as well as create opportunities.[160] As suggested earlier, the records of the Study Group on Security and Old Age highlight some of those constraints, a number being the result of decisions made in the past. A good example can be found in the Study Group's reluctant decision to advocate the introduction of a form of contracting-out. This decision was taken to limit electoral flack from, amongst others, the millions of workers who – unhappy at the prospect of a retire-ment funded solely by flat-rate state pensions and, perhaps, national assistance – had taken the opportunity to contribute towards a private second pension. This constraint was a weighty one in the late 1950s, but was not enough to deflect Labour's social policy-makers com-pletely from creating a scheme that would have seriously weakened the private pension industry. However, this was a constraint that was to become increasingly binding as the years went by, as ever growing numbers, encouraged by the Conservative pension reforms, took out occupational pensions.

Thus Crossman was lucky, at Labour Party level at least, both in championing a fashionable idea and in enjoying circumstances where, at this stage, opportunities outweighed constraints. He was, of course, rather unlucky that the Labour Party lost the 1959 election, and thus had no chance to implement this idea because a Conservative govern-ment was stubbornly in the way. This leads to another of Seldon's four factors, 'interests'. Seldon highlights the role of the Conservative Party as an 'external interest' of particular importance as it dominated British government in the late twentieth century.[161] And, though it tends to be regarded largely as a force blocking the implementation of national superannuation, it was a Conservative government that introduced to the UK important elements of the scheme, not least earnings-relation. However, as the previous section explained, the primary 'interest' behind this particular innovation was not Con-servative ministers but another group Seldon identifies as important, the civil service – in this case, officials at the Treasury. It also needs to be repeated that the earnings-relation introduced by the Conser-vatives was a version designed with ends very different to those of Labour's Study Group.

Returning to those developments in Labour's policy process, the most important interest group was another highlighted by Seldon, namely the trade unions. The influence of the unions is very clear throughout the development of the concept within the Study Group – a body that, of course, included union representation. As noted, the retention of national insurance was largely because of union pressure. It is also clear that support from the TUC was a necessary hurdle national superannuation had to clear in order for the concept to be acceptable to the wider Labour Party. However, it ought to be stressed that, although this support was forthcoming, notably from Sir Alfred Roberts, head of the TUC Social Insurance Committee, it was not of a terribly enthusiastic variety. Indeed, it was this hesitant level of support from the TUC, compared with the much more enthusiastic response of the Swedish wage-earners' trade union confederation, the Landsorganisationen (LO), that prompted Heclo's argument that 'the primary agents behind the creation of these new policy departures seem to have been the labo[u]r movements in Britain and Sweden'.[162] To briefly explain, in contrast to the TUC's position as 'at most a reluctant supporter of the proposed policy departure', the LO was a vital and unified force in leading the pressure on the Swedish government to introduce pension reform based on earnings-relation.[163] Nevertheless, despite Heclo's damning comparison, back in the UK, in 1957, at that crucial vote at the Labour Party Conference, key individuals from the TUC did provide vital support for Crossman's national superannuation project.

Another important interest in this story was the insurance industry. A little background is necessary here. At the time, private pension insurance for employees came in one of two main types: one of these was a pension plan internally administered by the company with its own independent fund; the other was an individual contract with one of the private insurance companies, the so-called life offices. The National Association of Pension Funds (NAPF) represented the interests of the former, and the Life Offices Association (LOA), the private insurance companies. Of these two groups, as Heclo notes, 'By far the most important, well-organised, and well-staffed interest group' were the latter, the LOA.[164] It was the LOA that organised a 'barrage of opposition' to Labour's scheme,[165] arguing that the state should stick to what it was doing, providing a flat-rate basic pension that left plenty of room on top for the private sector.

This noisy response was hardly surprising. The grave potential prospects for providers of private occupational pension schemes were quickly perceived in the City, as, on announcement of *National Superannuation*, 'the shares of the insurance companies fell sharply'.[166] The Prudential Insurance Company lost £2.4 million off the value of its shares within four days of publication.[167] However, the significant point about this response is that it was a reaction to proposals already made. Unlike the unions, the private pension industry had no representation on the Study Group, and was not integral to the policy-making process. As noted earlier, Crossman was more than happy to discuss plans with Frank Redington, and a few other 'of the highest-powered actuaries in the City' before the details of national superannuation had been completed.[168] And from them, Crossman claimed, he 'learned a tremendous lot'.[169] However, this did not sway the Study Group from its path of attempting to vigorously prune back the private pension industry.

Significantly, it was not until July 1957, a few weeks after the publication of *National Superannuation*, that the Study Group minutes record an 'Informal discussion with representatives of the Association of Superannuation and Pension Funds'.[170] These representatives included pension fund officials from the South Eastern Gas Board, Unilever, Courtaulds, Boots, and Pilkington Brothers. These pension fund officials offered 'to put their experience at the disposal of the Study Group', though they made it abundantly clear 'that their interest was primarily in the future status of private schemes'.[171] Their lack of delight with the plan was clear with their plea that some aspects of *National Superannuation* 'could lead to the collapse of many private schemes'.[172] However, despite the pension fund officials' entreaties, the Study Group offered little in the way of compromise. There was some, though. In the summer of 1959, the Study Group decided to drop the idea for the possibility of individual contracting-out, after pressure from the insurance industry and the Co-operative Movement.[173] However, the key industry-damaging pledge to make private sector products match the proposed inflation-proofed state second pension remained on the agenda. Thus, though the private pension industry might have made life difficult for a Labour government had it won the 1959 election, the wishes of the insurance industry could – as the Conservative government itself demonstrated – at that stage, largely be ignored. As suggested earlier, the expansion of this industry in the 1960s made this situation but a temporary one.

Back in the late 1950s, though, in terms of ideas, circumstances and interests, Crossman was, on the whole, in a good situation. He was championing an idea that was in vogue, circumstances were largely favourable, and the key interests were, if not wildly enthu-siastic, then they were, in the case of the unions, fairly positive or, in the case of the insurance industry, not yet powerful enough to do serious damage. The major obstacle was that one key interest opposed to the basic principle of national superannuation, the Conservative Party, was in power. Nevertheless, this did not prevent ideas Crossman was promoting from making a large mark on national politics. This just leaves one more of Seldon's factors to be examined: the role of the individual.

Before focusing on Crossman, the roles played by other key individuals need to be considered. Amongst others, Seldon himself and Heclo – when discussing the role of 'middlemen' in the policy process[174] – have drawn attention to figures such as Richard Titmuss, Brian Abel-Smith, and Peter Townsend, and, clearly, the contribution of this LSE 'skiffle group' needs to be recognised. It was, as the last chapter recounted, Abel-Smith who first articulated a left-wing case for an earnings-related scheme to replace the existing Beveridge-inspired flat-rate system, and it was his and Townsend's pamphlet, *New Pensions for the Old*, that Crossman drew on for his 1955 speech.[175] Unusually for academics, their role did not end at this initial stage of the policy process. With Titmuss, Abel-Smith and Townsend were co-opted into the Study Group and, as noted earlier, it was this trio that Crossman reckoned proved the 'dynamic' for the whole scheme. They were also able to work out many of the highly technical matters, a development that moved *National Superannuation* towards a degree of detail that placed it in a league above most traditional political party policy documents. Though similar ideas to those proselytised by Titmuss, Abel-Smith, and Townsend were circulating in the 1950s – as demonstrated by events in Sweden – it is safe to argue that without the efforts of these individuals, national superannuation would not have enjoyed the prominence in the British policy process that it gained. That Labour's scheme had the potential to place Britain 'among those European countries with the most advanced welfare states'[176] was also largely because of the contribution made by these particular academics.

As for Crossman, he never claimed to have invented national superannuation, only that he was a huckster, made good 'by borrowing ideas'.[177] Nevertheless, his role was crucial. He was, in John Kingdon's terminology, a 'policy entrepreneur'.[178] Kingdon defines these individuals as 'advocates who are willing to invest their resources – time, energy, reputation, money – to promote a position in return for anticipated future gain in the form of material, purposive, or solidary benefits'.[179] Crossman certainly believed his investment in the national superannuation idea provided rewards: regarding his work on this concept, he declared, 'I am now an obsessed man and, curiously enough, in the Commons this raises my status. . .'.[180]

In Kingdon's model, policy entrepreneurs – who can be from any place in the political system, from top-level politician to bureaucrat to academic – enjoy a number of crucial roles. One such role is that of 'softening up' policy communities and the wider public to get each accustomed to a new idea.[181] Another role is that of 'coupling solutions to problems and for coupling both problems and solutions to politics'.[182] Both roles are vital in the process of turning an idea into action.

Crossman was central to the process of 'softening up'. He was, as James Kincaid argues, 'one of the few professional politicians in Britain with sufficient stamina and agility of mind to grasp the more esoteric complexities of national insurance'.[183] Moreover, with his varied experiences as a lecturer, Crossman was one of even fewer able to explain national superannuation with sufficient coherence, simplicity and humour to engage a wide audience. For all its many merits *New Pensions for the Old* was not a bag of laughs, and it is fair to claim that the ideas this pamphlet contained would not have made a deep impact without its more populist spokesman. Turning to the second of the roles of the policy entrepreneur, it was Crossman, through his position on Labour's NEC, who was able to complete the coupling process. In the British context, it had been Abel-Smith who had first coupled the potential solution, a social security system based on some form of earnings-relation, to a particular problem, the perceived failure of the flat-rate regime. However, it was Crossman who first connected this to the political mainstream through his 1955 speech. Moreover, he fought gamely to keep this link alive through his vigorous chairing of the Study Group, and his cajoling of senior figures such as Gaitskell and Wilson.

Thus, though Crossman may only have been one factor amongst many that facilitated the arrival of national superannuation on the political agenda, he did play a substantial role in that process. As the man himself remarked:

> I can claim to have proved it is possible to make the Labour Party adopt a new policy, provided you have people outside Transport

House to do all the thinking, provided you do all the writing yourself and that you get the Shadow Chancellor on your side, and – most important of all – provided that nine-tenths of the Executive don't bother to read anything.[184]

4   THE RIVAL

The period between the 1959 general election and the next, in October 1964, tends to be regarded as being a relatively quiet one in the story of social reform in the UK. Certainly the Conservative government, led by Harold Macmillan until October 1963, and then, briefly, by Sir Alec Douglas-Home, appeared to do little to fire up the attention of those interested in social reform. Indeed, compared to the Profumo Affair of 1963, activities such as the starting up of the Boyd-Carpenter pension system lacked a certain pizzazz. Yet, behind the scenes, a social security policy-centred debate raged within the Conservative Party and in Whitehall. According to Lowe and Bridgen, this debate – which pitched those demanding an extension of earnings-related benefits against those calling for greater selectivity – led to a consensus in Whitehall 'that what was really required was an all-embracing and fundamental review of the National Insurance system – a "New Beveridge Report"'.[1] As part of this process, an internal Treasury working party was established in February 1963 to review the social security system.

One of the most significant aspects of this re-evaluation of the Beveridge system was increased consideration of a more selectivist system. A manifesto commitment from 1959 to preserve the universal system forced blatant proposals to expand national assistance off the agenda. However, other proposals aimed at targeting support were seriously considered. One of these suggestions was a plan to reintroduce a differential pension, with those aged over seventy – a group regarded as being in particular need – to be awarded more benefit. Another proposal considered was that of an income guarantee, an idea designed explicitly to avoid one of traditional problems identified with means-testing. As noted in an earlier chapter, back in the mid-1950s, Peter Townsend was one, of a number, who drew attention to the problem that many, particularly amongst the elderly, were too ashamed to take up the means-tested benefits to which they were entitled. They refused point-blank 'to plead poverty'.[2] Moreover, later surveys, such as that conducted by Dorothy Cole and J.E.G. Utting in 1962,[3] suggested that the scale of this take-up problem had been underestimated. Of those who supported a more selective welfare system, it was Enoch Powell who responded – initially in 1957 – with the most innovative potential solution to this problem. The idea was for the state to target provision by guaranteeing needy pensioners a minimum income well above subsistence without recourse to traditional means-testing procedures, with automatic use of income tax returns suggested as a possible, less demeaning, alternative. However, Powell's proposal did not progress any further along the policy process, under the Conservatives at least.[4] In the end, all of the Conservative government's efforts to construct a 'New Beveridge' ground to a halt when the Labour Party narrowly won the 1964 general election.

Interestingly, the Labour Party in Opposition mirrored the government during this period, in that little appeared to be happening on the social policy front. Indeed Fawcett has emphasised this impression of stability, arguing that national superannuation 'served as the corner-stone of Labour's social security planning from 1957 until it formed a government in 1964'.[5] And certainly the pledge to introduce an earnings-related pension scheme did indeed remain an integral part of the Labour Party's programme throughout this period. However, important intra-party debates took place – some echoing arguments taking place in Whitehall – and Labour's social security agenda became much more complicated. Two important additions to the programme were a proposed expansion of the earnings-relation concept to include groups in addition to the elderly and, more significantly, the Labour Party's very own income guarantee.

CROSSMAN'S RIVAL

Before examining these policy developments in detail, it is worth pointing out that Richard Crossman was still heavily involved in Labour's social policy process during this period. He continued to chair the Study Group; indeed he claimed, at one stage, that the work of the Study Group was, with only one other exception, 'the only constructive thinking in the Labour Party that has taken place since the election'.[6] He also continued to address the Labour Party Conference on social policy matters and, in addition, was deeply involved in drafting the social security passages in two important policy documents during this period: *Signposts for the Sixties* published in 1961, and *New Frontiers for Social Security* published in 1963. Moreover, Crossman claimed in March 1963 that he was 'still immersed in social security'.[7]

Yet, for all his efforts, Crossman was perhaps not quite the driving force on social security matters that he had been prior to the 1959 election. For a start, he had distractions. As noted in an earlier chapter, Crossman began the immediate post-election period with a promotion to the Front Bench as chief spokesperson on pensions and national insurance, but, as his relationship with Hugh Gaitskell rapidly deteriorated, this position quickly became untenable. In March 1960 Crossman was forced to resign his position and, in his own words, 'get back to my natural habitat on the backbenches'.[8] From then on, squabbles over issues such as the removal, or otherwise, of Clause 4 from Labour's constitution, defence policy, and Gaitskell's perceived deficiencies as a leader, all helped push deliberations on social security policy into the background. Indeed, it is telling that for nearly the whole of 1962, Crossman did not even bother with his *Backbench Diary*, stating that he 'felt less and less inclination to continue to record trivial details of frustration'.[9] Rather ghoulishly, it was Gaitskell's death in January 1963 that supplied the life-blood for Crossman's political revitalisation. After that, Crossman was engaged in helping his ally, Harold Wilson, to become party leader, and thence became Labour's Front Bench spokesperson on science and, later, education.

In addition to these distractions, after the 1959 election Crossman's domination of Labour's social policy process was challenged by the arrival of a fresh, though not young, face in the Study Group: a politician with his own ideas for social policy reform. His name was Douglas Houghton, and though a largely forgotten figure nowadays, he did play a distinctive and productive role in public life.[10] Almost a decade older than Crossman, Houghton had experienced the torment of Passchendaele before beginning a career in trade unionism. He became, in 1922, the General Secretary of the Association of Offices of Taxes, which he built into the formidable Inland Revenue Staff Federation. He retired from that post, nearly forty years later, in 1960. Back in the Second World War, Houghton became a familiar voice on the radio, first explaining tax problems and, later, more general queries on the popular programme, 'Can I Help You?'. Aged over fifty, Houghton's party political career began in 1949 after being persuaded to fight a by-election in Sowerby, in Yorkshire. After winning this contest, Houghton avoided much of the factional wrangling of the Labour Party of the 1950s, largely through being a busy member of the General Council of the TUC. It was in this position that Houghton first became involved in the Study Group on Security and Old Age, through joint meetings this body held with the TUC Social Insurance Committee.[11] He is recorded as a full member of the Study Group itself in July 1959,[12] though his main contributions were made from 1961 onwards. Houghton also became Crossman's deputy as a Front Bench spokesperson on pensions and national insurance in November 1959, taking his place on Crossman's resignation from the post in March 1960. As will be illustrated later, Houghton went on to become a Cabinet minister in 1964 with the tricky job of co-ordinating all the social security services. Incidentally, after leaving the Cabinet aged nearly seventy, Houghton proceeded to have one of the lengthiest and productive Indian summers in political history, both as chairman of the Parliamentary Labour Party and as an active member of the House of Lords. He died, aged 97, in May 1996, having made contributions to an astonishing range of issues: abortion reform, standards in public life, and animal rights being just three.

In terms of social policy reform, as will be made clear, Houghton's most significant idea reflected his long experience as a tax pro- fessional. He was one of the first politicians on the left to develop the idea linked to Powell that the Inland Revenue could be regarded as a potential means of delivering social services. Houghton was only starting the process of forming his ideas during this period, but it is worth highlighting at this stage his most developed statement on the subject. This came in a lecture from April 1967, which was published – interestingly – by the early right-wing think-tank, The Institute of Economic Affairs. In it, Houghton recorded that:

My own thoughts naturally turn to the use of the taxation system for social purposes. . . . Not only could the structure of PAYE and its ingenious and flexible coding system and tax tables be used to provide an automatic minimum income, it could be adapted to a scheme for payment for state services. An extension of the coding system below the point of no tax liability could be used to determine entitlement to supplementary cash benefit, graduated according to income assessment, and also for rate rebates, rent rebates, school meals, welfare services, and National Health Service.[13]

Houghton – the former civil servant and tax expert – summed up his high hopes for such a scheme with suitable restraint: 'the possibilities of using a standard system of income-assessment (code numbers for all of us) for taxation and certain social benefits will become quite exciting'.[14]

Thus Houghton and Crossman held some similar ideas regarding the need for reform of the social security system. They both believed that the flat-rate Beveridge system was well past its sell-by date. In Houghton's words, 'Beveridge's thinking was pre-war thinking'.[15] And both accepted that relying entirely on increased taxes and contributions to fund the expanding welfare state was not necessarily the way forward.[16] Crucially, though, they also held subtly different visions of the future. For Crossman, the primary solution remained a fundamental switch to a system which utilised earnings-related contributions and benefits, whereas, for Houghton, the answer was to lie in making more use of the income tax system.

On a personal level, the *Backbench Diaries* make it abundantly clear that Crossman regarded the arrival of Houghton on the scene as a threat. In November 1959, Gaitskell informed Crossman that Houghton was to be his 'Number Two' on the Front Bench. Crossman recorded that, in measured response to Gaitskell, he 'exploded down the phone'.[17] He explained this negative reaction by stating – with more than a trace of 'the pot calling the kettle black' – that he regarded Houghton as 'one of the most explosive, erratic men I know'. Crossman was also concerned that Houghton was a member of the General Council of the TUC, and generally felt that Houghton was 'the last thing I want near me if I am going to reconstruct our health and unemployment insurance'.[18] Gaitskell was unmoved, grumbling,

'I don't remember being consulted on who was my Number Two when I was offered a Cabinet job'.[19] The Crossman/Houghton relationship did not begin as a love match, and, as will become evident, it never became one.

WORK TO BE DONE

As the 1960s began, the engine room of Labour's social policy process remained the Study Group on Security and Old Age, and the composition of this working party remained largely familiar. The first meeting of 1960 included MPs who had been on the Study Group from the beginning: individuals such as James Griffiths, Margaret Herbison, Douglas Jay and, of course, Crossman himself, back to chair this Opposition 'policy community'.[20] C.R. Dale remained to represent the TUC, and Richard Titmuss, Brian Abel-Smith and Peter Townsend continued to provide academic substance. The LSE 'skiffle group' was to expand at the next meeting with the highly significant arrival of Tony Lynes, another of Titmuss's hugely talented young researchers who went on to make a lasting impact on the political world.[21] As noted earlier, one other prominent new figure in the Study Group was Douglas Houghton, who attended regularly from March 1961, and, went on, quite often, to chair meetings in Crossman's absence.[22]

As already suggested, some of the pressures prompting a move away from the rock-steady support of national superannuation involved the introduction of new individuals into the policy process. Other factors included the impact of the Conservative legislation, the lasting legacy of the Beveridge reforms, perceived weaknesses in the national superannuation scheme, lessons from successful social security systems elsewhere in Europe, and a general shift in the way the nature of poverty was perceived in Britain. Indeed, it is clear, from Study Group minutes from shortly after the 1959 election, that members of the committee were aware of these pressures, and there was no intention expressed to preserve national superannuation in some sort of policy aspic.

At the first Study Group meeting of the 1960s, it was Crossman himself who highlighted the perception that national superannuation was not the solution to all Britain's various social security ills. He did this by drawing attention to 'aspects of social security about which further thinking is urgently required'.[23] Heading Crossman's list of matters to be resolved was, 'To define what is meant by subsistence in relation to basic insurance benefits'. Reflecting changes to the perception of poverty which Abel-Smith and Townsend were to popularise a few years later, 'It was felt that this should no longer be considered as a purely physical calculation related to basic material needs, but should bear proper relation to the rising standards of a prosperous community'.[24] This suggested that, even if changes were to be made to national superannuation, then the concept of earnings-relation remained sacrosanct.

The second of Crossman's tasks for the Study Group was to 'review our own National Superannuation Scheme in the light of the development of the Government's scheme'.[25] It was acknowledged, as Oliver Poole had gleefully forecast, that the Conservative scheme prevented a future Labour government from introducing national superannuation *in toto*. With links to Rose and Davies' concept of policy inheritance – the idea that, 'Policymakers spend far more time living with the consequences of inherited commitments than with making choices that reflect their own initiatives'[26] – Crossman admitted that, once the Boyd-Carpenter system had been in operation for a few years, all that could be achieved was 'for the Labour Party to amend the Government scheme'.[27] As will be highlighted in a future chapter, changes to the Labour Party's policy on contracting-out were to be the most obvious consequence of inherited commitments.

Pre-empting debates about the increased role that selective benefits might play, the third of Crossman's issues to be reviewed was 'the application of National Assistance'.[28] Here, Crossman highlighted a particular weakness of national superannuation: that there would have to be a long transition period before fully earning-related benefits could be paid out, leading to a 'gap between the actual and proposed rates of benefit'. And it was in this role, to plug this forecast discrepancy, that Crossman grudgingly saw a possible limited role for means-tested support. As will be highlighted later in this chapter, a fresh concept did emerge which – though not based on the traditional means test – involved targeting the needy through the years of transition. This was the income guarantee.

Highlighting a further perceived problem with national superannuation, Crossman's final issue to be considered was 'the relationship between pensions and various other benefits'.[29] Crossman noted that the unemployed and the long-term sick were groups 'not considered in our National Superannuation scheme',[30] and, with poverty in the process of being 're-discovered', this exclusion was not something he wished to see maintained. Indeed, it is notable that, later that year, at the 1960 Labour Party Conference in Scarborough, Crossman highlighted the plight of '8 million people, men, women and children, in this country living at or near the poverty line'.[31] He added, 'on my rough calculation well over half those people are not old age pensioners and if we concentrate solely on the old age pension we are neglecting a large part of the problem of poverty'.[32] It was this particular problem – the perceived neglect in their earlier planning of those who were not elderly, but in need – with which the Study Group first seriously grappled.

EXPANDING EARNINGS-RELATION

One of the Study Group's earliest attempts to involve more groups in a coherent earnings-related scheme was the consideration, in July 1960, of a suggestion that the existing system of flat-rate contributions for sickness and unemployment benefits be abolished and 'all benefits paid for out of a single wage-related contribution'.[33] Crossman went on to mention the possibility of such a scheme at the Labour Party Conference in October 1960.[34] By March 1961, the policy was becoming more detailed, though far from finalised. It was proposed that the main benefits

> in respect of sickness, redundancy and retirement provided by good public and private employers should in principle be extended to the whole population. Thus benefits would take account of differences in earnings, but those on low wages would receive proportionally more.[35]

In justifying this expansion of the 1957 scheme, it was argued that as national superannuation had sought to 'bring together the "two nations" in old age, so in the sixties we must bring together the "two nations" at work'.[36]

This was not the end of the matter. It was noted that the trade union movement was 'vitally concerned' about any proposals affecting sick pay and unemployment benefit, and were pushing for 'the fullest consultation'.[37] Douglas Houghton was also mindful of union concerns, and suggested a number of revisions.[38] The minutes of a meeting of the Study Group in April record a division between those who felt that legislation to compel more support from the employer was the way forward, and those who supported the idea of a national contributory, earnings-related scheme.[39] This uncertainty meant that, when new social security proposals were published in the policy document *Signposts for the Sixties* there were no bold statements about cleaving together 'two nations at work'. Rather, the idea to include unemployment as part of the earnings-related scheme had vanished, replaced with some vague talk of nationalised industries setting 'a good example'.[40] For the long-term sick, there did remain a significant – if nebulous – proposal to create 'a State system of wage-related sickness contributions and sickness benefits, along the lines proposed for retirement pensions'.[41]

With this proposal for an extension of the state earnings-related scheme published, but with only the flimsiest of details, fleshing out this pledge became the top priority for the Study Group. Crossman suggested that 'National Superannuation, incorporating wage-related provisions for long term sickness, should be our basis for devising a comprehensive, and far simpler, social security scheme'.[42] To help prepare this new comprehensive scheme the Study Group made a detailed examination of relevant social security systems in existence outside the UK, looking for particular inspiration from Belgium, Germany, Sweden, and the United States.[43]

Following a very detailed examination of these four systems by Christine Cockburn of – inevitably – the LSE, the Study Group felt able, by January 1962, to agree on twelve principles that were to be the basis of further discussion.[44]

1. Any future scheme should be fully comprehensive, 'covering benefits for retirement, sickness, unemployment, maternity, widowhood, industrial industries, and a death grant',[45] and it should be universal in application;
2. Contributions to this scheme should be earnings-related, with a proportion paid by the employee, employer and the state;
3. The earnings-related formula used should allow for an element of redistribution;
4. Any retirement benefit should be based on an individual's most richly remunerated years, not just an average figure, and, thereafter, linked to rises in average earnings;

5. Both flat-rate benefits and, when in operation, wage-related ones should be index-linked;
6. Late-age entrants should be included within the scheme as soon as possible;
7. There should be provision for early retirement because of long-term unemployability or sickness;
8. Employers should pay in full, or supplement state benefits, to ensure an individual's normal level of earnings for the first weeks of sickness;
9. The possibility to abolish individual contribution records should be examined;
10. The possibility should be examined to introduce a non-means-tested benefit to assist pensioners with their rent through the transition period;
11. Occupational pension schemes should be expected to fit in with the state scheme;
12. Unemployment benefit should be earnings-related in the short-term, and flat-rate thereafter.

Having settled on these twelve principles – a combination of old and new – it was left to 'new boy' Tony Lynes to lead an attempt to develop these ideas into a practical social security scheme.[46]

If anything, the proposals that came out of the Lynes-led draft social security scheme made for a less coherent state of affairs than had existed previously.[47] The principle that contributions were to be made earnings-related remained, as did the planned comprehensive state scheme of earnings-related sickness and unemployment benefits. However, in this draft scheme, earnings-related benefits – in two parts, with a flat-rate benefit similar to the existing system augmented by an earnings-related supplement worth one quarter of the individual's average weekly income – were only to cover absence from work for the first year. After twelve months, the earning-related element would cease, and a new system of enhanced flat-rate benefits would kick in. The report admitted that the new policy 'may at first seem an untidy compromise'.[48]

Some of the factors noted as forcing this evident untidiness included practical problems such as not wishing to provide incentives for employers to discriminate against workers with poor health records and trying to cover trades with a tradition of rapid turnover of labour, such as construction.[49] However, topping the list of constraints, was the position of the trade unions. As was made very clear in a note for one of the regular meetings between representatives of the Study Group and the TUC Social Insurance Committee, the unions continued to remain 'apprehensive about the move away from a flat rate "subsistence" approach'.[50] The unions were also keen to ensure that the state left some scope for them to be able to negotiate sick pay arrangements 'to their own liking'.[51]

Eventually it was decided that the basic unemployment and sickness scheme designed by Lynes was 'broadly acceptable to the Study Group'.[52] However, there remained some divisions. Houghton objected to the proposal that sickness and unemployment benefit should be at the same rate, urging that unemployment benefit should be raised. This protest was dismissed by the Study Group. Following the unions' lead, Houghton also objected to the proposal to compel employers to pay full wages to their employees during the first ten weeks of sickness, 'since this would interfere unduly with conditions of service'.[53] This issue, the Study Group believed, was worth another look, after further examination of the German system.

In the end, however, the Study Group spent little more time debating the details of the proposals to extend earnings-relation to the unemployed and long-term sick. Much of Lynes' draft scheme was translated directly into a policy statement of the National Executive, *New Frontiers for Social Security*.[54] Furthermore, the Labour manifesto for the 1964 election did indeed promise – with very few details – to introduce a 'new wage-related scheme covering retirement, sickness and unemployment'.[55] As will be illustrated in the next chapter, only part of this pledge was implemented when Labour returned to power.

THE INCOME GUARANTEE

One of the reasons that the Study Group pushed this expansion of national superannuation rather to one side during the last few years of Labour's period in Opposition was the arrival of a new idea in Labour's policy process, one that came to dominate discussions from the spring of 1962 onwards. This idea arrived as a minor proposal to fix a perceived hole in the national superannuation scheme, but it very rapidly developed to become the centrepiece of Labour's plans for social security reform. This was the income guarantee.

The spark that lit this new policy appears not to have come from Powell and developments in the Conservative policy process, but, rather, emanated from Cockburn's examination of the four countries' social security systems noted earlier. As noted, one fresh idea outlined was that there 'should be some examination of the possibility of a non-means-tested form of financial aid to retirement pensioners in respect of their rent during the transitional period of flat-rate benefits'.[56] Though non-means-tested, there was a suggestion that only the most needy would receive the full benefit. Particular note was made in the document of the Swedish system of housing supplement. This suggests that that 'policy transfer' was at play, this being 'the process in which knowledge about policies, administrative arrangements, institutions etc. in one time and/or place is used in the development of policies, administrative arrangements, institutions etc. in another time and/or place'.[57] The Swedish system included a variable amount of supplement, available in bands up to a maximum of £100 for those households with a total annual income of less than £70. Very significantly, the Study Group lighted on the fact that eligibility for this supplement 'is decided on the basis of income tax assessment forms'.[58]

The impetus behind this examination of extra financial aid for some pensioners was concern that national superannuation failed to address the problem of existing pensioners in poverty. Indeed, from the beginnings of the national superannuation debate, one lingering problem had been the long transition period between the payment of old and new scheme benefits, one which potentially left large numbers of pensioners stuck on national assistance for many years. Indeed, this was, as mentioned earlier, one of the key problems Crossman had noted in that first Study Group of the 1960s.

This problem of existing pensioners in poverty was a particularly sore point for Labour's 'rank and file', as was repeatedly highlighted at the 1960 Labour Party Conference. That national assistance was deeply unpopular was evident, with one delegate expressing the mood of many by declaring that, 'I know that you will agree that it is entirely wrong that the old age pensioners should have to beg an existence'.[59] Another delegate made the point that whilst national superannuation scheme was fine as a method of guaranteeing future provision, 'what we are concerned with now is the immediate position of the old people as they are today'.[60] Thus the members of the Study Group were under pressure to find a method of creating an affordable system of support for existing pensioners for those years before national superannuation began to pay out generous benefits, without, if possible, having to resort to national assistance. Simply raising flat-rate benefits to a level that would remove all pensioners off national assistance was not an option the Study Group seriously considered. It would lead, it was reckoned, to 'an astronomical rise in contribution rates'.[61] Therefore this idea for a non-means-tested housing benefit targeted at retirement pensioners in need was, for the Study Group, very seductive. However, there was, as the Study Group acknow-ledged, a 'possibly fatal difficulty' in implementing such a scheme: rents varied much more in Britain, so creating a Swedish-like national level of housing supplement would have been 'impractical'.[62]

As before, it was left to Lynes and his team to create a practical proposition out of a hazy idea. In his draft social security plan of March 1962, Lynes sidestepped the problem of variable levels of rent by changing the proposed housing benefit into a general 'pension supplement', with this to be 'paid automatically to all retirement pensioners without any prior test of means in order to bring their pensions up to what we call a "guaranteed level"'.[63] There was general support in the Study Group for the idea of a pension supplement, but not for the complicated manner in which Lynes proposed that money would be recouped from those pensioners with an income in excess of the guaranteed level.[64] Indeed, one member remarked that the proposed 'recoupment tax' suggested of 'giving with one hand and taking away with another', and this was deemed a very unwelcome prospect.[65]

At the next meeting of the Study Group, in July 1962, discussion about the problems related to calculating the amount of pension supplement to be paid led to Crossman making a very significant intervention. He mused about the possible use of:

> some modified form of PAYE whereby the local office of the Ministry of Pensions and National Insurance would be supplied with a basic code number in respect of each retired person by the Board of Inland Revenue by means of which it would assess the supplement to be paid in each case.[66]

The Study Group was divided on the practicalities of this suggestion, so it was agreed that Houghton, the former tax specialist who happened to be absent from this particular meeting, be consulted on this issue. Houghton leapt at this opportunity.

Only weeks later, Houghton submitted a paper to the Study Group entitled 'The Guaranteed Income',[67] and introduced it by saying that the administrative difficulties of Lynes's scheme 'could be overcome by adopting the principles of income tax in calculating the supplement payable'. Houghton's idea was, theoretically at least, simple. Tax returns would be used to calculate how much an individual pensioner should receive from the state to make sure their total income reached a particular minimum level. This marked an important moment in the long, tortuous quest for social policy's 'holy grail': a scheme to combine tax and benefit into single transaction, taking from those who could afford, paying out to those who could not – the latter a kind of 'negative' income tax.

In his paper, Houghton recognised that this scheme he was proposing was, effectively, still based on a test of means. However, he argued,

> There will be great advantages in presentation if we say – as we reckon your income for tax, so we reckon it for this supplement. Whether you pay or receive, or even pay and receive (as some will!) we calculate your income in the same way'.[68]

He added that, 'If we take the tax system – its means test and its methods and principles of calculating total income for tax – only false pride will criticise this as "humiliating"'. Naturally, Houghton thought his proposal was better than Lynes's suggestion of uniform increases where some or all was clawed back. He also poked the Beveridge system in the eye by suggesting his scheme was preferable to general increases in flat-rate benefits 'which are inadequate for some and not needed by others'.[69]

The response from the Study Group was very positive, indeed Crossman 'congratulated Mr. Houghton on his paper and thanked him for it'.[70] From then on the income guarantee was at the forefront of the Study Group's activities. The public were made aware of the new approach in the policy document *New Frontiers for Social Security* where it was declared that it was necessary to mount 'a special rescue operation' to assist the increasingly large number of pensioners below the National Assistance level,[71] and it was admitted that this particular problem would remain throughout the first years of operation of the proposed national superannuation scheme. It was explained that the Labour Party's new way round this problem was:

> a quite novel kind of Income Guarantee which fixes a minimum income level and ensures that the necessary supplementary benefit will be paid as of right, and without investigation by the National Assistance Board, to everyone whose total income falls below that level.[72]

Details about this new policy were sketchy. For example, regarding the crucial matter of the level at which the income guarantee would be determined, *New Frontiers* merely suggested that, in the first year of operation, it would be 'fixed at a level well in excess of the present level of retirement pension'.[73] This lack of figures reflected the concept's newness, a matter Houghton himself addressed when writing, 'I am warned on all sides that the novelty of the operation is bound to raise snags galore'.[74] He was not kidding. These 'snags' included the administrative hurdle of re-engineering a system designed exclusively to take money in to achieve the opposite and give it out, and the issue of what to do about the wide disparity in the amount individuals paid in rent. Moreover, as the civil service were quick to demonstrate after the 1964 general election, despite spending much time discussing the income guarantee, Labour's policy-makers failed to resolve these difficulties by the time they were in a position to implement the scheme.[75]

Notwithstanding the income guarantee's unresolved 'snags', the concept figured prominently in Labour's manifesto for the 1964 general election.[76] Indeed widows, as well as those already retired, were promised a supplement, to be received 'without recourse to National Assistance', if their incomes failed to reach a particular – still unspecified – level. Furthermore, as Adrian Webb has suggested, it was the shiny new income guarantee, rather than dowdy old national superannuation, that received most attention during the campaign.[77] It made no odds though, because – as the next chapter will illustrate – the income guarantee wilted once a Labour government was in power, unable to cope with the political and economic environment of the 1960s.

SUMMARY

Despite an impression of sluggishness, the first half of the 1960s actually saw much activity in the social policy processes of both the government and the Opposition. Regarding the latter, the Labour Party, and, in particular, the influential Study Group on Security and Old Age, were not content merely to put national superannuation on the shelf in 1959 and dust it off again in time for the next election. As Crossman himself made clear, Labour's social policy had to move with the times. This meant more attention had to be paid to groups other than the elderly, such as the sick and the unemployed. It also meant that the attention that remained on the elderly focused more intently on those in immediate need, and on those who would remain in financial straits during the period before national superannuation could begin to cough up generous benefits.

The result of this refocusing of attention led to national super-annuation being joined on the Labour Party's policy agenda by commitments to extend earnings-related benefits to groups other than retired pensioners and by the rather radical income guarantee. Though laudable and imaginative in their own way, one ironic consequence of the development of new policies was that, as Bridgen has suggested, the work necessary to maintain the currency of Labour's core social policy, national superannuation, failed to be done, with serious consequences for later attempts to implement the scheme.[78]

Crossman was, of course, party to these developments; indeed it was he that made the key suggestion about using the machinery of the Inland Revenue to work out pension supplements which prompted Houghton to develop the income guarantee. However, Crossman did not dominate the Study Group as he had before the 1959 election. Houghton, with his vast knowledge of the tax system, became a rival political figure of authority and, just as Crossman had become the champion of the national superannuation policy in the late 1950s, so Houghton became the torch-bearer for the income guarantee. As the following chapters will elaborate, the overloaded policy agenda and rival political ambitions were important elements in the story of how this radical crusade which Crossman started – to break Britain free of the Beveridge system – slowed to a near halt during the second half of the 1960s.

5 INTO THE STORM[1]

The general election of 1964 began a period, which ran until June 1970, of continuous Labour administration – though one that began with a less than secure majority of four. As John Cole remembered, the Labour government of 1964 was one which 'took office on a wave of hope'.[2] Furthermore, the new Prime Minister, the relatively young Harold Wilson, had proved himself in the brief period from his election as Labour Party leader to be a very effective Leader of the Opposition, and began his premiership, in Peter Hennessy's opinion, as 'a genuinely shining figure'.[3] However, despite gaining a more secure ninety-seven seat majority in the spring of 1966, Wilson and his government quickly stopped glistening and began, in many ways, to look rather grubby.

Failure to deliver promised radical social reform was an important factor in the less than glowing collective memory of the first two Wilson governments. As hinted earlier, the two radical, Beveridge-busting social policy concepts – national superannuation and the income guarantee – simply failed to be implemented. Consequently Howard Glennerster has much evidence to back his claim that, on the social policy front, Wilson 'left office with very little credit'.[4] Others have been kinder. For example, Andrew Thorpe's verdict on the 1964–70 administrations' efforts is that 'given the constraints, we should perhaps be more surprised at what the government was able to do than condemnatory of what it failed to achieve in social policy'.[5]

Pat Thane makes a similar point, arguing that, 'Despite the economic difficulties and despite (and to some degree in response to) the criticisms of its own supporters, between 1964 and 1970 Labour presided over a notable expansion of state welfare'.[6] And, in terms of social security policy in particular, there clearly was some success in a difficult economic climate. Some of the radical thinking that had illuminated Labour's social policy process in the long years in Opposition did materialise, at least in a skewed form, as earnings-related supplements for widows, the sick, and unemployed were introduced. In addition, benefit rates were increased regularly and, at times, generously. Nevertheless, the loss of national superannuation and the income guarantee were grievous blows to the Party's radical reputation, and Crossman's longstanding goal of forcing the 'end of Beveridge' remained unfulfilled as he, and the rest of the Labour government, left office in 1970.

This chapter will largely be an account of how the wheels fell off Labour's social policy machine during its first few months in power. In particular, the spotlight will fall on the fate of the income guarantee, this proposal being simply abandoned in 1965. The saga of national superannuation, which was subject to a more lingering demise, will be examined in the following chapter.

CROSSMAN'S TEMPORARY EXILE

One intriguing element in this story of woe is the role played by Crossman. Initially, Wilson appeared reluctant for Crossman to be involved with implementing social security reforms. Crossman noted an interesting conversation he held with Wilson a few months prior to Labour's election victory in 1964. On being asked what position in government he would like if Labour won the election, Crossman replied,

> 'Well, I'd really like pensions, of course, because I would like to get that job done properly. It's not easy.' Here, Harold was quite impatient. 'Pensions? That's all finished. You've done that. No, no, that's not a job worth your while. I'll give that to someone quite junior. Try again.'[7]

From this it would appear that not only did Wilson want Crossman at a distance from the Ministry of Pensions, but also that the soon-to-be Prime Minister did not consider social security a particularly important issue. And Wilson was as good as his reported word, when, after the election, he gave Crossman the surprising position of Minister of Housing, and appointed Margaret Herbison as Minister of Pensions. Herbison was a stalwart of the Study Group on Security and Old Age and became a respected and able minister. However, during this period in Opposition, Herbison was not regarded a major figure, but rather as 'an unremarkable, mainstream loyalist'.[8] More significantly, Wilson did not grant Herbison the status of Cabinet Minister. Rather, Cabinet responsibility for social security, and health, fell on the shoulders of Douglas Houghton, the champion of the income guarantee. He was given the non-departmental post of Chancellor of the Duchy of Lancaster, and his role was to act as a social policy 'overlord'. This, as will be explained presently, was not an ideal organisational state of affairs.

Crossman, as a member of the Cabinet, did play some part in social security matters during the first couple of years of Wilson's administration, but this was largely confined to that of grumpy commentator. From January 1967, Crossman enjoyed a more active role in the social security policy process as chairperson of the Ministerial Sub-Committee on Earnings-Related Pensions. This situation was made more secure when Crossman – in the non-departmental position of Lord President of the Council – was created, like Houghton before him, 'overlord' of the separate ministries of social security and health. In November 1968 this position was rationalised when the ministries merged, and Crossman received the new title of Secretary of State for Social Services. However, as will be explained, Crossman claimed that his reaching of this central position – four years after achieving power – was 'too late', as the pace of government had become too sluggish to force through the radical ideas Crossman had in mind.[9]

CRISIS MANAGEMENT

After his disappointing experience during the 1964–70 Wilson governments, Crossman was particularly critical of the perceived waste of the first few months in office. He argued that, as Wilson himself believed, for a particular administration to achieve great things, it needed to rush out of the starting-gate with 'tremendous' gusto, emulating President Kennedy's 'hundred days'. What it should not do, Crossman suggested, was come up with 'a set of emergency programmes improvised on the spur of the moment'.[10] And the output, in terms of social security reform, in those crucial scene-setting first months certainly gave the impression of ministers reacting to events rather than one of rational policy-making.

One of the newly-elected Labour government's first actions was to announce a simple, if considerable, increase in national insurance benefits. This was a manifesto commitment, but it was hardly the stuff of radical reformers. Yet, as will be illustrated, even such a seemingly simple decision as this created havoc at the very highest level of government, and as Howard Glennerster has suggested, this decision – combined with a difficult financial situation – had unfortunate repercussions for other commitments.[11]

The 1964 Labour manifesto had promised that 'new and better levels of benefit' were dependent on 'the rate at which the British economy can advance', but that the income guarantee would go ahead regardless.[12] However, the minutes of the first meeting of Wilson's Cabinet recorded a change of plan, with a declaration that, 'It would be important to give as high a priority as possible to proposals for expenditure on social services'.[13] Thus, as an early signal of intent, it was agreed to increase national insurance benefits by an unprecedented 18.5 per cent, using the existing flat-rate system. This decision was made despite an earlier warning from First Secretary and Secretary of State at the newly formed Department of Economic Affairs, George Brown, that 'the economic situation was serious. It appeared to have been deteriorating for some time; and there was a prospect of a large and continuing deficit on the balance of payments'. The Chancellor of the Exchequer, James Callaghan, painted an even gloomier picture, to the point of warning, 'in the long term we might need to invoke our right to draw on the International Monetary Fund'.[14]

Such dismal predictions looked appropriate as the announcement of the benefit increase in November's Budget provoked a severe crisis of confidence in the British economy. This, in turn, led to a bizarre little episode involving truculent backbenchers, some rapidly and poorly cobbled-together plans to help pensioners, and an eventual U-turn in the face of impending devaluation. The catalyst for this crisis came from a surprising source. Swift on the heels of the budget, there arrived on the Cabinet agenda a report from the (Douglas-Home established) Lawrence Committee, which included a seemingly innocuous suggestion that MPs should receive a substantial salary increase backdated to the start of the session.[15] This particular recommendation was accepted, but, unexpectedly, it caused much grief. As Crossman ruefully noted in a footnote:

> Within a few days it became very clear that we had completely misjudged one thing. Whereas we had assumed that nobody could deny the right of MPs to a backdated pay award, there was in fact strong opposition to any increase for them and an unpleasant contrast made between our treatment of MPs and our treatment of old-age pensioners.[16]

As a result, many Labour backbenchers, alarmed at this apparent contrast between themselves and some of their less favoured constituents, began 'insisting that the pension increase should not be postponed until April but paid out much earlier'.[17] That Wilson's slender majority suggested an early election only intensified this call.

The Cabinet reacted sharply, if not wisely, to this new source of pressure. At a meeting on 19 November, the Cabinet agreed that something – anything – must be done to placate the backbenchers. The suggestions included bringing forward the date that national insurance benefits would be raised, despite 'the formidable administrative difficulties'. Desperation is evident in the suggestion that one possible means to expedite proceedings was to seek 'independent advice on the extent to which computer services might be used for this purpose'.[18] Astonishingly, Herbison, the minister responsible for national insurance – who, as a non-Cabinet Minister, could only attend when invited – was not present to discuss these suggestions.

However, it was Herbison's responsibility to return to the Cabinet, on 24 November, to explain how she was to respond to the suggestion to backdate national insurance benefits. Yet, in response to her plan to do exactly what the Cabinet had asked of her, she received, in Crossman's opinion, 'nothing but almost universal hostility'.[19] The reason for this reaction was that, by this stage, only days later, the situation had changed completely as a run on sterling had made the currency appear precariously vulnerable, and this, rather than angry backbenchers, became the Cabinet's paramount concern. As Crossman reported,

> The whole mood of the Cabinet last Thursday had been one of readiness to surrender and appease the backbenchers, but now, between the two Cabinet meetings, we had been faced with a sudden economic crisis and we could hardly fail to realise the obvious fact that if we implemented our decision of the previous Thursday we might well have a nine per cent bank rate or a devaluation.[20]

The Prime Minister's summing up of this sudden change of direction is illuminating, with the Cabinet minutes recording Wilson as stating that:

> in seeking to strike a balance between these conflicting considerations, the Cabinet should have due regard to the change in our economic circumstances which have taken place since their earlier discussion of the questions raised at this issue, as evidenced by the sharp increase in Bank Rate on the previous day. Rightly or wrongly, foreign holders of sterling would be considerably influenced by the extent to which they felt confidence in the Government's economic policies as a whole and by the Government's firmness in adhering to decisions once taken.[21]

Thus, to give at least an appearance of confidence, Wilson concluded that 'it appeared inevitable that the Cabinet's earlier decision [to delay the day of payment until spring] should stand'.[22]

To tie up this little saga, this decision not to backdate payments led to showdown at a Parliamentary Labour Party meeting that evening between the leadership – frantic about the possibility of devaluation – and the backbenchers, to whom this danger 'wasn't real' and were baying for more concessions for the pensioners.[23] In the end, George Brown managed to mollify the backbenchers by hinting at the potential danger and 'made them feel they had to accept the leadership of the Government and drop the idea of any further concessions to the pensioners'.[24]

Though this particular crisis had ended relatively calmly, damage had been done. Fear of the speculators – actual or imagined – became a major factor in the Prime Minister's future policy ambitions. As Wilson himself later bemoaned,

> We were soon to learn that decisions on pensions and taxation were no longer to be regarded, as in the past, as decisions for Parliament alone. The combination of tax increases with increased social security benefits provoked the first of a series of attacks on sterling, by speculators and others, which beset almost every action of the government for the next five years.[25]

Thus Labour's leadership was, from then on, very wary of any proposal that might again start the financial markets twitching. The changed atmosphere caused further suggestions for increasing public expenditure to be treated with extreme caution. This situation clearly had a major, and rather blunt, influence on plans for social security reform. It was certainly a major factor when, during the next crisis, the income guarantee was found dispensable. As Houghton himself put it, the income guarantee foundered 'on the rocks in the economic gales of July 1965'.[26]

DEEPER PROBLEMS

Clearly some unfortunate decision-making and the hairy financial situation during the first months of Wilson's administration did not help the implementation of the income guarantee. Crossman, as Glennerster highlights,[27] was in no doubt where the blame lay for the dismal turn of events. In his *Diaries*, Crossman claimed that Houghton and Herbison:

> got into a horrible mess and confirmed my fear that the whole strategy of our pensioneering, worked out for years before the election, had been jettisoned almost without noticing it by the Minister under the *diktat* of Douglas Houghton. The basic idea had been that we should switch as soon as possible from flat-rate to earnings-related contributions and in this way pile up enormous sums in the pension fund which we could use to dynamise the existing flat-rate pension. That was cardinal. However Douglas [Houghton] and Peggy [Herbison] had turned things upside down, by first of all conceding an enormously increased

flat-rate benefit financed by increased flat-rate contributions. The net result is the worst possible of all worlds as we can't raise the flat-rate contributions any higher without imposing an intolerable burden on the lower-paid worker. Even worse, the income guarantee which we had pledged ourselves to introduce would now be at an absurdly low level as the result of the money we had wasted on the huge initial increase of the flat-rate pension. . . . The least damaging thing we could do was probably to abandon the income guarantee because the pittance we could offer would make a mockery of the whole concept.[28]

However, there is more to the story than this. Crossman's account appears to suggest that the ministers had the freedom to introduce, or not, any policy they saw fit on entering office. This was not the case. As Houghton himself bitterly recalled in the aftermath of the abandonment of his pet scheme, he would have liked nothing better than to introduce the income guarantee as soon as possible: 'No Election pledge was more specific and unconditional than to introduce the Income Guarantee'.[29] However, as noted, the first action of the government was to increase existing cash benefits, and, as Houghton himself was willing to admit, this – and the unexpectedly expensive introduction of a redundancy pay scheme – helped stymie the introduction of the guarantee itself. Houghton, though, argued that there was little option but to introduce the benefits as soon as possible in order to achieve two important aims: 'i) to bring about a sharp improvement in real terms in the living standards of those receiving social payments; and ii) to "buy time" to formulate proposals for an Income Guarantee, and so pave the way for the major review'.[30] Moreover, these two aims reflect two major problems that have since been identified as significant factors in the Wilson governments' relatively miserable record on social security.

As noted, the first of the aims identified by Houghton was to improve the lot of those currently awarded benefits, particularly pensioners, and Helen Fawcett has argued that the struggle to achieve this aim has actually proved a perennial and debilitating influence on all post-war policy-makers wishing to transform the national insurance system. As explained earlier, using ideas taken from the concept of path dependency, Fawcett suggests that 'feedback effects generated by the Beveridge model itself were a barrier to long-term change',[31] and that this problem of existing pensioners – always pushing for improved benefits because of the scheme's inflexible and generally meagre nature – was, indeed, the most obvious 'legacy of Beveridge'.[32] Fawcett specifically highlights the situation in 1964, when increasing cash benefits became, almost inevitably, 'the government's first initiative' in order to placate growing pressure, with this, in turn, creating 'practical difficulties' for the implementation of the other more ambitious projects which had been planned.[33]

The argument that those attempting to reform social security during the 1964–70 period were heavily constrained by the various legacies of earlier policy-makers is a convincing one. In particular, the persistent inadequacy of the basic pension did indeed necessitate expedient measures to increase flat-rate levels in order to head off criticism, leaving more radical measures out in the cold. As noted in the previous chapter, for many in the Labour Party the plight of existing pensioners was their priority, and simply improving basic benefit rates was the obvious way forward. Constraints now associated with Fawcett's 'Beveridge Straitjacket' were a serious problem for Houghton and Herbison, and these were simply ignored in Crossman's account of policy failure.

In addition to these structural constraints, there is a further issue which Paul Bridgen has highlighted, and it is related to the second of Houghton's aims: the need to 'buy time' to formulate the income guarantee proposals. Quite simply, despite the time and effort devoted to the income guarantee during the final years in Opposition, Labour's policymakers did not have, by 1964, a scheme ready for implementation.[34] Indeed, this is an argument that Adrian Webb also made, many years before the archives revealed their secrets. Webb suggested that, during its gestation in Opposition,

> it is certainly possible that mistakes had been made about the cost and administrative feasibility of the income guarantee. It is also possible that too few decisions were made before coming into power about the details and that it subsequently became embroiled in the process of civil service consultations.[35]

Archives reveal Webb's argument to be based on fact. The civil service, in the form of the influential National Insurance Review

Committee, did indeed quickly identify a number of issues which supporters of the income guarantee scheme simply failed to address. One of the most important issues was that, as it stood, Labour's proposals failed to explain how the income guarantee could accommodate the huge variance in levels of rent, or even whether it should. The committee were convinced that, 'Variations here are so great that it seems inevitable on grounds of equity that rent above a reasonable minimum should be taken into account on an individual basis'.[36]

Another major stumbling block was that little thought appeared to have been given to the practicalities of involving an organisation that was designed to collect money, not give it out. As officials noted, with some forcefulness, 'it seems clear that the Inland Revenue machine is neither suitable nor readily adaptable to the collection of income returns from both taxpayers and non-taxpayers and the distribution of a social security benefit'.[37] There was a particular problem that, as tax returns were filled in annually, the proposed system simply could not deal with those whose income varied from week to week. There was also a cultural barrier: the Inland Revenue hated the idea. In an annexe to the Committee's report, originally prepared for the Chancellor of the Exchequer, a note from the Inland Revenue read: 'We hope the Chancellor will firmly resist any suggestion that the Inland Revenue should be concerned with the administration of an income guarantee'.[38] There were other problems as well. The officials noted that little detail was available regarding what was to become of groups such as the long-term sick and unemployed left to languish on means-tested national assistance. In short, the income guarantee was regarded as a seriously flawed policy proposal. As Webb has noted, this unsatisfactory situation was hardly surprising:

> however enthusiastic and expert they may be, a group of academics and politicians doubling up as part-time policy planners, [with] . . . a handful of staff servicing the whole range of policy proposals, cannot be expected to devise workable proposals; but they are expected to do so.[39]

Thus proposals for the income guarantee were deemed by officials as simply unworkable, and, even if the 'snags' discovered had been resolvable, time was indeed needed to sort them out, and, to link with Fawcett's thesis, using the existing system to improve benefits was the inevitable holding operation to assuage the pressure from existing pensioners. Thus, though Glennerster and Crossman were correct to mention the deleterious impact of making the increase in cash benefits, it does need to be stressed that the policymakers involved – notably Houghton and Herbison – had limited options available to them in 1964.

THE GARBAGE CAN

One other factor that has been identified as at least a minor factor in the failure of the Wilson government to implement radical reforms, such as the income guarantee, was, simply, poor organisation.[40] An effective lead from ministers might have rescued some manifesto pledges from the mire of official review. For this to occur, coherent organisational structure in the departments responsible for social security would have been necessary. Unfortunately, overall organisation during this period, and beyond, was very far from coherent.

Indeed, regarding this issue of organisation, it can be suggested that Labour's social security policy process bore, at times, a striking resemblance to that described by Michael Cohen, James March, and Johan Olsen in their 'garbage can' model of organisational choice.[41] To give some explanation, Cohen et al. have studied decision making behaviour in organisations they term 'organised anarchies'.[42] Within these 'organised anarchies', it is argued that decision-making is a semi-chaotic process characterised by ambiguity and confusion. They note that the participants who make up the organisation come and go, are often uncertain as to how their particular role fits into the whole, and often behave erratically, giving certain subjects more time than other ones, and perhaps contributing heavily to, or alternatively missing, critical meetings. Elaborating, they have argued that distinct 'streams' run through such organisations, separately carrying problems, solutions, participants, and opportunities, and which, if 'not completely independent of each other', only come together in 'fortuitous' circumstances.[43] Thus this model suggests that an organisation displaying traits of the garbage can is likely to possess an unpredictable decision-making system, where participants often make decisions without really knowing what they want, and where solutions are often discovered to problems not yet encountered.

Linking Cohen et al.'s work to Labour's social policy process, it appears that the stench of the 'garbage can' model was in the air during the Party's period in Opposition, particularly with the adoption of the income guarantee. This concept, as already noted, was designed to be a small-scale solution to a specific problem: that of improving the situation for existing pensioners during the transition years following the proposed introduction of national superannuation. However, with the enthusiastic patronage of one particular participant, Houghton, bringing with him ideas from a different environment, the tax office, the concept evolved to the extent that by the 1964 election some perceived it as the whole solution to the pensioners' problem – with this development diverting attention from the original 'solution', national superannuation. Indeed, as Webb notes, with strong hints of the garbage can, 'Harold Wilson seems to have taken a problem, pensioners' grievances, plus a ready-made but embryonic Labour solution, the income guarantee, and projected them into prominence during the heat of the election'.[44] However, as already noted, officials were easily able to demonstrate that, far than being an answer to a particular problem, the income guarantee merely provoked a whole set of new questions.

The Labour Party's years in government did not witness a sustained move away from 'garbage can' ways of making policy. Indeed, in some respects, the situation became even more chaotic, not least during the crucial first months in power. Hennessy, in particular, has suggested that Wilson's organisational incompetence was a general factor in that administration's relatively sorry performance. He mentions Peter Riddell's invocation of a 'still vivid political folk-memory . . . of the confusion and incoherence which so undermined Harold Wilson's Government' and claims himself that 'Wilson bids fair to be the untidiest of all the postwar premiers in administrative terms'.[45] Thus, despite Wilson's own claims of administrative prowess, many of his attempts to overhaul the machinery of government tend to be recalled unfavourably, resembling, as much as anything, the actions of an over-confident but under-prepared DIY enthusiast let loose with industrial power tools.

There were a number of illustrations of Wilson's wild organisational tendencies. His failed attempt to successfully establish the Department of Economic Affairs is perhaps the foremost example, but the ministries responsible for social policy were also the target for some Prime Ministerial meddling. One example of spectacular administrative clumsiness was Wilson's appointment of Houghton as non-departmental social policy 'overlord', responsible for two ministries. In terms of effectiveness, Crossman slyly noted that, 'As usual the arrangement worked very badly indeed'.[46] Moreover this comment was not simply a personal grudge against Houghton; Crossman later admitted that, when he himself was 'overlord', the situation remained 'hopeless'.[47] Ironically, Wilson himself later mused that a system of 'overlords', as used, again unsuccessfully, by Churchill and Attlee, was one that was 'unworkable under our administrative parliamentary system'.[48] Surprisingly, given its chequered history, politicians still occasionally feel the urge to revive the 'overlord' system. Providing a recent example, in 2003, the then-leader of the Conservative Party, Michael Howard, established an overlord system for his shadow cabinet. With deep awareness of British political history, Peter Riddell suggested that the structure Howard had in mind was 'a recipe for confusion'.[49]

Back in the 1960s, in assessing Houghton's 'overlord' role, Webb has noted particular weaknesses. Houghton only 'had a very small staff and was in the position of having to request information and papers from civil servants in the departments he was supposedly co-ordinating'.[50] Furthermore, Houghton, despite his seat in Cabinet, 'lacked the immediate access to ideas, opinions and data which departmental Ministers have. For example, Miss Herbison . . . had daily briefings with her departmental civil servants, but Houghton did not'. Further adding to the notion of potential organisational chaos, though Houghton was in charge of a wide-ranging social security review set up soon after the 1964 election, the officials who worked on it were only part of 'Houghton's own small office and were not attached to the Ministry of Pensions'. Unsurprisingly, Webb argues that Houghton's 'overlord' role was 'an area of some tension' possibly leading to a delay in the co-ordination of the various social security reforms.[51]

A further important aspect of the argument that poor organisation led to poor policy outcomes relates to the relationship between the Cabinet 'overlord', Houghton, and his social security 'underling', Herbison. To give some background, it is worth fleshing out another of these figures that seem unfairly to have been largely forgotten. Margaret – universally known as Peggy – Herbison was born in the same year as Crossman, 1907, in Shotts, Lanarkshire. The gifted daughter of a miner, Herbison's education was completed at Glasgow University, where she earned an MA, and chaired the university's Labour Party branch. She entered Parliament, like so many others, in 1945, becoming, briefly, Under-Secretary of State for Scotland from 1950 to 1951. As noted earlier, on Labour's return to office in 1964, Herbison became a 'quietly heroic' Minister of Pensions, which remained her position until 1966 when her title became Minister for Social Security.[52] She resigned from the government in 1967. During her period as a minister Herbison developed a distinctive reputation. Union leader, Jack Jones, remembered that she 'fought like a tiger for the pensioners',[53] and, more generally speaking, Barbara Castle commented that Herbison was 'widely esteemed for her conscientious-ness and integrity'.[54] Crossman, though Herbison's main ally in Cabinet, was not quite so complimentary, patronisingly declaring that, 'She's a darling and she fights for the old-age pensioners, but she's wholly in the hands of her officials'.[55] Herbison left Parliament in 1970, becoming Lord High Commissioner to the General Assembly of the Church of Scotland from 1970 to 1971. She made a few appearances in public life after this time, occasionally in tandem with her parliamentary successor, the late John Smith, and she died, in 1996, aged 89.[56]

Returning to 1964, regarding the critical relationship between Herbison and her immediate boss, Andrew Roth suggests that it could have been rosier. He notes – in the very first paragraph of her obituary – that Herbison fought 'many rounds of battles for pensioners and poor families against her hated "overlord", the late Douglas (later Lord) Houghton'.[57] More contemporaneously, Crossman also hinted at the frosty relations between the two most senior figures with responsibility for the government's social security policy, describing Houghton as 'the worst possible kind of overlord for Peggy Herbison'.[58] He also described heated arguments between the two, including during meetings of the Cabinet.[59]

Archive sources also hint at this lack of harmony. For example, there are notes of a considerable row that raged over the seemingly routine matter of whether the question of up-rating cash benefits should be considered by an official committee under the ambit of the

Ministry of Pensions or not. Herbison thought so, Houghton, not. Referring to this matter to Wilson, Sir Burke Trend, the Secretary to the Cabinet, remarked, with the air of an exasperated housemaster, 'As you know, there is a background of personal difficulty'. An equally frustrated Prime Minister responded with a hand-written comment at the top of the letter, 'This seems the most god-awful waste of time'.[60]

Thus, though perhaps not a major factor, it does appear that Wilson, in setting up the peculiar organisational structure for social security as he did – behaving, in Hennessy's pungent phrase, 'as if he were the bureaucratic equivalent of an experiment-crazed boffin'[61] – was not a helpful development on the road to implementing major social reform. It made the already potent constraints to social security reform even more difficult to surmount. Interestingly, there are parallels between the frosty relationship between Houghton and Herbison and another ill-starred couple supposedly in charge of social security some thirty years or so later.

In 1997 another shiny new, and New, Labour Prime Minister, this time Tony Blair, appointed Harriet Harman – then at the start of a very bumpy ministerial career – as Secretary of State for Social Security. The more maverick Frank Field was chosen to serve her as Minister for Welfare Reform. Harman was supposedly the senior figure, but Field was given a wider brief and, in addition, was given additional status by being made a Privy Councillor.[63] He was also, unlike Harman, given a seat on the Cabinet Committee dealing with public expenditure. Thus, in a twist on 1964, it was Field, from outside the Cabinet, who took on Houghton's more wide-ranging role, while Harman performed a more narrowly departmentally defined task, similar to that of Herbison. There was a similar result though: titanic clashes of personality, an organisational structure that left officials uncertain who was in charge, and precious little progress made in terms of welfare reform. Tony Blair's hopes of creating a social security 'dream team' were, in Nicholas Timmins' words, dashed as 'both the relationship [between Harman and Field] and the upside-down structure that had been created . . . proved a disaster'.[63] Both Harman and Field quickly left the government, Field never to return. Harman, though, staged a remarkable recovery, becoming Deputy Leader of the Labour Party in 2007, and holding Crossman's old position as Leader of the House of Commons.

Summary

Returning to the mid-1960s, the first few months in office proved a punishingly tough lesson in political and economic reality for those who had nurtured novel ideas in Opposition, and had hoped to implement them quickly. Douglas Houghton was the first to suffer as his income guarantee fell at virtually the first hurdle. He was not happy. Following the scheme's demise, Houghton took stock of what the government had achieved, including the 'conventional improvements in flat-rate pensions', and regarded the scene as 'depressing'.[64] However, not quite all was lost. As a more reflective Houghton remarked a few years later, one item that 'was salvaged from the wreck of the Income Guarantee' was the arrival of the supplementary benefits scheme in 1966.[65]

This new development in social policy was largely symbolic, with the National Assistance Board simply being replaced by the Supplementary Benefits Commission – with this, in turn, partially absorbed into a new Ministry of Social Security. The aim was to lessen the divide between means-tested and other benefits in order to reduce the stigma attached to the former and thus encourage take-up. In addition, a new and higher rate of benefit was introduced for pensioners who claimed. Some further changes simply involved changes to terms used, for example the transformation of the phrase 'test of need' into the less off-putting 'test of requirement'.[66] Still, to some extent, it worked and helped prompt a rise of 365,000 claimants within a year.[67] By scrapping the National Assistance Board, which enjoyed a relatively high level of discretion when awarding benefits, a further effect was, as Timmins notes, to 'set the means-tested benefits off down a more rights-based road'.[68]

As for the income guarantee itself, though Houghton accurately forecast that the immediate future for the concept was bleak,[69] ideas associated with it were revived many, many years later. In 1998, the Blair government announced that income support for the elderly was to cease, with problems of poor take-up due to stigma still cited as a major problem. Instead, the government announced, 'We are targeting help on those who need it most through a new minimum income guarantee'.[70] It was, as Alan Walker noted at the time, 'essentially a case of back to the future'.[71] It was certainly similarly vague in detail. But at least, unlike its predecessor, the 'income guarantee mark II' was implemented, though the policy, perhaps unsurprisingly, was beset with difficulties. Indeed after a few years in operation this reborn income guarantee was itself replaced, in 2003, with the Pensions Credit, though it remained basically the same: a means-tested device to bring pensioners up to a set level, though this time more explicitly rewarding those with modest savings or who had carried on working beyond retirement age.

The new minimum-income guarantee/pension credit, and other new benefits such as tax credits and the wider 'welfare to work' programmes, could be regarded as products of a very different social policy environment to that of the 1960s. There has been a declared shift away from universalism towards 'more sophisticated and better targeted' means of delivering benefits,[72] and policy is clearly driven by the Treasury to an unprecedented degree. As Timmins has noted, this department is currently in the position of 'shaping welfare reform and tax and benefit changes, and making policy on a scale in which it had never before indulged: creating it rather than merely funding and monitoring it'.[73] Some commentators have seen this turn in Labour policy as a case of 'policy transfer' from the USA,[74] which may indeed be the case. However, it is not necessary to look that far away, geographically at least, to find similar ideas being expressed.

As noted, Douglas Houghton was already trumpeting more sophisticated means of targeting benefits, with the goals of reducing stigma and managing costs, back in the 1960s. Significantly, Houghton also anticipated the current 'intricate relationship' between the departments responsible for revenue and for social spending.[75] Moreover, he also foreshadowed New Labour's priority of establishing strong and stable public finances before increasing social spending, arguing that, 'Redistribution of income as a measure of social change is possible if it is widely acceptable but the consequences in the steepening of the incidence of taxation must be carefully weighed in the balance of national benefit'.[76] He also questioned whether people would accept increased taxes and contributions 'for whatever worthy purposes, without loss of incentive to effort and efficiency'. In some ways, Houghton could, perhaps, be regarded as one of the few members of New Labour to have been born in the nineteenth century.[77]

6

A Story Rich
In Lessons[1]

Douglas Houghton left the Cabinet in January 1967 having nudged the social security regime towards a more targeted future, but having failed to usher in, in his own words, 'the coming of a new Beveridge'.[2] Some months later it was Richard Crossman's turn to attempt to put onto the Statute Book something that would prove 'as memorable as Beveridge'.[3] The vehicle for his hoped-for legacy was the national superannuation scheme with which he had been associated for over a decade. This ambition was thwarted, largely because it took an age for the national superannuation scheme to be made ready to form the basis of coherent legislation, and, as noted earlier, this legislation – the National Superannuation and Social Insurance Bill – fell with the Labour government in June 1970.

However, this tale of disappointment is worth telling for a number of reasons. It highlights the intricacies of the policy process, in particular, as Seldon has explained, the manner in which ideas, individuals, interests and circumstances must mesh in a certain way for progress to be made.[4] In this particular case, of course, these factors failed to interlock, and, despite expectation, promised policy did not materialise. In addition, following on from the previous chapter, similarities between Labour social policy in the 1960s and in the era of New Labour will be highlighted. Moves towards welcoming the private sector as a partner for the state in delivering benefits will be the particular focus of this investigation. Crucially, Crossman was at the heart of this development. As Noel Whiteside has argued, 'Old Labour he may well have been, but Richard Crossman could not have tried harder to shore up the private sector'.[5]

After a short section explaining the often difficult organisational situation in which social security found itself in the period from 1967 to 1970, and Crossman's position in it, this chapter will focus on those elements of the national superannuation scheme that were highlighted earlier: earnings-relation; the role of the private sector; and the funding mechanism. Each of these elements adds something different to the overall picture, and confirms that, in Crossman's words, this particular tale remains, to this day, 'a story rich in lessons'.[6]

CENTRE-STAGE, BUT TOO LATE

Douglas Houghton's departure from the Cabinet in January 1967 gave Crossman a chance to re-establish himself as the Labour Party's social security supremo. Unfortunately, for Crossman, the process was far from straightforward, and Wilson's strange organisational structure continued to cause problems. Focusing first on personnel changes at Cabinet level, it was Patrick Gordon Walker, not Crossman, who succeeded Houghton as social security 'overlord'. This was Gordon Walker's first ministerial position after regaining a seat, at the second attempt, following the 'Smethwick incident' of 1964.[7] As it was, only a few months later, in August 1967, Gordon Walker was moved to Education and Science, to be replaced as 'overlord' by Michael Stewart. However, less than a year later, in March 1968, Stewart – one of the most anonymous figures to grace the senior levels of British government – was abruptly moved back to the Foreign Office to fill the gap where the increasingly volatile George Brown had been until his sudden resignation. It was only then, in April 1967, that Crossman became the new 'overlord' of the separate Ministries of Social Security and Health, though retaining his old title as Lord President of the Council. This situation continued until November 1968 when the ministries merged and Crossman received the new title of Secretary of State for Social Services. This was a step towards organisational sanity, but it was rather late in the day, and, as noted earlier, Crossman argued that the government had, by then, lost any sense of dynamism it may have once possessed, making radical reform unlikely.[8]

Turning to Wilson's organisational structure, even after Houghton's departure the 'overlord' situation continued to create its own particular brand of confusion. Though the relationship between Herbison, still the Minister of Social Security, and Houghton's replacement was less poisonous – in Crossman's judgement, Herbison 'got on with him [Gordon Walker] rather better than with Douglas Houghton'[9] – there remained a striking lack of co-ordination. For example, on the issue of family allowances, Gordon Walker's *Diaries* indicate that he worked jointly with Callaghan, the Chancellor, rather than Herbison on one particular paper to be presented to Cabinet.[10] Herbison offered a very different proposal. Indeed, it is telling that Herbison, as well as loathing Houghton, 'equally detested' Callaghan, and she resigned in July 1967 following a dispute with the Treasury over benefit levels for pensioners and mothers.[11]

A further example of organisational muddle occurred during the creation of the Ministerial Sub-Committee set up in 1967 to review, again, the existing pension system. The 'overlord' Gordon Walker – after discussion with Crossman, who, as Lord President of the Council, was to chair this Sub-Committee – offered to become an ordinary member of this body; a set of affairs that was described by Burke Trend, with typical bureaucratic understatement, as 'a little anomalous'.[12] Even on this matter Herbison was not consulted. Gordon Walker, when explaining these negotiations to the Prime Minister, wrote: 'I take it that you have explained all this to the Minister of Social Security.'[13] The reply makes it clear that Wilson had not.[14] Moreover, with Herbison as Minister of Social Security, Gordon Walker as social security 'overlord', and Crossman as chair of this pensions Sub-Committee, there were now three senior ministers who could claim key responsibility for this central plank of Labour's social security reform agenda.

Herbison's resignation in the July of 1967 did little to improve matters. Judith Hart[15] replaced Herbison as Minister for Social Security, a position that remained outside the Cabinet. Michael Stewart took over from Gordon Walker in August, and Hart became the dominant ministerial force in social security, until Crossman's appointment as 'overlord' in April 1968. According to Crossman's account, Wilson assured Hart that her role in command of that department remained secure even after the arrival of Crossman. This, however, was not what Wilson had told Crossman. At a meal shared with Hart, within days of his appointment, Crossman noted that:

> as time passed it became clearer and clearer that the so-called clear understanding the PM had given me that I was to take over control of these two Departments [Social Security and Health] was something Judith and Kenneth Robinson had not been told themselves. She had the impression that I had accepted the position of a Michael Stewart co-ordinator.[16]

As Crossman later recalled himself thinking, regarding the same situation, 'my God, Harold's kindly indecision certainly creates problems'.[17]

Though not in the Herbison/Houghton league, there were tensions between Crossman and Hart. This was reflected in their differing priorities for social security reform. Soon after taking her post, Hart signalled a desire to break from past policy with the unambiguous declaration that 'I have been examining the implications of the present planning assumptions in the field of social security generally. They are unsatisfactory'.[18] She was unimpressed by the earnings-related pension scheme, and she suggested re-focusing on the problem of 'the pockets of poverty which have recently and rightly become the focus of pressure groups, and, therefore of the press and public attention'. Crossman, however, remained convinced that everyone, needy and affluent, should be at the heart of social reform. Regarding the issue of pension reform, Crossman suggested that Hart was keen 'to make the scheme more redistributive, i.e. to get more money for the bottom of the income scale'.[19] Crossman, on the other hand, thought the proposed superannuation scheme 'has to give value for money all the way through'.[20] As it turned out, there was little chance for Hart to consolidate her position in social security matters as she was promoted into the Cabinet, as Paymaster General, in November 1968.

Hart's promotion occurred at the same time as Crossman's new role as Secretary of State of the merged Department of Health and Social Security. Though there was less confusion over roles in the new giant department, there were still problems, not least the resultant relocation away from the heart of government to 'that dreary part of South London', the Elephant and Castle.[21] In terms of personnel,

Hart's replacement as Minister of State with responsibility for social security was the very competent Stephen Swingler, but he died only a few months later, in February 1969, his heart failing following a viral infection. David Ennals – who went on to head the department himself in 1976 – took Swingler's place until the 1970 election. As suggested in the previous chapter, the organisational structure during the 1964–70 governments, and the high level of personnel turnover, bears more than a passing resemblance to the 'garbage can model of organisational choice',[22] and this might have had some bearing on the administrations' relatively poor record on social security reform.

NATIONAL SUPERANNUATION AND SOCIAL INSURANCE

Despite the difficulties, a determined effort was made to introduce the remaining grand social security concept that remained up the Labour government's sleeve, national superannuation. Much work was done, by ministers and, crucially, by officials to adapt a scheme designed in the late 1950s for implementation towards the end of the following decade. However, this work took time. As Paul Bridgen has argued, for much of the period in Opposition, necessary updating work on national superannuation was, to a large extent, put on hold as other concepts, notably the income guarantee, took the lion's share of the attention.[23] As the previous chapter indicated, on gaining power in 1964, Labour's ministers were otherwise distracted for the first few months. Thus, the process of revision took a long time, even after Crossman had returned to the centre of Labour's social security policy process, and it was not until January 1969 that the relevant White Paper – *National Superannuation and Social Insurance*[24] – was published.

Possibly more significant than the delay itself were the many changes made to the scheme outlined in the 1969 White Paper compared to the one described in 1957's *National Superannuation: Labour's Policy For Security in Old Age*. One of the more eye-catching modifications related to the proposed structure of earnings-related benefits. In the original scheme, an earnings-related pension was designed as a supplement to an enhanced flat-rate benefit. In the White Paper, this two-tier benefit system had been replaced by a fully graded scheme. This, for Bryan Ellis, was the only 'striking' difference[25] between the 1969 and 1957 versions of national superannuation. The problem encountered in the 1950s, that a completely earnings-related benefit system maintained earnings differentials from work into retirement too obviously, was addressed, in the 1969 version, with the addition of a new concept, a two-banded pension formula which allowed for an element of redistribution, though, as Bridgen has highlighted, other changes greatly reduced the scale of this planned redistribution.[26] As will be explored, civil servants were the motor behind this important change.

Differences between the terms for accommodation with the private sector made in the 1969 scheme and those made in 1957 have also attracted comment. Helen Fawcett argues that, 'The most notable contrast between the 1957 proposals and the 1969 White Paper lay in the proposals for contracting-out',[27] a change that worked in the favour of the insurance industry. It was a conspicuous U-turn. As demonstrated in Chapter 3, though contracting-out was to be made permissible under the terms of the 1957 scheme, the conditions attached were extremely stringent and caused much alarm in the insurance industry. In 1969, it was proposed that, far from threatening this private industry, 'The State scheme will work in partnership with the occupational schemes'.[28] This was chiefly signalled by the dropping of the condition for occupational schemes to protect their pensions from inflation. In addition, in order to fit in with the plans for a fully graded scheme, the proposed mechanism for contracting-out was very different in 1969 to that of the original version. It involved a new approach to partial contracting-out, one dubbed 'abatement'. This will be examined later, along with a focus on the various factors that provoked the change of attitude towards the insurance industry.

One other area of contrast between the pension plans of 1957 and 1969 that has been singled out for attention was the manner in which the scheme was to be funded. As Hugh Heclo highlights, the 1969 White Paper 'carefully avoided any mention of "bold investment" for the superannuation fund'.[29] As noted earlier, in 1957 Crossman became very excited by the idea of a National Pensions Fund designed partially to fund future pensions; a device which would, serendipitously, also prove a 'most efficient and unobjectionable machine for buying up equities'.[30] In 1969 the White Paper prosaically explained that 'the new scheme will have two separate funds: a National Superannuation Fund and a Social Fund. Neither will be 'funded' in the technical sense in which most occupational schemes are funded'.[31] These National Superannuation Fund balances were still to be invested, creating a partially and temporarily funded scheme, but it was very far from the original concept, and, as will be illustrated, Crossman was livid that he was forced to drop this idea.

Clearly, much had changed between 1957 and 1969. Indeed, so different were these schemes that one former member of the Study Group on Security and Old Age, Tony Lynes, was moved to write – in the year the White Paper was published – that 'it is twelve years since proposals of this kind were first put forward by the Labour Party, and what was once a pioneering scheme will now do little more than bring Britain into line with our European neighbours'.[32] These changes will now be examined in detail.

EARNINGS-RELATION FOR ALL

To re-cap, as noted in Chapter 3, growing discontent with the Beveridge system of universal flat-rate contributions and benefits reached the Labour Party's policy-making machine in the mid-1950s. Crossman and academics such as Brian Abel-Smith were central to this development and, by 1957, the flat-rate approach was being publicly declared in a Labour Party policy pamphlet 'a dead end', a system that penalised the poorest.[33] However, many in the Labour Party were suspicious that the alternative to a flat-rate system, one based on earnings-relation, would preserve wage inequality into retirement. Others in the labour movement, particularly the trade unions, also retained a lingering fondness for the Beveridge system. These pressures were combined with the incessant need to provide more immediate help to existing pensioners. This led to a compromise, and the proposals announced in 1957's *National Superannuation* included one to preserve, and indeed increase, the existing flat-rate pension, with a level of earning-related benefits to be introduced later as a supplement.

A few years later members of the Study Group were still mulling over these issues. Moreover, with attention increasingly focusing on the plight of existing pensioners, the problem of how to accommodate them into a scheme basically designed for future generations continued to prove a major stumbling block. The Lynes-led draft social security plan of March 1962, that was mentioned in Chapter 4, suggested that the flat-rate pension would have to continue, though other proposed reforms such as the income guarantee, would, it was argued, allow this aspect of the pension to be kept 'at a lower level' than the existing system had allowed.[34] Public commitment to the flat-rate pension was re-stated the following year in *New Frontiers for Social Security*,[35] and again in the 1964 election manifesto.[36] Thus, though many of those working on pension policy for the Labour Party disliked the flat-rate element, they were still unable to conceive of a method of abolishing it completely in time for Labour's first election victory in thirteen years.

Soon after Labour's triumph, considerable changes occurred in the planning of pension policy. The first of these changes concerned the demise of the Labour Party's old Study Group. It did not, as such, vanish as the election results were announced, but, rather, some members remained to form the Social Policy Advisory Committee – again a sub-committee of the National Executive Committee's Home Policy Sub-Committee.[37] However, there is little evidence to suggest that this body played a significant role in the Labour government's social security policy process.

With the Social Policy Advisory Committee largely out of the picture, the scene was left clear for a new dominant force in the Labour government's pension policy community, and, as Bridgen has argued, it was certain interdepartmental committees of officials that strode up to the mark.[38] Moreover, on the particular issue of altering Labour Party policy from support for a two-tier pension system to support for a wholly earnings-related system, it would appear that it was civil service pressure which prompted this important change of policy.

It was before the 1964 general election that the civil service began in earnest to examine the Labour Party's policy on pensions. Indeed, archives contain a detailed review from March of that year, conducted by officials at the Ministry of Pensions and National Insurance (MPNI), in which a number of trenchant criticisms about the national superannuation scheme were made. These criticisms include 'the absence of detailed figures (e.g. on contribution rates)' and concern about 'the inflationary dangers' of the proposals.[39] Officials sagely commented that '"National Superannuation" was not then [in 1957 and 1958], and is even less now, an answer to all questions'. Later, in July 1964, a Working Group on Pensions was established, chaired by Sir Clifford Jarrett, Permanent Secretary at the MPNI. On this Working Group were four representatives from this particular ministry – including Jarrett – and these were supplemented by a smattering of representatives from the Treasury, the National Assistance Board, the Ministry of Labour, the Board of the Inland Revenue, the Ministry of Health, and the Government Actuary Department.[40]

The arrival of a new government in October 1964 did little to disrupt official activities. The Working Party disappeared, but was quickly replaced by the Official Committee on Social Security Review. Jarrett again chaired it, and it enjoyed a similar membership to that of the old Working Group.[41] A note found in the first set of minutes for the new Committee adds to this impression of near-seamless continuity. It states, 'Papers prepared for the Committee (but not those intended for Ministers) could, where convenient, refer to the papers of its predecessor, the Working Group on Pensions'.[42] Moreover, the Official Committee on Social Security Review – the Jarrett Committee, as it came to be called[43] – did not feel constrained by Labour's past policy proposals. As Jarrett noted:

> I shall emphasise that, while we must certainly take account of proposals put forward in Labour Party documents over the last few years, the subject is one of such intricacy that a proper examination of alternatives is needed and the answers should not be pre-judged.[44]

Regarding the issue of introducing a fully graded system, officials had begun to entertain this particular idea before the election. In one note for the Working Group on Pensions, from August 1964, it stated that, 'assuming graduation of both contributions and pensions has come to stay (an assumption which the working group should reflect on)', the question must be asked whether 'a separate flat-rate pension element is any longer called for'.[45] There were a number of reasons for officials to recommend the removal of the flat-rate pension. One obvious one was that its elimination might make the system appear more coherent. As it was noted, 'the simplest course on the benefit side, both administratively and presentationally, would be to replace the separate flat-rate and graduated pension elements by correspondingly fully graduated pensions'.[46]

There was, however, a further, weightier, reason for officials wishing to lose the flat-rate pension, and it related directly to a Treasury-led concern about future financial implications. The officials noted that the 'present system of intermittent and rather drastic increases of the standard rate necessitates a corresponding raising of the national assistance scale rates, if only to avoid the criticism that the increase is not given to those most in need'.[47] By removing the flat-rate element from pensions, from which the obvious comparison to flat-rate assistance rates could be made, the pressure to improve rates for – to use a phrase from another era – 'less deserving' recipients of the state's beneficence would be reduced. This would, in time, allow the vast majority of those retiring to do so with a pension which was above the national assistance level without provoking improvements in the situation for those on means-tested benefit.

In order to proceed with this removal of the flat-rate pension, officials realised that they needed to devise a solution to the problem whereby a completely earnings-related system would, inevitably, perpetuate wage inequalities. This, they reckoned, would present difficulties if it was to be introduced by a supposedly socialist government. A solution promptly appeared, with officials suggesting that a single graduated contribution system proportional to earnings up to a ceiling could be introduced, but, rather than one displaying a direct relationship between earnings and contributions, it could be based on a formula, one that 'if necessary [could be] weighted in favour of the lower paid'.[48]

Thus, even before the Labour Party had pulled on the boots of power, officials in the interdepartmental Working Group on Pensions had decided that the flat-rate pension had to go, and they had also devised a method to make a fully earnings-related system more attractive to those with socialist tendencies. They simply needed to convince ministers about the wisdom of their scheme. They had to wait around a while. The original Ministerial Sub-Committee that had been served by the Jarrett Committee had priorities other than pension reform, and was abolished when Douglas Houghton left the government. Its functions were transferred, in February 1967, to the Ministerial Sub-Committee on Earnings-Related Pensions.[49] As noted earlier, Crossman chaired this new body, and this brought a greater sense of urgency to the proceedings. As the re-styled 'Official Committee on Social Security', Jarrett and his team now served Crossman's committee.

It was in July 1967 that officials presented their thoughts to Crossman's committee on the matter of whether or not to continue with the flat-rate element.[50] In this paper, the officials made a strong case in support of a fully earnings-related system. It was argued that this type of system was 'likely to be able readily to provide whatever level of pension is required at different earnings levels' and it was also claimed that the calculation of the fully earnings-related pension, 'in normal cases at least, would be quite straightforward'.[51] The case for retaining the flat-rate element, the officials argued, was much weaker, and was based solely, it was claimed, on a few presentational factors. Officials also explained more fully their idea for a formula which allowed eventual benefits in a fully – if not purely – earnings-related pension scheme 'to be weighted in favour of the lower earner'.[52] It worked like this. The return on contributions on earnings up to half the national male average was to be calculated generously, with a premium rate benefit of 60 per cent of earnings suggested. The return on contributions on earnings in the 'upper band', of between half the national male average and a 'ceiling' of one and a half times, was not at the big-hearted 60 per cent rate, but one set at a relatively miserly 25 per cent. In short, the wealthy would have earned more benefit, but not a great deal more. Moreover, with contributions to be more obviously linked to earnings, this 60/25 benefit formula would have created a rather handy redistributive element.

In addition to the Jarrett Committee, there appears to have been another source of pressure advocating the flat-rate element's demise. At a crucial stage in the development of the pension scheme the Minister of Social Security was Judith Hart. As noted earlier, Crossman, at this stage, still lacked any departmental responsibility for social security, despite his chairing of the Ministerial Sub-Committee on Earnings-Related Pensions. In Judith Hart's papers at the Labour Party Archives in Manchester, there are many contributions from Theodora – known as Theo – Cooper, an Economics Fellow from Oxford seconded to the Cabinet Office from 1965 to 1969, and Cooper appears to have acted as Hart's special adviser on pension matters. Cooper was also a member of the Official Committee on Social Security and usefully provided background information about the thinking of her fellow Committee members. Regarding the officials' paper on whether to keep a flat-rate pension or not, Cooper argued that, 'There does not seem to be an overwhelming case either way, but I think that on balance the argument for full earnings relation is stronger'.[53] She agreed with the rest of the Official

Committee that a flat-rate pension free system would generally be less complicated, that it would not disadvantage low earners, and that it might promote administrative savings. Furthermore, with an awareness of what would eventually be dubbed 'spin', she argued – in support of full earnings-relation – that 'there are obvious advantages in making the scheme appear as clearly and distinctly as possible a radical reconstruction of the social security system'.[54]

With a background of such advice from the Official Committee, and from Theo Cooper in particular, by October 1967 Hart was writing a memorandum to the Ministerial Sub-Committee on 'why I support the Official Committee's provisional recommendation . . . against a flat-rate pension element in the new scheme'.[55] As Hart explained, she initially had reservations: 'One of my principal anxieties is that when the new scheme is introduced, old-scheme pensioners should not be unfavourably affected'. This was, after all, one of the key reasons that prevented the authors of *National Superannuation* from dropping the flat-rate element in 1957. However, in contrast to the framers of that earlier plan, Hart came to believe that 'Whether or not there is a flat-rate element in the new scheme was not a relevant factor'.[56] For her, a more important factor was to be the success with which both new- and old-style pensions kept up with inflation once they had been awarded. Certainly, in comparison to the 1957 plan, this was to be improved in the planning for the 1969 scheme. There was a proposal to review both sets of benefit payments every two years, and a promise eventually made that 'increases made will, as a minimum, compensate for any rise in prices during the two-year period'.[57] Thus, with this improvement, combined with the new banding concept, Hart was persuaded to follow the officials' line on the flat-rate element's abolition. By December 1967, in a review of conclusions reached, the Ministerial Sub-Committee reported that 'The pension formula should also be fully earnings-related, i.e. should contain no flat-rate or minimum element'.[58] In April of the following year, officials confirmed this by noting that 'only fully earnings-related formulae' were to be considered in future.[59]

This, however, was not the end of the matter. In April 1968 Crossman had his role in the social security policy process enhanced by becoming the non-departmental 'overlord' for social services. In the following month, he was flexing his new political muscle. In his

Diaries, Crossman mentioned the civil service-prompted policy change of removing the flat-rate element and introducing the banded system in its stead, and admitted that he was 'worried by this further complication'.[60] He even stated that he was still considering keeping 'a perfectly simple flat-rate pensions formula as part of our national insurance scheme'.[61] As a result of his doubts, Crossman put the issue on hold by referring it to his special band of pension advisers – the so-called 'Pensions Circus' of old Study Group stalwarts Abel-Smith, Titmuss and economics experts Thomas Balogh and Nicholas Kaldor.[62] Officials were particularly nervy about this development, particularly as Crossman had recently 'stood down' the Jarrett Committee, thus restricting the flow of official advice.[63]

However, it does seem unlikely that Crossman, at this stage, seriously intended to scrap the idea of a pension formula altogether. In a letter he sent to Balogh regarding this meeting of the 'circus', Crossman actually argued the official line that, regarding the existing contribution and benefit structure, to 'continue this combination of flat-rate and graded into the new superannuation scheme would bring grave administrative difficulties without any compensating pre-sentational advantages'.[64] However, at a meeting with officials at a similar time, Crossman – in typical contrary fashion – suggested radical changes to the pension formula, including dropping the '60/25' banding scheme.[65] Possibly this suggestion was not taken too seriously by officials, who felt that Crossman was 'perhaps speaking only in a Socratic vein'.[66]

In any event, on 16 May 1968, members of the 'circus' were joined by relevant ministers and officials at the first meeting of the 'Lord President's group of advisers'.[67] Crossman would have preferred to chair the meeting without the presence of the permanent secretaries, complaining that they 'always want to come to scotch good ideas'.[68] Correspondingly, the officials were less than thrilled at the idea of including 'some "outside" advisers' at this 'last-minute "think-in"'.[69]

Minutes of this first meeting of the 'circus' are missing, but it is clear from other documents in the relevant file that Crossman's protests achieved nothing in terms of changing the existing plans. A paper to be discussed at a further meeting of the 'circus' in June 1968 – by one of the 'outsiders', Brian Abel-Smith – includes the clear assumption that a fully graded system, based on the officials' 60/25 formula, was to be adopted.[70] Thus, Crossman's 'circus' was a interesting early experiment in the use of 'outside' political advisers, a development that has been expanded considerably under later governments, not least those that ply their trade under the New Labour label. The 'circus', however, did not play a significant part in the designing of the eventual superannuation plan.

Having survived the 'circus', the proposal to introduce a fully earnings-related pension scheme – including the '60/25' formula – appeared in the White Paper that was published in January 1969,[71] and then on Crossman's thwarted Bill. When the scheme was published, it appears that, despite claims that a wholly earnings-related system was presentationally simpler, Crossman had been correct to be concerned about the complexity of the scheme, as one result was near-universal bafflement. 'The great mass of the public, the Press, the House, the employers and the unions remain utterly bewildered by the scheme', complained Conservative social security spokesperson Lord Balniel partisanly but not inaccurately, adding, 'What a long way we have come from those simple phrases about half-pay on retirement!'.[72] This bewilderment – made greater still by some fiendishly complicated contracting-out arrangements – was one reason why, when a Labour government once again attempted to introduce a State Earnings-Related Pension Scheme, via Barbara Castle in 1975, the banded scheme was dropped, and policy reverted to support for a two-tier system.[73]

One other interesting aspect of policy to note was the fact that, for those receiving pensions, whether the system was to be wholly earnings-related or a two-tier system was not an issue that would have made a significant difference. As Bryan Ellis – an official involved in the pension policy process in the late 1960s – has highlighted, because of the 'over-compensatory' benefits for the lower income groups, there would have been, even in the fully earnings-related scheme, a near-universal *de facto* basic level of benefit for the least economically secure.[74] Thus there would have been a fairly seamless continuation of the existing flat-rate basic pension even if the fully earnings-related scheme had been introduced. The only significant difference, as the officials acknowledged way back in August 1964, would have been the severing of the notional link between pensions and means-tested supplementary benefits, thus separating the elderly from those deemed 'less worthy' of generous state support and minimising future financial commitments.

LOWERING THE 'CEILING'

For Bridgen, one of the most important modifications to proposals from 1957 to 1969 was the change in the original scheme's earnings limit for employees' contributions – the so-called 'ceiling'. This, Bridgen argues, was one factor that indicated that the 1969 scheme was 'considerably less ambitious than that outlined in 1957'.[75] This ceiling was the point in an individual's earnings beyond which contributions would not be payable, and, likewise, benefits would not be available. As noted earlier, one reason presented for introducing a ceiling was that it was a device to prevent the payment of very high pensions to a few in a scheme designed, primarily, to lessen pension inequality.

As noted in Chapter 3, in 1957 the suggested ceiling for contributions was one of 'four times the average wage',[76] which, when combined with the proposed 'floor' below which no pension would be permitted to fall, would have left considerable scope for redistribution within the scheme. Little changed in the next few years, with Lynes, in 1963, mentioning that Labour's pension plans still included this relatively high ceiling of 'possibly four times the average wage'.[77] However, by 1969, this ceiling of four times the average wage had been lowered considerably to one 'of about 1½ times national average earnings';[78] though there was to be no ceiling for employers. The proposed lowering of the employees' ceiling was highly significant because, in Lynes' words, it would 'reduce to some extent the redistributive nature of the scheme [because] [t]he higher the contribution ceiling, the bigger the 'profit' available to subsidise the pensions of the low paid workers'.[79]

As with the proposal to introduce a fully graded scheme, the role of certain official committees appears significant in the change of policy. As early as March 1964, in that examination of Labour's plans for social security reform mentioned earlier, officials were warning that 'an earnings ceiling for contributions of anything like four times average earnings was higher than was proper or necessary'.[80] Soon after the Labour Party came to power, the Jarrett Committee was quick to come up with an alternative figure, asking, rhetorically, 'need it be more than 1½ times average earnings?'.[81]

There were a number of reasons why officials were keen to lower the ceiling. There was a practical consideration that relatively little was gained by extending the ceiling much beyond the 1½ times average earnings mark.[82] Even Lynes – not a regular sympathiser with attempts to water down the 1957 scheme – concurred with this view, remarking that:

> At first sight, the proposed ceiling may seem disappointingly low. In fact, however, a higher ceiling would make surprisingly little difference to the scheme. As we have already noted, only 7 per cent of employees earn more than one and a half times average industrial earnings. Of those 7 per cent, probably the majority earn only a few pounds a week more'.[83]

However, there were others factors lurking. As Bridgen has noticed, Treasury officials in particular were troubled by the potential effect of the pension plan's redistributive elements.[84] These officials argued that Labour's suggested scheme 'penalised the higher paid relative to the lower paid [and this] might tend to discourage higher earnings'.[85] On the interdepartmental Official Committee on Social Security Review this point was made rather differently. There too was concern that a high ceiling would penalise high earners. However, the main problem as perceived by this body was not that this was an unwise decision, but rather – if redistribution was wanted – then there were better ways of going about it. As they noted, 'if it is considered desirable to raise more revenue from high earners taxation is a more direct and straightforward source'.[86]

Thus there was concern about the potential effects of redistribution, although it is difficult to argue that this was the main reason for official disinclination to suggest a high ceiling. What appears more pressing was the potential effect such a ceiling would have on private occupational pensions. As the Jarrett Committee clearly admitted, 'one of the greatest drawbacks of a high ceiling is the damage it would inflict on occupational pension schemes'.[87] To explain, in what will become a major theme of the next section, it had become patently clear by 1965 that the private pension sector was here to stay and could not be treated lightly. The Jarrett Committee thus concluded that a state pension scheme should concentrate on providing for what Crossman later described as the 'ground floor',[88] leaving the top floors, where the wealthy went shopping, to the private sector. The rationale was that, at this higher level, 'adequate facilities already exist through occupational schemes or individual private insurance'.[89]

In the archives, one paper by Theo Cooper is particularly helpful as a guide to the thinking behind the setting of the ceiling.[90] Balancing the debate, Cooper noted that one of the perceived benefits of a high ceiling was that it would help maintain the ideal concept of a state scheme with 'fully transferable, dynamised pensions that provide a reasonable degree of earnings relation, and therefore protection of living standards at retirement, for people over a wide range of earnings levels'. She also pointed to the 'economic advantage of the extra revenue' a higher ceiling would generate, though she did also note, as mentioned earlier, that little extra would be gained by increasing the ceiling beyond 1½ times average earnings.

On the other side of the debate, in favour of a lower ceiling, Cooper expressed concern that a high ceiling would create difficulties in setting a suitable level of contribution acceptable to all employees. Furthermore, and critically, she also made the point that the 'higher the ceiling, the more damage is done to occupational pension schemes and the more difficult it is to deal satisfactorily with their adjustment problems'.[91] She concluded by arguing that the points in favour of a lower ceiling outweighed those that supported the contrary position. Thus Cooper closed, commenting that 'I think it would be sensible to decide against a 'high' ceiling, as the Official Committee suggests' – though she was concerned that aim should not be much below the 1½ level as that 'would seem to involve rather too much whittling down of a scheme planned as a very long term one because of transitional problems'. The very next day, Crossman – chairing the Ministerial Sub-Committee on Earnings-Related Pensions – found the officials' argument 'conclusive', and thus it was agreed that there should be a 'moderate ceiling' which covered 'the span of 1¼ and 1½ times average earnings'.[92] In the end, the slightly larger figure – one worth £75 million in extra contribution income – was the one chosen.

Thus, again under pressure from the civil service, Labour Party pension policy was altered. Some of the impetus behind the official recommendation to lower the ceiling can be attributed to apprehension that the originally considerable redistributive element of the pension scheme would damage incentives. However, most of the evidence suggests that the prime factor behind the setting of a lower ceiling in 1969 was that, by this stage, private sector accommodation was regarded a prerequisite for a successful state pension scheme, and this made a high ceiling an impossibility. This acceptance of the private sector was not one that filled officials with glee, but rather, as will be examined more closely in the next section, was regarded as a sad inevitability.

TOWARDS PUBLIC-PRIVATE PARTNERSHIP

Though the influence of the civil service, and in particular the Jarrett Committee, was a major factor in the remodelling of Labour's national superannuation scheme, its arrival on the scene does not, on its own, tell the whole story. There was one area in particular where, though officials had an influence, it was not a decisive one. It was also an aspect Crossman singled out as a 'really formidable problem'.[93] This problem concerned contracting-out, which, as explained earlier, was the mechanism by which an individual could contribute less to a state scheme – and thus receive less benefit in return – providing that s/he had an adequate alternative provided by the private pensions sector. With occupational pensions then providing the vast majority of pensions outside the state system, the stringency of conditions for contracting-out was the most important influence on the relationship between the public and private sectors. The changes to the policy on contracting-out made during the late 1960s were amongst the most significant attempted. This is because – decades before New Labour – they explicitly marked the Labour Party's acceptance that a significant role ought to be played by the private sector in the delivery of social security.

As noted in Chapter 3, the framers of the original national superannuation scheme had little love for the insurance industry. Though it was accepted, grudgingly, that some form of contracting-out should be allowed, the conditions necessary were deliberately designed to be exceptionally tough to fulfil, and it was hoped, in the words of Titmuss, that the scheme would, eventually, 'break the power of private insurance'.[94] However, in the end, Labour's plan merely spurred the Conservative government into action, and, subsequently, reforms were introduced that included a contracting-out system which, rather than threatening the insurance industry, actually gave it quite a fillip.

In Opposition again, the Labour Party continued, for a while, to harbour a flinty attitude towards the private sector, despite the outcry from the insurance industry about the 1957 scheme. Although, as mentioned earlier, in the summer of 1959 the Study Group dropped the proposal to introduce individual contracting-out, the potentially most damaging condition – to force the private sector to match the proposed inflation-proofed state second pension – remained. Indeed, in the draft social security plan from March 1962, there were renewed threats of 'very severe conditions for contracting-out of National Superannuation'.[95] Nevertheless, as the 1964 election approached, there was a slight softening of Labour's stance. For example, in *New Frontiers in Social Security* of 1963 a significant passage reads: 'We are in no way opposed to the provision by progressive employers – whether private or public – of their own superannuation, redundancy and sickness schemes. Indeed, we regard such provision as a useful addition to any really adequate state system'.[96] The 1964 Labour manifesto continued in a similar vein, promising that, 'Provision will be made for "contracting-out" of good private schemes'.[97] Sadly, the all-important adjectives in these two pledges, 'progressive' and 'good', were left undefined, leaving considerable confusion in their wake.

By January 1969 the situation was much clearer, and the government's position of accommodation with the private sector was confirmed. In stark contrast to the hardly veiled threats in the 1957 scheme, twelve years later the government declared that 'there is no question of the State provision replacing occupational schemes. On the contrary, its structure will leave ample scope for their continued development'.[98] This continued development was to be achieved by dint of presenting a state scheme which was less generous than that proposed in 1957, particularly for the more affluent, thus lessening potential competition for the private sector, and by the introduction of a unique system of contracting-out known as abatement; a system that, crucially, did not require the private pension sector to 'inflation-proof' its wares. Indeed, it was proposed the state would actually step in, if necessary, to guarantee the standard of contracted-out employees' pension.[99] Crossman could rightly boast that, 'No Government have taken more trouble than we have to protect the pension interests in introducing a new State scheme'.[100]

Many existing explanations for the Labour Party's volte-face regarding accommodation with the private sector have focused on developments in the world of private pension provision, and with good reason. Sustained by the inadequacies of the Beveridge system, and encouraged by the Conservative reforms, private sector pension coverage expanded considerably, with the numbers with pension scheme membership outside the state sector increasing by over four million between 1956 and 1967.[101] Indeed, by the mid-1960s, almost half the national workforce was contributing towards an occupational pension. A little later, it was accurately stated that 'Britain has one of the most highly developed systems of occupational pensions to be found anywhere in the world'.[102] This expansion of the occupational pension market is another important aspect of Fawcett's concept of the Beveridge 'straitjacket'. She argues that the Beveridge-inspired reforms, *inter alia*, provoked this expansion, and this, in turn, established a number of 'lock-in' effects. These made it increasingly difficult for policy-makers to deflect the path in which UK pension policy was following; a path which, at the time, was paved by an expanding occupational pensions sector. As Fawcett explains, 'efforts the Labour party made to protect those covered by occupational schemes indicates the importance of policy "lock-in". Government action was strongly influenced by the sheer numbers of employees covered by the private sector'.[103] Hiroshi Araki makes a similar point, arguing that structural obstacles forced Labour policy-makers to accept the private sector, though Araki puts greater stress on the actions of the Macmillan government hastening private sector expansion.[104]

Aside from the pressure from sheer numbers involved, another significant element of this private sector expansion was the growing strength of those various groups committed to maintaining a viable occupational pensions sector, and this has been the focus of interest in other accounts. As noted in Chapter 3, the insurance industry itself became a powerful pressure group as more and more people took out occupational pensions. However, not all the pressure to safeguard occupational schemes came from business groups. As Leslie Hannah argues, Crossman was forced to become 'very aware that any new scheme would have to take note of the now clearly established pensioning institutions, if only because the white collar unions within the TUC would insist on it'.[105] Heclo, like Hannah, is also keen to highlight the role of the unions pressing Labour's policy-makers to support a viable contracting-out system.[106] And, in support of this view, it is clear that the TUC – through the medium of its Social Insurance Committee which continued to hold regular meetings with representatives of the Labour Party's Study Group during the years up to Labour's 1964 election victory – did increasingly raise concern about the future of occupational pension provision. For example, in 1963, the successor to Alfred Roberts as chairperson of the Social Insurance Committee, Harold Collison, insisted that a section in an early draft of *New Frontiers for Social Security* be amended, because, he argued, it 'could be interpreted as expressing hostility to employers' supplementary schemes'.[107] He suggested 'that it should be made clear that the Labour Party was in favour of occupational schemes in addition – and not as an alternative – to adequate state provision'.

Approaching the 1964 election, of these two sorts of pressure – the general concern about the growing masses that enjoyed membership of occupational pension schemes and the more focused demands from groups keen to safeguard such schemes – it seems it was the former that most disturbed Crossman. Though union pressure did press the same way, the reason stated in *New Frontiers* for the gradual acceptance of private provision was, simply, the 'growth of private superannuation'.[108] To be more specific, what really bothered Crossman was one particular, slightly esoteric, development in the expansion of the private pensions' market. In a newspaper article written in December 1963 – one that caught the eye of officials at the MPNI – Crossman noted the presence of a 'small but important segment' of the population covered by occupational pension provision that was more generous than the state could hope to offer, particularly during the inevitable transition period following the introduction of a new scheme.[109] As Crossman explained, 'For at least ten to fifteen years, employers like ICI will pay better pensions than the State can provide, even in a good State graded scheme'. This had severe implications for policy on contracting-out, because, as officials noted, 'if a scheme could not see a way to continue to be contracted out, it would have, in most cases, either to be severely cut back or abandoned altogether';[110] and this, in turn, had political consequences. As Crossman later commented, 'If ICI workers could be told by their firm, or by the trustees of their pension scheme, that we were requiring their pensions to be cut by 40 per cent, I did not see much chance of winning the election'.[111] As will be illustrated, it was indeed Crossman's – and officials' – realisation that electoral harm was a possible consequence of introducing a pension scheme without a viable system of contracting-out that drove the Wilson government's reluctant accommodation with the private pension sector.

With Labour's victory in the 1964 election, officials who – as noted – had been closely studying the Labour Party's activities in Opposition, began to play their part in the decision-making process over potential accommodation with the private sector. Interestingly, the attitude of most civil servants to the private sector was not one of abundant warmth. As noted in Chapter 3, officials – particularly those working at the Treasury – had illustrated their antipathy to the idea of extending the role played by the private sector during the compromised creation of the 1959 National Insurance Act. This frostiness continued into the Wilson era: the Official Committee on Social Security declaring that, 'it might be necessary to consider the practicality (in both administrative and political terms) of not merely curbing the growth of occupational schemes but virtually bringing them to an end over a period – if that is the desired objective'.[112] To give a little more colour to this point, Crossman noted the desire of certain officials to tell representatives from the occupational pensions industry to 'go to hell'.[113]

Despite this hostility to the private pensions sector, officials found themselves in a similar position to that of Crossman. Initially they supported the idea that – if contracting-out was to continue – then it should only be with stringent terms attached in order to guarantee that occupational schemes matched equivalent state provision.[114] However, again, practicalities blocked the way. As Theo Cooper ruefully conceded:

> if only pension schemes that were satisfactory in these respects were allowed to exist, some schemes might be wound up or fail to be established either because of the cost of these improvements was so great that the contributions employers were willing to pay and to require their employees to pay would not be sufficient to finance a basic pension that looked like a worthwhile amount, or because of the administrative complications'.[115]

As a result, the politically unpalatable situation would exist where 'there would be several decades before the major part of the improvement in pension provision took effect'. As a result of this dilemma, doing nothing was an option seriously considered.[116]

Thus, in contrast to the situation regarding whether or not to introduce a fully graded pension, Jarrett's various committees were unable to settle the issue of contracting-out, and this issue was thrust back to Crossman's Ministerial Sub-Committee, which appeared in no hurry to tackle it. As late as March 1968, Crossman was still pre-varicating. In a letter to the Prime Minister, Crossman admitted that,

> The Committee tends to the view that instead of trying to resolve this issue at this stage it might be wise to envisage a presentation in the White Paper next Autumn which sets out the two alter-natives [a scheme including contracting-out and one without], invites public discussion and reserves the final decision until all the interests concerned have had an opportunity to give their views.[117]

However, in a rhetorical question to complete this letter's final paragraph, Crossman indicated that he realised which direction the wind would blow by embarking on this consultation exercise by asking 'would this in fact commit us willy-nilly to contracting-out?'.

In an ideal world, Crossman would have discontinued contracting-out, and he was clearly envious of countries like Sweden that had been able to set up an earnings-related pension system without resorting to contracting-out.[118] As he explained to Wilson:

> if we were starting de novo we would design a universal State scheme covering every employed worker up to 1½ times the average male earnings; and we should limit private schemes to the useful purpose of providing extra cover beyond the level and on top of benefits of the State scheme for any groups of workers the firm might wish to benefit in this way.[119]

However, as Crossman was only too well aware, he could not start de novo; the existing extent of private pension coverage prevented it. Moreover, Crossman simply could not overcome his original problem that contracting-out

> was developed as an important safeguard designed both to allay the fears of workers (in I.C.I. for example) about the future of their pension schemes and also to reduce the danger of an all out

propaganda campaign by the insurance interests which could easily panic the electorate.[120]

With a viable system of contracting-out reluctantly accepted as inevitable, one task remaining was to decide on what form it would take. It proved to be very difficult, as determination to create a wholly earnings-related scheme prevented easy adaptation of the existing contracting-out system. To explain, the National Insurance Act of 1959 had introduced the concept of *partial* contracting-out, whereby it was only possible to 'opt out' from one particular portion of a multi-part state pension scheme – the 'graduated' pension in this instance. This maintained an element of universal contribution in the scheme and allowed for the possibility of redistribution.[121] A similar system – though with considerably less friendly conditions attached – had been proposed in Labour's 1957 pension scheme. However, because of the proposed abolition of the flat-rate standard pension, the model introduced in the 1969 White Paper had no handy 'part' from which partial contracting-out could take place.

Discussion on the way forward focused on a new variation on the partial contracting-out theme, one termed 'abatement'. The plan here was for contracted-out employees, and their employers, to pay a lower percentage of contribution than those who did not contract out. In return, the contracted-out employee, when retired, would be awarded a reduced state pension, with the approved occupational pension available to at least make up the shortfall. According to Heclo, this abatement idea had been floating around – to borrow again John Kingdon's useful phrase – the 'policy primeval soup' since 1959, when it 'was created by a senior representative of the insurance companies' interests, and through a series of informal talks within the close network of London actuaries, the idea gradually spread among experts'.[122] Civil servants were 'quick to seize on the new approach', though insurance interest groups were less easily convinced, and it took until the mid-to-late 1960s before abatement became an integral element of pensions policy. By March 1967, the Jarrett Committee automatically assumed that if a system of contracting-out was deemed necessary, then it would 'be based on an abatement formula'.[123]

Thus, to summarise, if pension policy-makers of the late 1960s believed contracting-out inevitable, then, because of 'spill-over' from the proposal to abolish the flat-rate element, the system proposed had to be one based on the abatement concept, as this was the only method yet conceived in which partial contracting-out would work in a wholly earnings-related pension scheme. Crossman accepted this argument, but was far from happy with it, admitting that these new terms for contracting-out were 'feasible, though enormously complicated'.[124] With considerable significance, Crossman also realised that accepting this scheme ended hopes of forcing the private sector to protect their products from inflation. He remarked that this scheme 'requires the State to bear the full cost of any dynamic element in the pension of those contracted out, since dynamism [in other words, inflation-proofing] is the one feature of our State scheme which cannot be reproduced in a private scheme'.[125]

After considerable agonising, it took until September 1969 for Crossman – by this stage Secretary of State at the newly created DHSS – to inform the Cabinet of the decision to plump for a pension scheme that included abatement. In so doing, he made it clear that he had not solved the problem he mentioned in the newspaper article way back in 1963. Having noted the sharp rise in the number of occupational pension schemes, Crossman declared:

> It was undesirable – and would not in any case be politically acceptable – for the Government to compel those in charge of occupational schemes to wind them up when the State scheme was introduced and it would accordingly be necessary to take them into partnership'.[126]

Once the decision to include a contracting-out option had been made, the only matters left to consider were the details of the scheme – though, as usual, details proved devilish. The most important of these details concerned the levels to be set for pension abatement and contribution rates for those contracted out. This was significant because, as Heclo highlights, the gap between abatement rate and contribution 'was the economic breathing space that would make private schemes profitable or unprofitable'.[127] Crossman's *Diaries* suggest negotiations to set the tightness of this breathing space were fraught. It was certainly the battleground for the revival of a long-running departmental division of opinion over contracting-out, which had its roots in the preparations for the 1959 Act. Crossman explained:

The Department of Health and Social Security was anxious to give generous terms so that the existing private occupational schemes would not campaign against the state scheme but the Treasury wished the terms to be stiff because they had in mind the effect on government revenue.[128]

When it came to actual figures, the influential figure of the Government Actuary – the joyously named Sir Herbert Tetley – made calculations that initially led to the suggestion that an occupational scheme would provide its members a pension of 1 per cent of each year's earnings for men in return for a reduction of 1.25 per cent from both employees' and employers' national superannuation contributions.[129] This became known as the 1:1.25 ratio, and was a figure with which the Treasury was content.[130] Calculations based on women's relative longevity, earlier pensionable age, and earning patterns led to the Government Actuary's frugal recommendation that 'the pension abatement for women (corresponding to 1 per cent for men) is 0.55 per cent of earnings'.[131]

Though they accepted the calculations for the reduced rate for women, groups with an interest in maintaining occupational pension profitability were unhappy with the proposed male ratio of 1:1.25. Bodies such as the Life Offices, the Confederation of British Industries (CBI) and the nationalised industries were angling for a more generous one of 1:1.5.[132] Crossman had already noted that 'the pressures from the occupational pension schemes and the representatives of the TUC are now becoming formidable'.[133] He had been particularly unnerved by the TUC Conference in September 1969, noting at Cabinet level that it 'had been shown by debates at the recent Trade Union Congress the earnings-related scheme was not popular and there were serious political objections to fixing the ratio at less than 1:1.3'.[134]

Thus Crossman, and officials in his department, were keen to come a little closer to the 1:1.5 mark than the Treasury wanted. Crossman was, in his words, willing 'to pay a little more danegeld to get agreement'.[135] A figure of 1:1.3 was agreed at the 11 September Cabinet meeting,[136] Crossman having negotiated with Roy Jenkins, the Chancellor of the Exchequer, a few days earlier.[137] Ironically though, Crossman discovered in the month following this Cabinet meeting that the TUC, as a whole, was not all that enthusiastic about generous abatement terms, despite 'certain anxieties from the Firemen and from NALGO'.[138] To explain, white collar unions, such as the National Association of Local Government Officers (NALGO), ran their own schemes, and, as a result, proved far more hostile than other unions to any perceived threats to these schemes. NALGO was particularly vocal, with a shrill plea to Crossman to 'avoid the risk of "castration" of existing schemes' typical of their viewpoint.[139]

Despite the interminable debates, when the National Super-annuation and Social Insurance Bill was introduced, on 17 December 1969, it did indeed include a viable system of contracting-out. It was based on a unique system of abatement set at a (male) abatement ratio of 1:1.3, and, crucially, it did not require the private pension sector to 'inflation-proof' its products. Indeed, so unique was the scheme that Crossman proudly remarked that it 'had not been attempted in any other country', adding for effect, 'I challenge the Opposition to give me any example, even from Venezuela'.[140]

The reaction of the insurance industry to these terms was in marked contrast to the 'panic in the City' response of 1957. As Crossman ruefully commented, following the announcement of the new details:

> the whole idea that our terms would be so unworkable, harsh and damaging to the pensions interests has been quietly dropped. Even the other day at a meeting of the National Association of Pension Funds, Mr. Michael Pilch of Noble Lowndes – and one cannot have a bigger pensions pundit than Mr. Michael Pilch – made an informed guess that the number contracted out would be 7 million, compared with the 5½ million contracted out today.[141]

Of course, the opportunity to test the validity of Mr. Pilch's prediction never arose as Crossman's scheme failed to leave the debating chamber. However, despite the pension plan falling at the final fence, it is clear that the changes made during the 1964–70 period to the Labour Party's policy towards the private sector – exemplified by the more accommodating terms for contracting-out in 1969 compared with those from 1957 – were set to become permanent. This was confirmed once Wilson and his government returned to power in February 1974 – though, of course, without Crossman, who was, by this stage, a dying man.

In 1975, only two decades after the Labour Party Conference had decided that an earnings-related pension scheme was an idea worth exploring, Barbara Castle successfully introduced the State Earnings-Related Pension Scheme (SERPS). Though, in this version, the abatement system was ditched – being deemed 'both complex and artificial'[142] – a key aspect that did remain from the 1969 plan was the promised 'partnership with well-founded occupational schemes'.[143] In a reflection of the policy process of the 1960s, Labour's policy-makers in the 1970s found much at fault with the private sector but – like Crossman – were forced to concede that, 'A crucial factor in determining the future pattern of pension provision is the existence in this country of thriving occupational pension arrangements'.[144]

Bringing this aspect of Labour policy up to date, the accommodation grudgingly pledged in the 1960s and 1970s has evolved into something more explicit. Following another long period in Opposition, recent New Labour governments have had to adjust to a near two-decade period in which the already secure position of private pensions industry has been heartily bolstered, not least by the drastic weakening of the Castle's pension scheme. This era also witnessed the dominant position of occupational pensions challenged by an expansion in private personal pensions, a development heavily promoted by Conservative governments in the 1980s. In such circumstances, Labour's pension reform proposals for the twenty-first century possess strong echoes of Crossman's acceptance of the virtual inevitable. However, where in 1969 Labour's proposed partnership with the occupational pension sector was clearly an uncomfortable marriage of convenience, this relationship with a now much more diverse private sector has become passionate. For example, the re-styled Department of Work and Pensions (DWP) has triumphantly announced that the UK is in a relatively rosy position, in terms of future financial sustainability of the pension system, 'because of its system of targeted state support coupled with a well-developed, funded private pensions system'.[145] The DWP adds that, 'The continued success of the UK approach to pension provision relies on the renewal of the partnership between the Government, individuals and employers, underpinned by a competitive and accessible financial services industry'. However, though the rhetoric is now a little more effusive, as this section has illustrated, and as Whiteside has rightly highlighted, 'such arrangements are hardly new'.[146]

No 'bold investment' after all

Labour's removal of designs for using a National Pensions Fund to finance 'bold investment'[147] in the British economy might be regarded as a surprise. As noted in Chapter 3, this novel form of nationalisation was seized upon with enthusiasm by the Labour Party's elite, not least by the then-leader Hugh Gaitskell. This was largely because as it fitted so snugly into Gaitskell's 'philosophy that the road to further nationalisation lies through the buying up of equity shares through great public companies'.[148] However, as noted, not everyone was as enthusiastic. Insurance companies, understandably, were aghast, but figures such as Abel-Smith were also alarmed, fearing that people would suspect a Labour government of 'gambling with the savings for their old age pensions'.[149] Significantly, it was this concern that the Conservatives seized upon in the 1959 election, accusing the Labour Party of planning 'nationalisation by stealth'[150] via their new-fangled pension scheme.

During the next period in Opposition, the Labour Party, its fingers burned, became a little more bashful about their idea for bold investment. Gaitskell's successor, Wilson, was particularly cautious, warning Crossman, in March 1963, to 'be careful about talk of investing in equities. We don't want to resurrect the trouble we had with the 600 firms'.[151] Crossman, however, remained keen on the idea. He wrote, 'We reached the issue of whether the funding proposals of National Superannuation should be included in the new draft. . . . I strongly felt that they should'.[152] Moreover, *New Frontiers* did include a section about the National Pensions Fund which remained in line with that proposed in 1957:

> [The National Pensions Fund] will be controlled by trustees appointed by the Government who will have the same opportunities to carry out profitable investment of their funds as trustees of private pension schemes and insurance companies. Thus they will be able to ensure that the national savings piling up in the Pensions Fund will be used to help our national capital investment programme.[153]

Yet, as noted earlier, by the 1969 White Paper, plans for the type of National Pensions Scheme Crossman wanted had disappeared. And, as with the earlier tale of the dropping of the proposals for two-tier benefit structure, it seems as though the impetus behind this change of policy was the arrival on the scene of the civil service, in particular the series of interdepartmental official committees chaired by Clifford Jarrett.

It is clear that, months before the Wilson government was elected, officials were putting the evil eye on Crossman's fund. In the list of 'main criticisms' of national superannuation that officials at the MPNI made in March 1964, one important criticism mentioned was 'the danger that most of the investment in the National Pensions Fund would simply be diverted from existing sources and that the investment in equities would be back door nationalisation'.[154] Later, in the document, officials noted a letter in *The Guardian* from April 1963, sent by the almost omnipresent Brian Abel-Smith. This letter suggested that the investment policy was under review, and officials took this to indicate 'that the Labour Party now realise the potential danger of advocating such an investment programme and are seeking to minimise it'.[155] The officials were indeed correct to deduce that figures such as Abel-Smith and, indeed, Wilson were wary of this programme; Crossman though, as will be illustrated, remained his adventurous self.

The first of the interdepartmental committees chaired by Jarrett, the Working Group on Pensions, continued to be highly critical of the whole concept of the National Pension Fund. It noted a whole series of issues that the Labour Party's pension policy planners should have dealt with during those long years in Opposition, but had not. It was pointed out that:

> it would be no easy matter to find buyers for long-dated Government Securities on this scale. Equally, it would not be easy, without considerable disruption of existing price rela-tionships, for a Government agency to acquire £850 million in equity shares.[156]

A further point made was that 'such a course would imply lack of confidence in Government obligations, confess inability to control inflation and suggest that all pension rights should be geared not to fixed interest stocks but to equities'. Another issue was that the 'switch of existing reserves into equities would raise interest rates and inflate equity prices', and there were further anxieties including the impact on the market in company securities. There was also the vital point, one which more recent policy-makers might have included higher up the list, that 'there is always the possibility that investments in equities would not show a profit but a loss'.[157] Thus, a whole catalogue of abuse was heaped on the idea of a National Pension Fund by the Working Group.

Unsurprisingly, when the Official Committee on Social Security began making detailed proposals to present to its ministerial counterpart, it was simply assumed that the scheme would be funded using the existing pay-as-you-go system.[158] It was not, though, quite a forgone conclusion at this stage. Whiteside has suggested that some officials at the new Ministry of Social Security were friendlier to Crossman's idea than civil servants elsewhere, not least the Treasury.[159] Moreover, Theo Cooper, in a note for ministers in May 1967, suggested that – though she did not consider the matter 'at all urgent' – 'More work should be done by officials on the question of investment of part of the "fund" in equities'.[160] Furthermore, she thought, like Crossman, that this investment 'could make the scheme look more attractive'.

Urgency did arrive shortly after Crossman took over Cabinet responsibility for social security in April 1968 when, as with the situation over the two-banded formula, he started to throw his ministerial weight around. In July, Crossman, with Judith Hart in support, led 'a fairly tough discussion' with representatives of the Treasury, a department which had assumed national superannuation was to be based on a pay-as-you-go scheme.[161] Crossman suggested the Treasury ought to re-assess that assumption pronto. He expressed his reasoning for his preference by stating, 'To my mind, national superannuation is a system of deferred pay and the essential thing is to convince the working class that this is a genuine pension plan'. He added, 'If it's simply a pay-as-you-go scheme . . . where each year you're just collecting enough money to pay out again that's another version of the Tory swindle and it's ridiculous to use thousands of officials for such a bogus pretence of a pensions scheme'.[162] Crossman achieved a small victory in getting the issue reviewed by the Treasury.

Crossman may have won that particular battle, but he lost the war. The civil service closed ranks. As Crossman lamented in August 1968, 'I have found (it's a sad thing to have to admit) that my own personal position has been fatally undermined. I am fighting both the

Ministry [of Social Security] and the Treasury in support of a properly funded scheme'.[163] He went on to explain:

> Alas, the unanswerable Treasury argument is that if we piled up millions in the fund it would only be appropriated for the existing pensioners. We must therefore really accept pay-as-you-go. This is a tremendous blow for me since I have spent twelve hours arguing with my officials and now I've been beaten by them.[164]

As Janet Morgan – Crossman's editor – pointed out in a footnote, the argument that eventually floored Crossman did not actually make sense. Existing pensioners would not have had the opportunity to contribute into a funded scheme, and so would not have been entitled to benefits from it and, anyway, pay-as-you-go would have remained the primary financing vehicle for many years ahead, even if a decision to proceed with full funding had gone through. Morgan expands on this point explaining that 'Mr Crossman does not make it clear whether the "Treasury argument" concerns the public presentation of the scheme or the assessment of the appropriate rate of contributions in the early years of the new scheme'.[165] She concluded by admitting that Crossman 'may not have entirely appreciated the Treasury's economic argument'. As Crossman himself admitted at one point, 'I am not numerate, only literate'.[166]

Having gathered his thoughts a little, in June 1969 Crossman publicly explained the abandonment of the original scheme was for two reasons. Firstly, he argued that getting the scheme working properly would have meant levying higher contributions than he thought many employees would accept. Secondly, because of the expansion in occupational schemes, Crossman suggested that the original promise of extra savings had evaporated as most workers would simply be transferring savings from private schemes to the government fund.[167] He added:

> We decided, therefore, that what was needed in the present situation was not competition for savings between a funded Government scheme and funded private schemes, but a partnership between the funded schemes of the private sector and the pay as you go of National Superannuation.

Thus, again, structural constraints appear to have been a major influence pushing Crossman towards revising the original plan in a manner that made the scheme much more accepting of the private sector.

That was largely that, though Crossman did mount a late charge to amend the National Superannuation and Social Insurance Bill at the committee stage to permit, subject to Treasury control, some investment of the funds in equities.[168] The Treasury remained unmoved. Secretary of the Cabinet, Burke Trend, also dismissed Crossman's idea. In words that encapsulated the particular concern figures such as Abel-Smith and Wilson had been making for many years, Trend asked, rhetorically, 'would it really be helpful at this juncture to provoke further speculation about government intervention and back-door nationalisation?'.[169]

As noted earlier, not quite everything was lost from Crossman's original vision. A separate National Superannuation Fund did make it on to the Statute Book, though with precious few details about its operation. And, as Whiteside has highlighted, a combination of recently agreed benefit up-ratings and potential income lost through contracting-out meant that the future balances left for investment would, in any case, have been seriously eroded.[170] Thus, even if the legislation had survived, this National Superannuation Fund would have proved a terribly thin version of Crossman's original aspiration. This was, it should be recalled, for the state to harness the 'enormous economic power that those who invest in these private insurance schemes exert on the community'.[171] From the mid-1950s onwards, that enormous power only increased, and, despite Crossman's efforts, it remained firmly in the hands of the private sector. And, as the 1980s approached, this situation only intensified. From information gathered during a post-premiership position chairing a committee charged with investigating the role and function of the City of London, Harold Wilson, no less, was moved to remark that the 'growth of pension funds during and since the middle 1970s has created the biggest revolution in the British financial scene in this century'.[172] He went on to remark of pension funds:

> they are so powerful that they do not know how powerful they are. They could very well be, for example, transforming the

nature of our society more than any Government would dare to do even if it had a large majority in Parliament.[173]

Until recently, the only promise to introduce a government fund came, oddly enough, from the Conservatives. During Edward Heath's 1970–74 administration, Crossman's successor at the DHSS, Sir Keith Joseph introduced yet another pension scheme. Despite earlier jibes about 'nationalisation by the backdoor', part of this 'Joseph plan' was a proposal to create an independent Reserve Scheme Fund to finance a state earnings-related second pension for those unable to find suitable cover from occupational schemes.[174] The Board of Management for this scheme – which was to include representatives of the CBI and TUC – was to be allowed similar investment freedoms to those enjoyed by occupational schemes. Regarding this Fund, there were estimates of there being between £5 and 7 billion accrued by the end of the twentieth century – though, intriguingly, the considerable potential political and economic consequences of this form of Conservative-sponsored nationalisation were hardly discussed at the time.[175] It hardly mattered. When the Heath government fell in February 1974, so did Joseph's scheme.

A more recent state challenge to the private sector has come from New Labour. As part of a wholesale review of pensions, in December 2002 the government established the Pensions Commission. This was an independent body chaired by Lord Turner, who – when plain Adair Turner – was director-general of the CBI. One of the many recommendations of the Turner Commission was that the government establish a National Pensions Savings Scheme into which people would be automatically enrolled, but had the right to opt-out.[176] It was designed for those on low income, without easy access to a private pension, in order to provide automatic entitlement to a pension that would be run centrally, by a single agency, with money collected directly from salaries, with this, in turn, to be channelled into vast pooled investment funds. There is, as Hugh Pemberton has high-lighted, in many respects 'a striking resemblance' between this proposal and the scheme outlined back in 1957 by Crossman and his team, for the state to invest in stocks and shares to build up a National Pensions Fund.[177] After initial concerns, the government decided to plough ahead with the National Pensions Savings Scheme – though re-styled 'personal accounts' – with the expectation that between six and ten million people would take out these personal accounts, and generate £4–5 billion pounds in the process.[178] To enhance this feeling of déjà vu, one major fund manager activist has already warned that the 'state pension fund could allow back-door national-isation'.[179]

SUMMARY

In attempting to sum up the story of the delays and changes to the Labour Party's old plans for establishing a national superannuation scheme, it would be helpful to return to Seldon's four factors: ideas, individuals, circumstances, and interests. Regarding the first of these factors, one important feature was a significant adjustment in the manner in which the national superannuation idea itself was generally perceived. As noted earlier, in the late 1950s, national superannuation appeared, in the UK at least, to be a fresh idea; a brilliant potential solution that seemed to offer hope to a situation that was becoming ever more problematic. By the 1960s, though, as was highlighted in Chapter 4, national superannuation was, for many, not in step with the times, and other concepts took precedence. In particular, the income guarantee appeared a more subtle and targeted measure for tackling the more modish problems illuminated by the so-called 'rediscovery of poverty'. Thus, as Bridgen has highlighted, remedial work that should have been done on the original national super-annuation concept was ignored, contributing to delays when Labour came to power in 1964. The officials at the MPNI were correct in their assessment that national superannuation had not been 'an answer to all questions' in the late 1950s, and was even less so nearly a decade later. Furthermore, as highlighted in this chapter, even as the 1960s progressed, and Crossman managed to tug the spotlight back on to national superannuation, important players in the policy process, such as Minister for Social Security, Judith Hart, were of the opinion that this pension scheme was not the answer to the main social problems of the day. As noted, for Hart, it was those immediate 'pockets of poverty' that Abel-Smith and Townsend had 're-discovered' that were the paramount issue, and the superannuation scheme was, basically, a distraction.

As was demonstrated in the previous section, one particular aspect of national superannuation that fell out of fashion with a thud was the notion of using a National Pensions Fund as a vehicle for bold investment. In the time of Gaitskell, this was one of the most attractive components of the whole scheme for the Labour Party elite as it fitted in with the conceptual movement away from overt nationalisation towards a more subtle revisionist stance. Under Wilson, any notions about nationalisation, subtle or otherwise, were largely swept under the carpet as the Labour Party embraced less divisive ideas, such as the much-hyped science and technology-led 'revolution'. Conservative taunts about 'nationalisation by the backdoor' helped this process. It is significant that, as the response to Abel-Smith's letter to *The Guardian* demonstrated, officials had noticed this development, and were aware, by March 1964, that the funding idea was losing ground in the Labour Party. Thus, using Seldon's model,[180] it could be argued that, as the 1960s progressed, the 'lower level' idea of 'bold investment' contained within the original version of national superannuation fell out of sympathy with the 'dominant' ideas of the new Labour regime. Consequently, when Crossman continued to fight for a funded pension scheme, he was at a disadvantage compared to the situation in 1957 when the idea enjoyed wider support. Thus, isolated, Crossman was easily defeated.

Leaving the role of individuals until later, 'circumstances' are the next of Seldon's four factors to examine. In one obvious respect, compared to the situation in the late 1950s, one changed circumstance worked strongly in the favour of those who hoped that the ideas Crossman was articulating might be implemented. This was the election, in October 1964, of a Labour government – albeit one that initially operated with a tiny majority. It was also a major advantage that the new Prime Minister, Wilson, was something close to a friend of Crossman's, and was willing to let him into the Cabinet. And there the helpful circumstances end.

As was illustrated in Chapter 5, though Crossman was in the Cabinet, he was not, initially, in a position in which he could, to any great extent, influence social security policy. Furthermore, the organisational structure itself made the planning of radical social policy reform more difficult than strictly necessary. The 'overlord' situation was particularly unhelpful in this respect, leading to comparison to Cohen, March and Olsen's garbage can model of organisational choice. In addition, the economic circumstances during this period were, for the most part, some distance from obliging.

However, probably the most serious constraining circumstance was the growth in numbers of those with a stake in the occupational pension industry, and this expansion – encouraged by the weaknesses in the Beveridge system and intensified by Conservative reforms – is, as noted earlier, a central component of Fawcett's concept of the 'Beveridge straitjacket'. This model does appear to be particularly useful when explaining the difficulties faced when negotiating the contracting-out conditions in the 1960s, and, in particular, under-standing why these conditions became markedly less stringent. To be a little more specific, the single biggest constraint acting on Crossman was the political problem that, by the mid-1960s, many thousands of occupational scheme members, working for munificent firms such as ICI, would almost inevitably become worse off during the first years of the planned new state pension scheme if, as seemed likely, those running the occupational schemes felt compelled to close them or make them less generous. These thousands of members, Crossman feared, would make the government responsible pay dearly. As he claimed, 'Unless we made special arrangements with the private schemes, they would tell their members that the wicked Labour Government was depriving them of their pensions. So this was politically very, very dangerous indeed'.[181]

Crossman certainly did not like the confusion that contracting-out created. As he mentioned in that note to Wilson, he would have abolished the device, if granted the opportunity to start *de novo*. However, that was simply not an option available, and a gesture of partnership to the occupational pension industry was deemed a political inevitability, by Crossman, and by the officials in Jarrett's committees. And this was a significant compromise from the position back in 1957 when, had its terms been implemented, *National Superannuation* threatened to 'kill the bulk of their [the insur-ance companies'] expanding business in pensions'.[182] This offer of partnership made by Crossman in 1969 is, as Whiteside has high-lighted, an important demonstration that the distinction between Old and New Labour is not at all clear-cut.[183]

Turning to the role of 'interests', three groups in particular appear particularly significant in this episode: the insurance industry, the trade unions, and the civil service. Regarding the first two of these groups, it appears that the aspect of national superannuation on which they had the greatest influence during Labour's period in power was the tortuous matter of negotiating the conditions for contracting-out. Here, representatives of both business and the workers were largely pushing in the same direction, that of protecting the existing generous contracting-out terms established by the Conservatives. And there is some evidence to suggest that these groups made some impression. For a start, Crossman was keen to listen to what these groups had to say. Heclo suggests that Crossman 'went much further than any of his Conservative counterparts in seeking early consultation with the groups concerned'.[184] Crossman himself backed this view, expressing with pride, that 'we have consulted the vested interests, briefed them before legislation, brought them right in – the TUC, the CBI, above all, the Institute of Actuaries and the Life Association people'.[185] Crossman was particularly impressed by representatives of the Life Offices. He judged them to be 'brilliant, cool, able, collected'[186] and 'the people I least want to quarrel with, the nicest people involved'.[187] He was, however, probably more concerned about the unions, as suggested by his comment at the Cabinet meeting on 11 September 1969 regarding the setting of the abatement rate.[188]

Nevertheless, for all this combined power of industry and unions, it is worth stressing again the point that Crossman had – before 1964 – come to the conclusion that national superannuation needed to be adapted in order to accommodate the thousands already covered by good occupational schemes. The Life Offices and unions such as NALGO were, effectively, pushing at an open door when pressing for reasonable contracting-out conditions. It is also worth highlighting that, when the vested interests were invited into discussion, it was often simply to fine-tune decisions already made. For example, when a group such as Life Offices was allowed in – interestingly before talks with the TUC and CBI – officials at the Ministry of Social Security made certain that it was for '*technical* discussions' only, 'not negotiations'.[189] Thus, though important as the business and union interests were, there was one other group that appeared to make an even greater impression on the development of the plans for national superannuation during this period, and that was the civil service.

It would be inaccurate to argue that this particular 'interest', the civil service completely changed the direction of Labour's superannuation policy during the period between 1964 and 1970; there were many other factors involved, not least the impact of past policy decisions. Nevertheless, for particular aspects of the scheme, such as the decision to include a wholly earnings-related scheme, it is clear that the civil service did act in a co-ordinated manner to provoke a change to party policy, and vigorously maintained this approach throughout Crossman's attempt to limit the influence of the Official Committee on Social Security in May 1968.

As noted, the main agent of official influence in the pension reform policy process was the succession of interdepartmental committees chaired by the MPNI's Permanent Secretary, Sir Clifford Jarrett. On the matter of introducing a wholly earnings-related pension, it is clear that Jarrett's team had decided that abolition of the flat-rate element was the correct course to take before the Wilson government had been elected. This was largely because, without a flat-rate level, when pensioners were granted an increase in benefits, it was less likely to provoke calls to improve other types of benefit. To achieve their end, officials created the 'banded' earnings-related formula to mitigate the least welcome aspects of a wholly earnings-related benefit scheme, and persuaded ministers, such as Judith Hart, of the benefits of pursuing the policy they had devised. Officials then managed to hold their nerve when Crossman decided to establish his 'Pensions' Circus' to review the matter. Officials proved to be equally dogged in their efforts to remove any plans for bold investment in the economy, and, as the previous chapter demonstrated, to ditch the income guarantee.

For all this, it would be incorrect to argue that the officials involved were all reactionaries, motivated solely by economic concerns, eager to overturn the overall thrust of Labour's plans for social security reform. Indeed, the concept of a fully graded pension scheme was, in some ways, more coherent than the earlier two-tier proposal, and, as noted in Chapter 2, something similar to such a scheme had been suggested by Abel-Smith and Townsend as a possible option way back in 1955. Also, as Bridgen has noted, the officials that made up Jarrett's committees did adopt 'a more progressive approach than the Treasury-dominated reform process of the late 1950s'.[190] Crossman also made a similar point, claiming that, at certain points, civil servants actually proved to be 'tremendous radicals'.[191]

Perhaps the most poignant demonstration of the devotion some civil servants felt for national superannuation was the very sad case of Herbert Lewin, one-time Assistant Secretary at the DHSS. Lewin was an important member of Jarrett's committees, a key contributor to the 1969 White Paper and, in Crossman's own words, 'the brain behind the whole pensions plan'.[192] The extent of Lewin's obsession with the scheme was made tragically clear in his obituary, written by Crossman, not long after pension legislation had fallen at the 1970 election. Entitled 'Mr Herbert Lewin – Creating Labour pensions plan', Crossman wrote:

> very occasionally a civil servant so identifies himself with a particular piece of legislation that its fate becomes for him almost a matter of life and death. That, I feel, was the case with Herbert Lewin whose brilliant intellectual qualities in the last period of his life were wholly dedicated to the Labour Government's National Superannuation Bill.[193]

Crossman went on to state that in his years as a minister, he had 'never met another civil servant who showed himself such a master of detail and clarifier of complexity, while never losing sight of the basic objectives we were seeking to achieve'. Lewin was forty-eight.

Thus some civil servants, typically those working at the MPNI and its successor departments, were sympathetic to Crossman's plan. Moreover, it is the case that some of the changes to policy prompted by officials were often simply a response to weaknesses in the original design or were reactions to developments that had overtaken the 1957 scheme, not least the growth in numbers in occupational schemes. For example, the officials' recommendation to lower the ceiling appears to be as a much a response to this expansion of the private sector as to concern about what some considered potentially excessive redistribution. Therefore, though officials did play a very important role in the development of national superannuation, their influence was not necessarily all-pervasive or malign. Tellingly, Crossman himself did not blame officials for the scheme's demise in 1970: 'The fault, dear Brutus, lies not in our civil servants but in ourselves'.[194]

Thus, for the period between 1964 and 1970, with the obvious exception that the party that had championed national superannuation was, at last, in government, many of the other factors were working against the prospects for the successful implementation of national superannuation. The idea itself was becoming less interesting to Labour's elite, not only was it associated with defeat in 1959, but it seemed less and less the answer to the problems of the day. This meant that, for much of the 1960s, little work was carried out to keep national superannuation as coherent as it needed to be, and this was picked up by the civil service when they became involved in the policy process. The other main interests involved – including Labour's traditional supporters, the unions – remained, at best, ambivalent towards the project. The economic situation was, for the most part, unfavourable and, most significantly, the growth in the numbers involved in occupational pensions had expanded to the point where the options of the policymakers were heavily circumscribed. In these circumstances, perhaps the wonder is less that national superannuation failed to be implemented and more that certain individuals were able to drag the scheme as far as they did along the legislative conveyor-belt.

The individual who did much of the heavy pulling was, of course, Crossman. It is too much to claim that national superannuation would have materialised that much sooner had Crossman been in control of social security policy from the start. As Bridgen has explained, 'Even if *National Superannuation* had been given priority by Labour in 1964 . . . considerable work – both technical and political – would still have been required to make its introduction a practicable proposition'.[195] Nevertheless, Crossman was there to rescue the plans for national superannuation from the mire of official review, and, more than anyone else, Crossman hauled the concept back into the political mainstream.

Politically, national superannuation had ceased to be a priority issue soon after the 1959 election. This was illustrated by the rise to prominence of the income guarantee concept during the early 1960s. Once the Labour Party attained power, Wilson appointed Douglas Houghton, the income guarantee's loudest cheerleader, to be the main player in social security, and it was clear that implementing national superannuation was not at the top of Houghton's to-do list. It was only when Crossman re-appeared as a major player in this story, by chairing the Ministerial Sub-Committee on Earnings-Related Pensions, that the process towards implementation was given any degree of political momentum. Furthermore, the process was given an even greater shunt when Crossman was given Cabinet responsibility for social security in April 1968. This ended the confusion over responsibility for pension policy, and sidelined Judith Hart who, like Houghton, thought national superannuation should not be the foremost of Labour's social security priorities. As the episodes involving abatement and funding demonstrate, Crossman, in comparison to Hart, felt more able to challenge – albeit with limited success – the views of the Jarrett Committee.

It needs to be stressed that Crossman was not alone in carrying the torch for national superannuation; other individuals played their part. As Crossman's obituary to him suggested, the unfortunate Herbert Lewin was important. He possessed the particular talent of being an ingenious problem-solver; as Crossman put it, 'we came to think of him as the genie – the fragile, dark-eyed slave of the lamp who would appear at a moment's notice with all the answers ready'.[196] In particular, Lewin appears central to the creation of the crafty two-banded formula that allowed a wholly earnings-related scheme to possess an element of redistribution.[197]

There were also roles for some members of the original LSE 'skiffle group'. Indeed, as demonstrated in the previous chapter, during the years leading up to 1964, the numbers of academics involved actually increased with the addition of Tony Lynes to the Study Group. However, once the Labour Party attained power, this influence lessened, and it did not take very long for the academics to submit to a sense of disenchantment. Lynes, after a brief period as advisor to Margaret Herbison, left government and academia to become, in 1966, the first director of the Child Poverty Action Group (CPAG). In the same year, Brian Abel-Smith and Peter Townsend, to Crossman's considerable displeasure, 'launched a tremendous attack on the Government for its failure to abolish poverty'.[198] Townsend was back on the attack towards the end of the Wilson government when, as chairman of CPAG, the pressure group claimed, with more public effect than statistical accuracy, that 'the poor get poorer under Labour'.[199] This also failed to please Crossman.

However, not all bridges were burned. As the 'Pension Circus' episode displayed, Crossman was still willing to heed the advice of figures such as Richard Titmuss and Abel-Smith. Moreover, as mentioned in Chapter 1, in 1968 Titmuss was happy to serve Crossman as Deputy Chairman of the Supplementary Benefits Commission and, more significantly here, in the same year, Abel-Smith became Crossman's Senior Advisor at the DHSS. Indeed, as Timmins archly notes, when Townsend as chairman of CPAG came to meet an incandescent Secretary of State about the pressure group's 'poor get poorer' claim, Abel-Smith was actually part of Crossman's team, 'so the joint authors of *The Poor and the Poorest* were on the opposite sides of the table'.[200] Abel-Smith was Crossman's closest ally at the DHSS, and Crossman – who did have trouble with his sums – found him indispensable. As Crossman remarked towards the end of his time in office, 'He [Abel-Smith] has been my closest personal friend and without him I could have done very little in the past two years'.[201]

Incidentally, Crossman also recommended to Abel-Smith that, if the opportunity arose for him to serve Barbara Castle at the DHSS, he should take it. This Abel-Smith did, though not until Wilson's re-election in 1974, and he went on to prove as indispensable to Castle as he had to Crossman, becoming one of the main architects of SERPS. Indeed, he survived Castle's abrupt departure from government in 1976. As Townsend noted in his colleague's obituary, Abel-Smith became, 'probably the most influential political adviser appointed by successive Labour governments, first in 1968 to Crossman, and then, in turn, to Barbara Castle, David Ennals and finally Peter Shore'.[202] Moreover, all the while, Abel-Smith maintained his academic career in social administration at the LSE. Abel-Smith was, thus, the epitome of a phenomenon Kingdon identified whereby, in order to make an impact on the political agenda, 'some researchers and academics build 'inner–outer' careers in which they travel between academia and government'.[203] He was also, in the end, the only policy actor to remain on stage throughout national superannuation's tortuous twenty-year evolution from academic idea to, in some measure, legislative reality.

CONCLUSION:
CROSSMAN'S LEGACY

Towards the end, Richard Crossman became strangely detached from the project with which he had been associated for fifteen years, and with which he had made his political reputation. In the last days of the Wilson government – in 'a dying House of Commons'[1] – Crossman noted, almost in passing, that,

> During the past three days we have been winding up a whole mass of business, getting all the Bills through with the agreement of the Opposition, including Barbara's [Castle] Equal Pay Bill. But my Superannuation Bill and the Ports Bill have fallen by the way and we will have to start all over again'.[2]

Crossman knew, though, that this process of re-assembly was not one in which he would play a leading role. Even had the Labour Party won the forthcoming election – as seemed likely at the time – he was off to edit the *New Statesman*. Thus, by 1970, with new horizons ahead, even Crossman was susceptible to a trace of ennui regarding the issue of pension reform.

However there was still some energy left in Crossman's national superannuation idea, as demonstrated by the introduction of the State Earnings-Related Pension Scheme in 1975, at a time when Crossman's friend Barbara Castle led the DHSS. SERPS offered, to those who did not contract out, a supplementary pension based on the accrual of an index-linked one-eightieth of earnings each year, for twenty years, to a maximum pension equivalent of 25 per cent of earnings in the additional pension range. One generous touch was that, once twenty years of contribution had elapsed, the top-up pension would be derived from a worker's best twenty years' earnings.

However, in the 1980s, the ideological mood changed. Thatcherism proved an inhospitable atmosphere for a relatively generous centralised system of benefit delivery. Having only been in operation for a few years, SERPS had yet to establish itself, and was an easy target. Abolition was proposed,[3] but, instead, in 1986, SERPS was made much less generous: the replacement value of 25 per cent of earnings was reduced to just 20 per cent; the 'Twenty Best Years' formula was replaced with a calculation based over the lifetime average; and widows lost half their husbands' pension rights. The private sector – particularly through the fresh option of personal pensions – was supposed fill the gap that once, very briefly, was occupied by the promise of a decent state second pension for all.

Ironically it was a Labour government, under Tony Blair, that appeared to apply the *coup de grace*, with its decision to phase out SERPS for good. Its direct state replacement was the State Second Pension, to which contributions could be paid from April 2002. This was expressly designed for lower earners, and, though an earnings-related pension, the government stated its intention that, before long, it would simply become a flat-rate supplement to the basic state pension.[4] In addition, by this stage, individuals had long since had the option of not merely opting out of the state supplementary scheme by joining occupational schemes, but also by opening their own personal pension. In April 2001 the Labour government added to the already complicated mix with the extra option of allowing individuals to contribute towards a Stakeholder Pension, a personal pension in which the state regulates the cost and charging structure.[5] This policy was an astonishingly long way from the pledge made by Richard Titmuss to break the power of the insurance industry. This was acknowledged by Barbara Castle, who fought to the end of her life to keep some of Crossman's dream alive by calling for the restoration of SERPS. She did this with assistance from what she called 'my little band of pension experts'.[6] Displaying remarkable tenacity, this 'band' included Study Group survivors Peter Townsend and Tony Lynes, and they, unimpressed, dubbed stakeholder pensions 'little more than modified Personal Pension schemes'.[7]

Thus it looked as though Crossman's concept of an earnings-related pension scheme run by the state to cover all classes had disappeared for good. However, once an idea is out there, the chance always remains that, to use Kingdon's phrase, it may 'flower anew' in a friendlier political environment.[8] Indeed Peter Townsend has stated that:

> Sooner or later, a British government will be forced, because of increasing poverty and inequality among the late middle-aged and elderly in a global market, to bring back the key features of national superannuation – an earnings-related pension – to repair the damage now being made to the pensions system, and to the living standard of millions of people.[9]

And lo, in 2005, the Turner Commission was recommending that the Labour government introduce a 'new policy for earnings-related provision'.[10] The proposed National Pension Savings Scheme was the result of this 'new' thinking. Moreover, it could be argued that this new scheme, now drearily called personal accounts, though adapted for the circumstances of the twenty-first century, has, at its core, a similar goal. In providing the foreword to the White Paper, the then Prime Minister, Tony Blair, explained that 'personal accounts will extend the benefits of low-cost saving to those without access to a good occupational pension'.[11] This is very much in the tradition of Crossman's 'M&S' socialism examined in Chapter 1, that of basically ignoring redistribution, and concentrating instead on the solidaristic goal of enabling a privilege for a few to become the right of the many.

Therefore, to some extent, consciously or otherwise, ideas Crossman nurtured all those years ago are still informing the policy process today. So, though Crossman was not a great minister – he said himself, 'Intellectuals, the exciting people, aren't necessarily the best Parliamentary Secretaries or the best Ministers'[12] – and he failed to introduce that single killer piece of legislation that would have put a stake through the heart of the Beveridge system, Crossman did make an impressive mark on the British system of social security through his propagation of particular ideas. Throughout the second half of the twentieth century, and beyond, various governments, Labour

(Old and New) and Conservative, freely borrowed and adapted these ideas to reshape British social policy. That these reforms have been of an incremental nature – rather than the 'fresh start' Crossman recommended way back in 1954 – has helped to create a system of social security, particularly of pensions, that is breathtakingly complicated.[13] Nevertheless these reforms have, at least, helped to drag the regime away from the flat-rate straitjacket of the Beveridge system, and Crossman should now be recognised as a serious political figure in British post-war social history.

In a sense, Crossman's most significant role in social policy relates to the metaphor used originally by Crossman's biographer. As noted in the first paragraph of this book, Anthony Howard described Crossman as 'one of those meteors' that occasionally light the political scene.[14] Howard was suggesting that Crossman's personality was such that he was able, briefly, to 'bring a glow to the normally grey and dingy skies of British politics'. Indeed the impression of many – though, in fairness, not Howard – was that Crossman was indeed much like a meteor, dazzling but, ultimately, useless. However, there is a theory that meteors can create more than a pretty light-show as they burn up in the Earth's atmosphere. The theory of panspermia, associated in recent times with the late Sir Fred Hoyle and Chandra Wickramasinghe, is that life did not evolve independently on earth, but was derived from importation of viable cells from space through vehicles such as comets or meteors.[15] It could be argued that Crossman, in a similar manner, took ideas from outside the political world and, in a dazzling display, imported them into the heart of the British policy process. As with life, these ideas Crossman carried mutated and evolved into forms very different to their origins,[16] but that should not detract from the significance of that first contact.

NOTES

INTRODUCTION

1. For example, Catherine Bochel and Hugh Bochel, *The UK Social Policy Process*, (Basingstoke, 2004); Peter Dorey, *Policy Making in Britain*, (London, 2005); Kevin Theakston, 'Richard Crossman: The Diaries of a Cabinet Minister', *Public Policy and Administration*, 2003, vol 18, no 4, pp. 20–40. A new biography of Crossman by Victoria Honeyman was published by IB Tauris in December 2007, sadly too late to inform this particular book.
2. Kevin Jefferys (ed.), *Labour Forces: From Ernest Bevan to Gordon Brown*, (London, 2002).
3. Kevin Hickson, 'Review: *Labour Forces* by Kevin Jefferys (ed.)', *Political Studies Review*, 2003, vol 1 no 3, p. 389.
4. Anthony Howard (ed.), *The Crossman Diaries*, (London, 1979), p. 9.
5. Richard Crossman, *The Diaries of a Cabinet Minister, vol 1: Minister of Housing 1964–66* (London, 1975); Richard Crossman, *The Diaries of a Cabinet Minister, vol 2: Lord President of Council and Leader of the House of Commons 1966–68* (London, 1976); Richard Crossman, *The Diaries of a Cabinet Minister, vol 3: Secretary of State for Social Services 1968–70*, (London, 1976).
6. Janet Morgan (ed.), *The Backbench Diaries of Richard Crossman* (London, 1981).
7. Anthony Howard, *Crossman: The Pursuit of Power*, (London, 1990), pp. 1–2.
8. Ibid, p. 1.
9. Richard Crossman, *The Politics of Pensions*, Eleanor Rathbone Memorial Lectures no 19 (Liverpool, 1972), p. 6.
10. Ibid.
11. Ibid, p. 26.

12. Martin Powell and John Stewart, 'Themed Section on History and Policy: Introduction', *Social Policy and Society*, 2005, vol 4 no 3, p. 293.
13. Glen O'Hara and Helen Parr, 'Conclusions: Harold Wilson's 1964–70 Governments and the Heritage of "New" Labour', *The Wilson Governments 1964–1970 Reconsidered*, ed. G. O'Hara and H. Parr, (Abingdon, 2006), p. 171.
14. Tony Blair quoted in O'Hara and Parr, 'Conclusions', p. 171.
15. Anthony Seldon, 'Ideas are not Enough', *The Ideas That Shaped Post-War Britain*, ed. D. Marquand and A. Seldon, (London, 1996).
16. Labour Party, *National Superannuation: Labour's Policy for Security in Old Age*, (London, 1957), p. 5.
17. Howard, *Crossman*, p. 290.

Chapter 1 – Ideas, Individuals, Circumstances and Interests

1. Seldon, 'Ideas'.
2. W.H. Auden quoted in Edward Mendelson (ed.), *W.H Auden: Selected Poems* (London, 1979), p. 32.
3. Howard, *Crossman*.
4. Tam Dalyell, *Dick Crossman: A Portrait*, (London, 1989).
5. Hugo Young, *The Crossman Affair*, (London, 1976).
6. See Theakston, 'Richard Crossman: The Diaries of a Cabinet Minister'.
7. Howard, *Crossman*, p. 11.
8. Crossman, *Diaries*, vol 2, p. 190, diary entry for 8 January 1967.
9. Dalyell, *Dick Crossman*, p. 7.
10. Ibid.
11. Howard, *Crossman*, p. 22.
12. Ibid, p. 14.
13. Dalyell, *Dick Crossman*, p. 16.
14. Richard Crossman, 'The Wykehamist' *New Statesman and Nation*, 18 September 1954, p. 328.
15. Ibid.
16. Ibid.
17. Howard, *Crossman*, pp. 25–38.
18. Ibid, pp. 83–107.
19. Lockhart quoted in Howard, *Crossman*, p. 107.
20. Howard, *Crossman*, p. 105.
21. Ibid, pp. 108–26.
22. Crossman quoted in Keith Laybourn, *A Century of Labour: A History of the Labour Party 1900–2000* (Stroud, 2000), p. 79.
23. Laybourn, *A Century*, p. 80.
24. Ibid, p. 81.
25. Howard, *Crossman*, p. 153.
26. Ibid, pp. 166–7.
27. Dalyell, *Dick Crossman*, p. 87.
28. Ibid.
29. Tragically, Crossman's son, Patrick, took his own life in 1975, aged 17.
30. Howard, *Crossman*, pp. 184–7.

31. Ibid, pp. 198–9.
32. Ibid, p. 210.
33. Lisa Martineau, *Politics and Power: Barbara Castle* (London, 2000), p. 138.
34. Crossman, *vol 1*, p. 11.
35. Howard, *Crossman, Diaries*, p. 250.
36. Crossman, *Diaries, vol 1*, p. 12.
37. Bob Mellish quoted in Ben Pimlott, *Harold Wilson* (London, 1992), p. 328.
38. Keith Banting, *Poverty, Politics and Policy* (London and Basingstoke, 1979), pp. 14–65.
39. Dame Evelyn Sharp quoted in Howard, *Crossman*, p. 267.
40. Howard, *Crossman*, p. 279.
41. Harold Wilson, *The Labour Government 1964–1970: A Personal Record* (London, 1971), p. 521.
42. Howard, *Crossman*, p. 296.
43. Crossman, *Diaries, vol 2*, p. 722, diary entry for 19 March 1968.
44. Young, *Crossman Affair*, p. 11.
45. Ibid, p. 195.
46. Denis Healey, *The Time Of My Life* (London, 1989), pp. 107–8.
47. Douglas Jay quoted in Pimlott, *Wilson*, p. 212.
48. Jack Jones, *Union Man* (London, 1986), p. 175.
49. Healey, *Time of My Life*, p. 108.
50. John Cole, *As It Seemed To Me*, revised paperback edition (London, 1996), p. 65.
51. Morgan, *Backbench*, p. 11.
52. Ibid.
53. Theakston, 'Richard Crossman: The Diaries of a Cabinet Minister', p. 22.
54. Crossman, *Diaries, vol 2*, p. 190, diary entry for 8 January 1967.
55. Crossman, *Pensions*, p. 10.
56. Richard Crossman, *Paying For The Social Services*, Fabian Tract 399 (London, 1969), p. 6.
57. Ibid.
58. Ibid, p. 9.
59. Theakston, 'Richard Crossman: The Diaries of a Cabinet Minister', p. 22.
60. Edward Pearce, 'Denis Healey', *Labour Forces*, ed. Kevin Jefferys (London, 2002), p. 146.
61. Crossman quoted in Howard, *Crossman*, p. 199.
62. Pimlott, *Wilson*, p. 335.
63. Eric Shragge, *Pensions Policy in Britain* (London, 1984).
64. Banting, *Poverty, Politics and Policy*, pp. 139–40.
65. Ibid, p. 4.
66. Hugh Heclo, *Modern Social Politics in Britain and Sweden* (New Haven and London, 1974).
67. Ibid, p. 308.
68. Ibid, p. 308–9.
69. Howard, *Crossman*, p. 170.
70. Crossman, *Pensions*, p. 5.
71. Ibid, p. 1.
72. Seldon, 'Ideas', p. 289.
73. Ibid.
74. See Dorey, *Policy Making*, pp. 13–27.

75. Seldon, 'Ideas', p. 259.
76. Dahrendorf quoted in Seldon, 'Ideas', p. 263.
77. Ibid, p. 264.
78. Ibid.
79. Dorey, Policy Making, p. 13.
80. Seldon, 'Ideas', p. 264.
81. Ibid, p. 266.
82. Roger Cobb and Charles Elder, Participation in American Politics: The Dynamics of Agenda-building (Boston, 1972).
83. Ibid, p. 85.
84. Crossman quoted in Morgan, Backbench, p. 584; diary entry for 3 May 1957.
85. Seldon, 'Ideas', p. 267.
86. Ibid.
87. Ibid.
88. For example Banting, Poverty, Politics and Policy; Heclo, Modern Social Politics; Grant Jordan and Jeremy Richardson, 'The British policy style or the logic of negotiation', Policy Styles in Western Europe, ed. J. Richardson (London, 1982); David Donnison, 'The academic contribution to social reform', Social Policy and Administration, 2000, vol 34 no 1, pp. 26–43.
89. David Reisman, Richard Titmuss: Welfare and Society, (London, 1977), pp. 2–5.
90. Richard Titmuss, The Gift Relationship (London, 1970).
91. Robert Page, 'A Guide to the Literature', The Student's Companion to Social Policy, ed. P. Alcock, A. Erskine, and M. May (Oxford, 1998), p. 335.
92. Reisman, Titmuss, p. 5.
93. Crossman quoted in Morgan, Backbench, p. 75, footnotes to diary entry for 14 February 1952.
94. Peter Townsend, 'Obituary: Professor Brian Abel-Smith', The Independent, 9 April 1996.
95. Ibid.
96. Julian Le Grand, 'A Religion of Doing Good – Obituary: Brian Abel-Smith', The Guardian, 9 April 1996.
97. Paul Thompson, 'Reflections on becoming a researcher: Peter Townsend interviewed by Paul Thompson', Social Research Methodology, 2004, vol 7 no 1, pp. 85–95.
98. John Kingdon, Agendas, Alternatives and Public Policies, 2nd ed. (New York, 1995), p. 19.
99. Ibid, p. 20.
100. Ibid.
101. Seldon, 'Ideas', p. 276.
102. Ibid, p. 276–7.
103. Ibid, p. 278.
104. Richard Titmuss, Problems of Social Policy, (London, 1950); Titmuss, Essays on the Welfare State (London, 1958).
105. Seldon, 'Ideas', p. 278.
106. Report of the Committee on the Economic and Financial Problems of Old Age, Cmd. 9333 (London, 1954), p. 14.
107. Pensions Commission, A New Pension Settlement for the Twenty-First Century: The Second Report of the Pensions Commission (London, 2005), p. 4.

108. Richard Rose and Philip Davies, *Inheritance in Public Policy: Change Without Choice in Britain*, (New Haven, 1994), p. 4.
109. Stephen Krasner, 'Approaches to the State', *Comparative Politics*, 1984, vol 16 no 2, pp. 218–30.
110. Paul Pierson, *Dismantling the Welfare State: Reagan, Thatcher, and the Politics of Retrenchment* (Cambridge, 1994).
111. Ibid, p. 39.
112. Ibid, p. 42.
113. Ibid.
114. Helen Fawcett, 'The Beveridge Straitjacket: Policy Formation and the Problem of Poverty in Old Age', *Contemporary British History*, 1996, vol 10 no 1, p. 22.
115. Ibid, p. 20.
116. John Myles and Paul Pierson, 'The Comparative Political Economy of Pension Reform', *The New Politics of the Welfare State*, ed. P. Pierson (Oxford, 2001), p. 306.
117. Seldon, 'Ideas', p. 279.
118. Ibid.
119. Heclo, *Modern Social Politics*, p. 263.
120. Leslie Hannah, *Inventing Retirement: The development of occupational pensions in Britain* (Cambridge, 1986), p. 56.
121. Seldon, 'Ideas', p. 279.
122. Hiroshi Araki, 'Ideas and Welfare: The Conservative Transformation of the British Pension Regime', *Journal of Social Policy*, 2000, vol. 29 no. 4, p. 599.
123. Ibid, pp. 616–19.
124. Seldon, 'Ideas', p. 280.
125. Crossman quoted in Kevin Theakston, 'Ministers and Civil Servants', *United Kingdom Governance*, ed. R. Pyper and L. Robins (Basingstoke, 2000), p. 46.
126. Crossman, 'Politics of Pensions, p. 26.
127. Ibid.
128. Gabriel Chavallier, *Clochemerle* (London, 2004; originally published 1934).
129. Seldon , 'Ideas', p. 276.

CHAPTER 2 – CHALLENGING BEVERIDGE

1. Crossman in Morgan, *Backbench*, p. 449; diary entry for 15 October 1955.
2. Jose Harris, *William Beveridge: A Biography*, 2nd ed. (Oxford, 1997), p. 363.
3. Ibid, p. 452.
4. Ibid, p. 365.
5. John Macnicol, *The Politics of Retirement in Britain, 1878–1948* (Cambridge, 1998).
6. William Beveridge, *Social Insurance and Allied Services*, Cmd. 6404 (London, 1942), p. 6.
7. Ibid, p. 120.
8. Ibid, p. 121.
9. Ibid, p. 11.

10. Ibid, p. 141.
11. Ibid, p. 8.
12. Nicholas Timmins, *The Five Giants*, revised edition (London, 2001), p. 23.
13. Pat Thane, *Foundations of the Welfare State*, 2nd ed. (London, 1996), p. 237.
14. Harris, *Beveridge*, p. 1.
15. James Griffiths quoted in Timmins, *Giants*, p. 136.
16. Rodney Lowe, 'A Prophet Dishonoured in his Own Country? The Rejection of Beveridge in Britain, 1945–1970', *Beveridge and Social Security*, ed. J. Hills, J. Ditch and H. Glennerster (Oxford, 1994), p. 123.
17. Ibid, p. 120.
18. Fawcett, 'Beveridge Straitjacket'.
19. Hannah, *Inventing Retirement*, p. 19–21.
20. Beveridge, *Social Insurance*, p. 93.
21. Ibid, pp. 6–7.
22. Hannah, *Inventing Retirement*, p. 67.
23. Beveridge, *House of Lords Debates*, 5th series, vol 182, col 676, 20 May 1953.
24. Ibid.
25. Iain Macleod and Enoch Powell, *The Social Services: Needs and Means*, (London, 1952), p. 32.
26. Ibid, p. 5.
27. Crossman, *Pensions*, p. 11.
28. Brian Abel-Smith, *The Reform of Social Security*, Fabian Research Series no 161 (London, 1953), p. 41.
29. Ibid, p. 12.
30. Ibid, p. 39.
31. Ibid, p. 14.
32. Ibid, p. 25.
33. Ibid.
34. Richard Titmuss, 'The Age of Pensions: Superannuation and Social Policy', *The Times*, 30 December 1953.
35. Ibid.
36. Ibid.
37. Abel-Smith, *Social Security*, p. 26.
38. Ibid, p. 39.
39. Ibid, p. 40.
40. Barbara Wootton quoted in Abel-Smith, *Social Security*, p. 40.
41. Brian Abel-Smith and Peter Townsend, *New Pensions for the Old*, Fabian Research Series no 171, (London, 1955).
42. *Report of the Committee on the Economic and Financial Problems of Old Age*, Cmd. 9333, p. 56.
43. Abel-Smith and Townsend, *New Pensions*, p. 21.
44. Ibid.
45. Ibid, p. 26.
46. Ibid, p. 21.
47. Ibid, p. 25.
48. Ibid.
49. Ibid.
50. Ibid, p. 23.

51. Kingdon, *Agendas*, p. 116.
52. Crossman, *Pensions*, p. 11.
53. Ibid, pp. 11–12.
54. Ibid, p. 12.
55. Ibid.
56. Ibid.
57. Ibid.
58. Crossman quoted in Morgan, *Backbench*, p. 448, diary entry for 15 October 1955.
59. Mike McBeth, 'Traditional theories of welfare', *Introducing Social Policy*, revised edition, ed. C. Alcock, S. Payne, M. Sullivan, (Harlow, 2004), p. 123.
60. Ibid, pp. 116–21.
61. Richard Crossman, 'Towards a Philosophy of Socialism', *New Fabian Essays*, ed, R. Crossman (London, 1970; first published 1952), p. 25.
62. Ibid, p. 26.
63. Michael Sullivan, *The Development of the British Welfare State* (Hemel Hempstead, 1996), p. 15.
64. Crossman, 'Towards', p. 27.
65. Ibid, p. 28.
66. Ibid, p. 29.
67. Ibid, pp. 28–9.
68. Crossman, *Pensions*, p. 10.
69. Ibid.
70. Morgan, *Backbench*, p. 448, footnote for entry of the 15 October 1955.
71. Labour Party Archives, John Rylands Library Manchester (hereafter LPA), Social Services Sub-Committee, minutes, 17 December 1953.
72. Richard Crossman, 'The End of Beveridge', *New Statesman and Nation*, 11 December 1954, p. 772.
73. Ibid.
74. Ibid.
75. Ibid.
76. Ibid.
77. Ibid.
78. Ibid.
79. Ibid.
80. Crossman quoted in Morgan, *Backbench*, p. 449, diary entry for 15 October 1955.
81. Crossman quoted in Labour Party, *Report of the 54th Annual Conference* (London, 1955), p. 201.
82. Ibid, p. 202.
83. Ibid.
84. Heclo, *Modern Social Politics*, p. 262.
85. Crossman quoted in Labour Party, *54th Annual Conference*, p. 201.
86. Aneurin Bevan, *In Place of Fear* (London, 1952), p. 79.
87. Bevan quoted in Labour Party, *54th Annual Conference*, p. 196.
88. Sir Alfred Roberts quoted in *54th Annual Conference*, pp. 197–8.
89. Heclo, *Modern Social Politics*, p. 262.
90. Crossman, *Pensions*, p. 13.

CHAPTER 3 – THE CUNNING PLAN

1. Cobb and Elder, *Participation in American Politics*, p. 85.
2. Crossman quoted in Morgan, *Backbench*, p. 584, diary entry for 3 May 1957.
3. LPA, Study Group on Security and Old Age, minutes, 16 April 1956.
4. LPA, Study Group on Security and Old Age, minutes, 20 November 1956.
5. Morgan, *Backbench*, pp. 578–81, diary entry for 29 March 1957.
6. Ibid.
7. Fawcett, 'Beveridge Straitjacket', p. 21.
8. Labour Party, *Superannuation*, p. 2.
9. Crossman quoted in Morgan, *Backbench*, p. 581, diary entry for 29 March 1957.
10. Ibid, p. 584, diary entry for 3 May 1957.
11. Ibid, p. 621, diary entry for 24 October 1957.
12. Helen Fawcett, 'The Privatisation of Welfare: The Impact of Parties on the Private/Public Mix in Pension Provision', *West European Politics*, 1995, vol 18 no 4, p. 157.
13. Crossman, *Pensions*, p. 13.
14. LPA, Study Group on Security and Old Age, minutes, 4 July 1956.
15. Ibid.
16. Ibid.
17. LPA, Study Group on Security and Old Age, minutes, 25 September 1956.
18. LPA, Study Group on Security and Old Age, minutes, 4 July 1956.
19. Ibid.
20. LPA, Study Group on Security and Old Age, minutes, 27 June 1956.
21. LPA, Study Group on Security and Old Age, minutes, 27 June 1956, amended in the 4 July 1956 minutes.
22. LPA, Study Group on Security and Old Age, minutes, 25 September 1956.
23. Labour Party, *Superannuation*, p. 73.
24. Crossman quoted in Morgan, *Backbench*, p. 584, diary entry for 3 May 1957.
25. Labour Party, *Superannuation*, p. 22.
26. Ibid, p. 10.
27. Ibid, p. 23.
28. LPA, Study Group on Security and Old Age, minutes, 25 September 1956.
29. Labour Party, *Superannuation*, p. 22.
30. Ibid, pp. 22–3.
31. Fawcett, 'Beveridge Straitjacket', p. 29.
32. Crossman quoted in Labour Party, *54th Annual Conference*, p. 202.
33. Crossman quoted in Morgan, *Backbench*, p. 578, diary entry for 14 February.
34. Ibid, pp. 577–8, diary entry for 14 February.
35. Ibid, p. 578, diary entry for 14 February.
36. Ibid.
37. See LPA, Minutes of a Joint Meeting between Representatives of the TUC Social Insurance Committee and the Labour Party Study Group on Security and Old Age, 22 May 1957.

38. Roberts quoted in Labour Party, *Report of the 56th Annual Conference*, (London, 1957), p. 115.
39. Ibid.
40. Labour Party, *Superannuation*, pp. 8–9.
41. James Griffiths quoted in LPA, Study Group on Security and Old Age, minutes, 27 June 1956.
42. Titmuss quoted in LPA, Study Group on Security and Old Age, minutes, 4 July 1956.
43. Crossman quoted in LPA, Study Group on Security and Old Age, minutes, 4 July 1956.
44. W.H. Clough quoted in LPA, Study Group on Security and Old Age, minutes, 4 July 1956.
45. LPA, Study Group on Security and Old Age, minutes, 4 July 1956.
46. Labour Party, *Superannuation*, pp. 24–5.
47. Ibid, p. 64.
48. Ibid.
49. Fawcett, 'Beveridge Straitjacket', p. 31.
50. Labour Party, *Superannuation*, p. 30.
51. C.N. Scott quoted in Labour Party, *56th Annual Conference*, p. 114.
52. Author's emphasis; Crossman quoted in Labour Party, *56th Annual Conference*, p. 122.
53. Roberts quoted in Labour Party, *56th Annual Conference*, p. 116.
54. Crossman, *Pensions*, p. 13.
55. Hannah, *Inventing Retirement*, p. 149.
56. John Atkinson, 'The Developing Relationship Between the State Pension Scheme and Occupational Pension Schemes', *Social and Economic Administration*, 1977, vol 11 no 3, p. 216.
57. Crossman quoted in LPA, Study Group on Security and Old Age, minutes, 27 June 1956.
58. Titmuss quoted in LPA, Study Group on Security and Old Age, minutes, 27 June 1956.
59. Ibid.
60. Jay quoted in LPA, Study Group on Security and Old Age, minutes, 4 July 1956.
61. Ibid.
62. Titmuss quoted in LPA, Study Group on Security and Old Age, minutes, 4 July 1956.
63. Reisman, *Titmuss*, p. 2.
64. Labour Party, *Superannuation*, p. 12.
65. Ibid, p. 14.
66. See LPA, Minutes of a Joint Meeting between Representatives of the TUC Social Insurance Committee and the Labour Party Study Group on Security and Old Age, 22 May 1957.
67. David Ginsburg quoted in LPA, Study Group on Security and Old Age, minutes, 4 July 1956.
68. Jay quoted in LPA, Study Group on Security and Old Age, minutes, 4 July 1956.
69. Gerald Reynolds quoted in LPA, Study Group on Security and Old Age, minutes, 4 July 1956.
70. LPA, Study Group on Security and Old Age, minutes, 4 July 1956.

71. Atkinson, 'Developing Relationship', pp. 219–20.
72. Titmuss quoted in LPA, Study Group on Security and Old Age, minutes, 4 July 1956.
73. Labour Party, *Superannuation*, p. 40.
74. Ibid, p. 54.
75. Fawcett, 'Privatisation of Welfare', p. 157.
76. Labour Party, *Superannuation*, p. 54.
77. Ibid.
78. Ibid, p. 55.
79. Hannah, *Inventing Retirement*, p. 56.
80. Labour Party, *Superannuation*, p. 90.
81. LPA, Study Group on Security and Old Age, 19 September 1956.
82. Labour Party, *Superannuation*, p. 42.
83. Ibid, pp. 49–51.
84. Ibid, p. 50.
85. Ibid.
86. Redington, as recorded by Crossman, quoted in Morgan, *Backbench*, p. 579, diary entry for 29 March 1957.
87. Crossman quoted in Labour Party, *54th Annual Conference*, p. 202.
88. Jay quoted in LPA, Study Group on Security and Old Age, minutes, 27 June 1956.
89. Morgan, *Backbench*, p. 578, diary entry for 29 March 1957.
90. Ibid, pp. 578–80.
91. Crossman quoted in Morgan, *Backbench*, p. 580, diary entry for 29 March 1957.
92. Ibid.
93. Seldon, 'Ideas', pp. 265–7.
94. Crossman quoted in Morgan, *Backbench*, p. 580, diary entry for 29 March 1957.
95. Morgan, *Backbench*, pp. 579–80, diary entry for 29 March 1957.
96. Jay quoted in *Backbench*, p. 580, diary entry for 29 March 1957.
97. Crossman quoted in *Backbench*, p. 580, diary entry for 29 March 1957.
98. Labour Party, *Superannuation*, p. 89.
99. Ibid, p. 91.
100. Ibid, p. 96.
101. Ibid, p. 90.
102. Ibid.
103. Heclo, *Modern Social Politics*, p. 266.
104. Crossman in Morgan, *Backbench*, p. 581, diary entry for 29 March 1957.
105. Paul Bridgen and Rodney Lowe, *Welfare Policy Under the Conservatives 1951–1964* (London, 1998), pp. 104–12.
106. Paul Bridgen, 'The One Nation Idea and State Welfare', *Contemporary British History*, 2000, vol 14 no 3, pp. 83–104.
107. Hugh Pemberton, 'Politics and Pensions in Post-war Britain', *Britain's Pension Crisis: History and Policy*, ed. H. Pemberton, P. Thane and N. Whiteside (Oxford, 2006), pp. 49–53.
108. Oliver Poole quoted in Heclo, *Modern Social Politics*, p. 266.
109. Bridgen, 'One Nation', p. 92.
110. Crossman quoted in Morgan, *Backbench*, p. 596, diary entry for 23 May 1957.

111. Bridgen and Lowe, *Welfare*, p. 96.
112. Ibid, p. 105.
113. Ibid.
114. Harold Macmillan quoted in Bridgen and Lowe 1998, p. 105.
115. Bridgen and Lowe, *Welfare*, p. 105.
116. Bridgen, 'One Nation', p. 94.
117. Ibid, p. 93.
118. Ibid, p. 96.
119. Alan Deacon and Jonathan Bradshaw, *Reserved for the Poor: The Means Test in British Social Policy* (Oxford, 1983), p. 55.
120. Iain Macleod quoted in Bridgen and Lowe, *Welfare*, p. 108.
121. Bridgen and Lowe, *Welfare*, p. 106.
122. Bridgen, 'One Nation', p. 96.
123. Macleod quoted in Bridgen and Lowe, *Welfare*, p. 108.
124. Bridgen, 'One Nation', p. 99.
125. Ministry of Pensions and National Insurance (hereafter MPNI), *Provision for Old Age*, Cmnd. 538 (London, 1958), p. 13.
126. Ibid, p. 9.
127. Ibid, p. 13.
128. John Boyd-Carpenter, *Way of Life: the memoirs of John Boyd-Carpenter*, (London, 1980), p. 135.
129. Author's emphasis; MPNI, *Provision for Old Age*, p. 11.
130. Boyd-Carpenter, *Way of Life*, p. 135.
131. Bridgen and Lowe, *Welfare*, p. 109.
132. MPNI, *Provision for Old Age*, 1958, p. 16.
133. Labour Party, *Superannuation*, 1957, p. 54.
134. Fawcett, 'Privatisation of Welfare', p. 154.
135. MPNI, *Provision for Old Age*, pp. 13–16.
136. Heclo, *Modern Social Politics*, p. 273.
137. Hannah, *Inventing Retirement*, p. 58.
138. LPA, Study Group on Security and Old Age, minutes, 2 March 1961.
139. Bridgen and Lowe, *Welfare*, p. 111.
140. Macleod quoted in Timmins, *Giants*, p. 192.
141. Timmins, *Giants*, p. 196.
142. Hannah, *Inventing Retirement*, p. 58.
143. Ibid, p. 145.
144. Fawcett, 'Privatisation of Welfare', p. 155.
145. David Butler and Richard Rose, *The British General Election of 1959* (London, 1960), p. 56.
146. Crossman, *Pensions*, p. 13.
147. Tony Benn, *Years of Hope: Diaries, Papers and Letters 1940–62* (London: 1995), p. 236, diary entry for 21 May 1957.
148. Author's emphasis, Kingdon, *Agendas*, p. 131.
149. Lowe, 'Prophet', p. 121.
150. Crossman quoted in Howard, *Crossman*, p. 199.
151. Lowe, 'Prophet', pp. 131–2.
152. Michael O'Higgins, 'Public/Private Interaction and Pension Provision', *Public/ Private Interplay in Social Protection: A Comparative Study*, ed. M. Rein and L. Rainwater (Armonk, NY, 1986), p. 105.
153. Seldon, 'Ideas', p. 264.

154. Deacon and Bradshaw, *Reserved for the Poor*, p. 60.
155. Brian Abel-Smith and Peter Townsend, *The Poor and The Poorest*, LSE Occasional Papers on Social Administration no 17 (London, 1965), p. 63.
156. Ibid.
157. Labour Party, *Superannuation*, pp. 30–1.
158. Crossman quoted in Morgan, *Backbench*, p. 584, diary entry for 3 May 1957.
159. Frank Baumgartner and Bryan Jones, *Agenda and Instability in American Politics* (Chicago, 1993).
160. Seldon, 'Ideas', p. 276.
161. Ibid, p. 279.
162. Heclo, *Modern Social Politics*, p. 228.
163. Ibid, p. 263.
164. Ibid, p. 267.
165. Hannah, *Inventing Retirement*, p. 56.
166. Ibid.
167. Heclo, *Modern Social Politics*, p. 266.
168. Crossman quoted in Morgan, *Backbench*, p. 579, diary entry for 29 March 1957.
169. Ibid.
170. LPA, Study Group on Security and Old Age, minutes, 1 July 1957.
171. Ibid.
172. Ibid.
173. See LPA, Study Group on Security and Old Age, minutes, 14 July 1959.
174. Heclo, *Modern Social Politics*, pp. 308–9.
175. Crossman, *Pensions*, pp. 11–12.
176. Fawcett, 'Beveridge Strait-jacket', p. 26.
177. Crossman, *Pensions*, p. 1.
178. Kingdon, *Agendas*, p. 179.
179. Ibid.
180. Crossman quoted in Morgan, *Backbench*, p. 581, diary entry for 29 March 1957.
181. Kingdon, *Agendas*, p. 127.
182. Ibid, p. 20.
183. James Kincaid, *Poverty and Equality in Britain*, rev. ed. (Harmondsworth, 1975), p. 116.
184. Crossman quoted in Morgan, *Backbench*, p. 585, diary entry for 3 May 1957.

CHAPTER 4 – THE RIVAL

1. Bridgen and Lowe, *Welfare*, p. 113.
2. Abel-Smith and Townsend, *New Pensions*, p. 21.
3. Dorothy Cole and J.E.G. Utting, *The Economic Circumstances of Old People*, Occasional Papers on Social Administration no 4 (London, 1962).
4. Bridgen and Lowe, *Welfare*, p. 123.
5. Fawcett, 'Beveridge Straitjacket', p. 25.
6. Crossman quoted in Morgan, *Backbench*, p. 848, diary entry for 20 May 1960.
7. Ibid, p. 987, diary entry for 5 March 1963.

8. Ibid, p. 823, diary entry for 8 March 1960.
9. Ibid, p. 969, diary entry for 8 February 1963.
10. See obituaries for Lord (Douglas) Houghton in *The Guardian*, *The Independent*, and *The Times*, all 3 May 1996.
11. LPA, Study Group on Security and Old Age, minutes for 22 May 1957 and passim.
12. Ibid, minutes, 28 July 1959.
13. Douglas Houghton, *Paying for the Social Services* (London, 1967), pp. 17–18.
14. Ibid, p. 18.
15. Ibid, p. 14.
16. Compare Houghton's *Paying for the Social Services* with Richard Crossman's identically titled *Paying for the Social Services*, Fabian Tract 399 (London, 1969).
17. Crossman quoted in Morgan, *Backbench*, p. 800, diary entry for 13 November 1959.
18. Ibid.
19. Ibid.
20. LPA, Study Group on Security and Old Age, minutes, 6 April 1960.
21. Ibid, minutes, 27 April 1960.
22. Ibid, minutes, 23 March 1961, 6 March 1962, 23 March 1962.
23. Ibid, minutes, 6 April 1960.
24. Ibid.
25. Ibid.
26. Rose and Davies, *Inheritance*, p. 4.
27. LPA, Study Group on Security and Old Age, minutes, 6 April 1960.
28. Ibid.
29. Ibid.
30. Ibid.
31. Crossman quoted in Labour Party, *Annual Report of the 59th Annual Conference* (London, 1960), p. 104.
32. Ibid, pp. 104–5.
33. LPA, Study Group on Security and Old Age, minutes, 13 July 1960.
34. Labour Party, *59th Annual Conference*, pp. 106–7.
35. LPA, Study Group on Security and Old Age, RD. 132, 'New Needs In Social Policy', March 1961.
36. Ibid.
37. LPA, Study Group on Security and Old Age, minutes, 20 April 1961.
38. LPA, Study Group on Security and Old Age, RD. 136, 'Suggested Re-draft of New Needs in Welfare' by Douglas Houghton, April 1961.
39. LPA, Study Group on Security and Old Age, minutes, 13 April 1961.
40. Labour Party, *Signposts for the Sixties* (London, 1961), p. 26.
41. Ibid.
42. LPA, Study Group on Security and Old Age, RD. 181, 'Future Work', November 1961.
43. LPA, Study Group on Security and Old Age, minutes, 28 November 1961.
44. LPA, Study Group on Security and Old Age, RD. 198, 'Aide Memoire on principles to be incorporated in Labour's social security scheme with special reference to the application of such principles in the schemes of Belgium, Germany, Sweden and U.S.A.', January 1962.
45. Ibid.

46. Ibid.
47. LPA, Study Group on Security and Old Age, RD. 216 (revised), 'A Draft Social Security Plan', March 1962.
48. Ibid.
49. Ibid.
50. LPA, 'A Note for the Meeting between the TUC Social Insurance Committee and Representatives of the Labour Party's Study Group on Security and Old Age', 14 February, 1962.
51. LPA, Study Group on Security and Old Age, RD. 216 (rev.).
52. LPA, Study Group on Security and Old Age, minutes, 11 December 1962.
53. Ibid.
54. Labour Party, *New Frontiers for Social Security*, (London, 1963), pp. 15–16.
55. Fred Craig, *British General Election Manifestos 1900–1974*, (Basingstoke, 1975), p. 265.
56. LPA, Study Group on Security and Old Age, RD. 198, January 1962.
57. David Dolowitz and David Marsh, 'Who learns what from whom: a review of the policy transfer literature', *Political Studies*, vol 44 no 2, p. 344.
58. LPA, Study Group on Security and Old Age, RD. 198, January 1962.
59. C.P. Shopland quoted in Labour Party, *59th Annual Conference*, p. 99.
60. E. Roberts quoted in Labour Party, *59th Annual Conference*, p. 102.
61. LPA, Study Group on Security and Old Age, RD. 291, 'The Guarantee', June 1962.
62. LPA, Study Group on Security and Old Age, RD. 198, January 1962.
63. LPA, Study Group on Security and Old Age, RD. 216 (rev.).
64. LPA, Study Group on Security and Old Age, minutes, 29 May 1962.
65. G. Lowthian quoted in LPA, Study Group on Security and Old Age, minutes, 29 May 1962.
66. Crossman quoted in LPA, Study Group on Security and Old Age, minutes, 27 June 1962.
67. LPA, Study Group on Security and Old Age, minutes, 17 July 1962.
68. LPA, Study Group on Security and Old Age, RD. 307, 'The Income Guarantee: Memorandum from Douglas Houghton M.P.', July 1962.
69. Ibid.
70. LPA, Study Group on Security and Old Age, minutes, 17 July 1962.
71. Labour Party, *New Frontiers*, p. 6.
72. Ibid.
73. Ibid, p. 19.
74. LPA, Study Group on Security and Old Age, RD. 743, Income Guarantee by Douglas Houghton, March 1964.
75. National Archives, Kew (hereafter NA PRO) T 227/2216, National Insurance Review Committee, 20 November 1964.
76. Craig, *Manifestos*, p. 265.
77. Adrian Webb, 'The Abolition of National Assistance: Policy Changes in the Administration of Assistance Benefits', *Change, Choice and Conflict in Social Policy*, P. Hall, H. Land, R. Parker, and A. Webb, (London, 1975), p. 451.
78. Paul Bridgen, 'Remedy For All Ills: Earnings-Relation and the Politics of Pensions 1950s/1960s', an unpublished paper given at the conference 'Relative decline and relative poverty: signposts to the sixties?' at the University of Bristol, 13 May 1999.

CHAPTER 5 – INTO THE STORM

1. A version of this chapter has already appeared in Stephen Thornton, 'A Case of Confusion and Incoherence: Social Security under Wilson, 1964–70', *Wilson Governments 1964–1970 Reconsidered.*
2. Cole, *As It Seemed To Me*, p. 45.
3. Peter Hennessy, *The Prime Minister: The Office and its Holders since 1945* (London, 2000), p. 288.
4. Howard Glennerster, *British Social Policy Since 1945* (Oxford, 1995), p. 121.
5. Andrew Thorpe, *History of the Labour Party* (Basingstoke, 1997), p. 167.
6. Pat Thane, 'Labour and Welfare', *Labour's First Century*, ed. D. Tanner, P. Thane and N. Tiratsoo (Cambridge, 2000), pp. 109–10.
7. Crossman quoted in Morgan, *Backbench*, p. 1014, diary entry for 17 July 1964.
8. Andrew Roth, 'Obituary – A Politician of Quiet Integrity: Peggy Herbison', *The Guardian*, 31 December 1996.
9. Crossman, *Pensions*, p. 25.
10. Ibid.
11. Glennerster, *Social Policy*, p. 121.
12. Craig, *Manifestos*, p. 266.
13. NA PRO CAB 128/39, 1st conclusions, 19 October 1964.
14. Ibid.
15. Crossman, *Diaries, vol 1*, p. 54, diary entry for 12 November 1964.
16. Ibid, p. 62, diary entry for 19 November 1964.
17. Ibid.
18. NA PRO CAB 128/39, 9th conclusions, 19 November 1964.
19. Crossman, *Diaries, vol 1*, p. 70, entry for 24 November 1964.
20. Ibid.
21. NA PRO CAB 128/39, 10th conclusions, 24 November 1964.
22. Ibid.
23. Crossman, *Diaries, vol 1*, p. 70, diary entry for 24 November 1964.
24. Ibid, p. 71, diary entry for 24 November 1964.
25. Wilson, *The Labour Government 1964–1970*, p. 31.
26. Houghton, *Paying for the Social Services*, p. 12.
27. Glennerster, *Social Policy*, p. 121.
28. Crossman, *Diaries, vol 1*, pp. 276–7, diary entry for 17 July 1965.
29. NA PRO CAB 147/125, 'A Re-appraisal of Social Policy' by Douglas Houghton, n.d. but sent to Wilson on 22 December 1965.
30. Ibid.
31. Fawcett, 'Beveridge Straitjacket', p. 20.
32. Ibid, p. 35.
33. Ibid.
34. Bridgen, 'Remedy For All Ills', p. 13.
35. Webb, 'The Abolition of National Assistance', p. 445–6.
36. NA PRO T 227/2216, National Insurance Review Committee, 20 November 1964.
37. Ibid.
38. Ibid.
39. Webb, 'The Abolition of National Assistance', p. 451.

40. Thornton, 'Confusion'.
41. Michael Cohen, James March and Johan Olsen, 'A garbage can model of organisational choice', *Administrative Science Quarterly*, 1972, vol 17, pp. 1–25.
42. Ibid, p. 1.
43. Michael Cohen, James March, and Johan Olsen, 'People, Problems, Solutions and the Ambiguity of Relevance', *Ambiguity and Choice in Organizations*, 2nd ed., ed. J. March and J. Olsen (Oslo, 1979), p. 27.
44. Webb, 'The Abolition of National Assistance', p. 456.
45. Hennessy, *The Prime Minister*, p. 310.
46. Crossman, *Diaries, vol 1*, p. 34, diary entry for 28 October 1964.
47. Crossman, *Pensions*, p. 17.
48. Wilson, *The Labour Government 1964–1970*, p. 711.
49. Peter Riddell, 'Slimline team of 12 is recipe for confusion', *The Times*, 11 November 2003.
50. Webb, 'The Abolition of National Assistance', p. 447.
51. Ibid.
52. Roth, 'Obituary: Peggy Herbison'.
53. Jack Jones, *Union Man* (London, 1986), p. 169.
54. Barbara Castle, *The Castle Diaries 1964–70* (London, 1984), p. 76, footnote of the diary entry for 7 December 1965.
55. Crossman, *Diaries, vol 2*, p. 429, diary entry for 17 July 1967.
56. Roth, 'Obituary: Peggy Herbison'.
57. Ibid.
58. Crossman, *Diaries, vol 1*, p. 283, diary entry for 21 July 1965.
59. Ibid, p. 362, diary entry for 26 October 1965.
60. NA PRO PREM 13/1209, Trend to Wilson, 18 May 1966 and Wilson note on MS.
61. Hennessy, *The Prime Minister*, p. 310.
62. Andrew Rawnsley, *Servants of the People*, rev. ed. (London, 2001), p. 106.
63. Timmins, *Five Giants*, p. 562.
64. NA PRO CAB 147/125, 'A Re-appraisal of Social Policy'.
65. Houghton, *Paying for the Social Services*, p. 12.
66. Ibid.
67. Timmins, *Five Giants*, p. 227.
68. Ibid, p. 226.
69. NA PRO CAB 147/125, 'A Re-appraisal of Social Policy'.
70. Department of Social Security, *A New Contract for Welfare: Partnership in Pensions*, Cm 4179 (London, 1998), p. 33.
71. Alan Walker, 'The third way for pensions (by way of Thatcherism and avoiding today's pensioners)', *Critical Social Policy*, 1999, vol 19 no 4, p. 519.
72. Tony Blair quoted in Gerard Seenan, 'Blair answers Booth on pensions', *The Guardian*, 2 September 2000.
73. Timmins, *Five Giants*, p. 560.
74. For example, Desmond King and Mark Wickham-Jones, 'Bridging the Atlantic: The Democratic (Party) Origins of Welfare to Work', *New Labour, New Welfare State? The Third Way in British Social Policy*, ed. M. Powell (Bristol, 1999).
75. Houghton, *Paying for the Social Services*, p. 13.

76. Ibid, p. 23.
77. Only in some ways though. Houghton was clearly 'Old Labour' in terms of industrial relations policy, as most famously evinced by his significant role in the scuppering of Barbara Castle's attempt to strap the unions into a legislative framework ('In Place of Strife') in 1969.

CHAPTER 6 – A STORY RICH IN LESSONS

1. Aspects of this chapter have appeared in Stephen Thornton, 'Richard Crossman, the Civil Service, and the Case of the Disappearing Pension; *Public Policy and Administration*, 2005, vol 20 no 2, pp. 67–80; and Thornton, 'Towards public-private partnership: Labour and pensions policy', *The Labour Governments 1964–1970*, ed. P. Dorey (London, 2006), pp. 292–308.
2. Houghton, *Paying for the Social Services*, p. 14.
3. Crossman, *Diaries, vol 2*, p. 722, diary entry for 19 March 1968.
4. Seldon, 'Ideas'.
5. Noel Whiteside, 'Historical Perspectives and the Politics of Pension Reform', *Pension Security in the 21st Century*, ed. G. Clark and N. Whiteside (Oxford, 2003), pp. 30–1.
6. Crossman, *Pensions*, p. 26.
7. Gordon Walker lost his seat in Smethwick at the 1964 election in a contest tainted by racism. Wilson appointed him Foreign Secretary anyway, but the unlucky Gordon Walker lost the by-election engineered for him to return to the Commons. He did return in 1966, following another by-election, but, by then, his political career had stalled.
8. Crossman, *Pensions*, p. 25.
9. Crossman, *Diaries, vol 2*, p. 444, diary entry for 26 July 1967.
10. Patrick Gordon Walker, *Political Diaries*, ed. R. Pearce, (London, 1991), p. 308, diary entry for 24 February 1967.
11. Roth, 'Obituary: Peggy Herbison'.
12. NA PRO CAB 165/605, Trend to Wilson, 27 January 1967.
13. NA PRO PREM 13/2394, Gordon Walker to Wilson, 24 January 1967.
14. NA PRO PREM 13/2394, Wilson to Gordon Walker.
15. Judith Hart was born in Burnley in 1924, and became an MP for Lanark in 1959. Before becoming Minister of Social Security in 1967 she had worked at the Scottish Office and Commonwealth Office. Promoted to the Cabinet in 1968, Hart became Paymaster General. Dropped from the Cabinet, she became Minister of Overseas Development from 1969–70 and again, intermittently, throughout the 1974–6 government. She died in 1991. In Crossman's view – which, as ever, says as much about Crossman as the individual being reviewed – Hart was 'a competent, efficient woman, not tremendously creative in mind, lacking many good ideas and a bit slapdash, but she is dashing, courageous, with a good political instinct for being on the right side' (quoted in Duncan Sutherland, Oxford Dictionary of National Biography, available at http://www.oxforddnb.com/view/article/49767?_fromAuth=1)
16. Crossman, *Diaries, vol 2*, p. 767, diary entry for 8 April 1968.
17. Ibid, p. 769, diary entry for 9 April 1968.

18. NA PRO CAB 147/125, 'Social Security: A New Strategy', undated, appears to have been written September 1968.
19. Crossman, *Diaries, vol 3*, pp. 52–3, diary entry for 8 May 1968.
20. Ibid, p. 53, diary entry for 8 May 1968.
21. Ibid, p. 225, diary entry for 16 October 1968.
22. Cohen et al's, 'garbage can model'. In addition to the Harman/Field incident, the Blair/Brown governments also possess additional 'garbage can' characteristics. For example, in terms of staff turnover at the DSS/DWP, since 1997 there have been no less than eight secretaries of state (as of February 2008). Furthermore, until his dramatic resignation from government in 2008, Peter Hain, Brown's first Secretary of State at Work and Pensions, also had a part-time job as Secretary of State for Wales.
23. Bridgen, 'Remedy For All Ills', p. 13.
24. Department of Health and Social Security (hereafter DHSS), *National Superannuation and Social Insurance*, Cmnd. 3883 (London, 1969).
25. Bryan Ellis, *Pensions in Britain 1955–1975* (London, 1989), p. 23.
26. Bridgen, 'Remedy For All Ills', p. 12.
27. Fawcett, 'Privatisation of Welfare', p. 158.
28. DHSS, *National Superannuation*, p. 12.
29. Heclo, *Modern Social Politics*, p. 274.
30. Crossman quoted in Morgan, *Backbench*, p. 580, diary entry for 29 March 1957.
31. DHSS, *National Superannuation*, p. 16.
32. Tony Lynes, *Labour's Pension Plan*, Fabian Tract 396 (London, 1969), p. 31.
33. Labour Party, *Superannuation*, p. 11.
34. LPA, Study Group on Security and Old Age, RD. 216 (rev.), March 1962.
35. Labour Party, *New Frontiers*, p. 15.
36. Craig, *Manifestos*, p. 239.
37. LPA, Social Policy Advisory Committee, Res. 12, 'Programme of Work', February 1965.
38. Bridgen, 'Remedy For All Ills', p. 12.
39. NA PRO PIN 47/141, 'Matters Relating to the Labour Party', 13 March 1964.
40. NA PRO T/227 2216, Working Group on Pensions, 14 July 1964.
41. NA PRO T 227/2216, Official Committee on Social Security Review, 5 February 1965.
42. NA PRO T 227/2216, Official Committee on Social Security Review, 12 February 1965.
43. NA PRO PREM 13/1209, note by Burke Trend to Wilson, 18 May 1966.
44. NA PRO T 227/2216, Official Committee on Social Security Review, 5 February 1965.
45. NA PRO PIN 47/147, Working Group on Pensions, 'The flat-rate and graduated pension elements', note by the Ministry of Pensions and National Insurance, 18 August 1964.
46. Ibid.
47. Ibid.
48. Ibid.
49. NA PRO CAB 165/133, Ministerial Committee on Social Services Sub-Committee on Social Security Cash Benefits, 13 March 1967.

50. NA PRO CAB 134/3303, Ministerial Sub-Committee on Earnings-Related Pensions, 'The Question Whether New Scheme Pensions Should Contain A Flat-rate Element Or Be Fully Earnings-related', note by the Secretaries, 24 July 1967.
51. Ibid.
52. Ibid.
53. LPA, HART 11/3, 'The Pension Formula for the New Scheme', 27 July 1967.
54. Ibid.
55. NA PRO CAB 134/3303, Ministerial Sub-Committee on Earnings-Related Pensions, 12 October 1967.
56. Ibid.
57. DHSS, National Superannuation, p. 6.
58. NA PRO CAB 134/3303, Ministerial Sub-Committee on Earnings-Related Pensions, 5 December 1967.
59. NA PRO CAB 134/3304, Ministerial Sub-Committee on Earnings-Related Pensions, Memorandum by the Official Committee on Social Security, 30 April 1968.
60. Crossman, Diaries, vol 3, p. 52, diary entry for 8 May 1968.
61. Ibid, p. 53, diary entry for 8 May 1968.
62. Ibid.
63. NA PRO T227/2589, Earnings Related Pension Scheme 1968; Discussions with: 1) The Lord President's Group of Academic Experts, 2) Confederation of British Industry and the Trade Union Congress, letter from Serpell to Houghton, 10 May 1968.
64. NA PRO T227/2589, letter from Crossman to Balogh, 7 May 1968.
65. NA PRO T227/2589, official briefs related to the Lord President's Meeting on 16 May 1968, 15 May 1968.
66. Ibid.
67. Ibid; Crossman, Diaries, vol 3, pp. 66–7, diary entry for 16 May 1968.
68. Crossman, Diaries, vol 3, p. 66, diary entry for 16 May 1968.
69. NA PRO T227/2589, Earnings Related Pension Scheme 1968 Discussions.
70. NA PRO T227/2589, 'TWO social security funds?', note by Professor Brian Abel-Smith, 18 June 1968.
71. DHSS, National Superannuation, p. 23.
72. Lord Balniel quoted in Ellis, Pensions in Britain, p. 29.
73. DHSS, Better Pensions, Cmnd. 5713 (London, 1974), p. 15.
74. Ellis, Pensions in Britain, p. 24.
75. Bridgen, 'Remedy For All Ills', p. 12.
76. Labour Party, Superannuation, p. 25.
77. Tony Lynes, Pension Rights and Wrongs: A Critique of the Conservative Scheme, Fabian Tract 348 (London, 1963), p. 15.
78. DHSS, National Superannuation, p. 20.
79. Lynes, Labour's Pension Plan, p. 31.
80. NA PRO PIN 47/141, 'Matters Relating to the Labour Party', 13 March 1964.
81. NA PRO T 227/2216, Official Committee on Social Security Review, 5 February 1965.
82. Ibid.
83. Lynes, Labour's Pension Plan, p. 21.

84. Bridgen, 'Remedy For All Ills', p. 13.
85. NA PRO T 227/2217, National Insurance Review Committee, 23 June 1966.
86. NA PRO T 227/2217, Official Committee on Social Security Review, 1 June 1965.
87. Ibid.
88. Crossman, *Pensions*, p. 21.
89. NA PRO T 227/2216, Official Committee on Social Security Review, 12 February 1965.
90. LPA HART/11/3, 'Major Considerations relevant to the Choice of the Ceiling for Reckonable Earnings in the New Pension Scheme', 6 June 1967.
91. Ibid.
92. NA PRO CAB 134/3303, Ministerial Sub-Committee on Earnings-Related Pensions, 7 June 1967.
93. Crossman, *Pensions*, p. 20.
94. LPA, Study Group on Security and Old Age, minutes, 4 July 1956.
95. LPA, Study Group on Security and Old Age, RD. 216 (rev), March 1962.
96. Labour Party, *New Frontiers*, p. 9.
97. Craig, *Manifestos*, p. 265.
98. DHSS, *National Superannuation*, p. 38.
99. DHSS, *National Superannuation: Terms for Partial Contracting-out of the National Superannuation Scheme*, Cmnd. 4195 (London, 1969), p. 5.
100. Crossman, *House of Commons Debates*, 5th series, vol 794, col 61, 19 January 1970.
101. Hannah, *Inventing Retirement*, p. 145.
102. National Association of Pension Funds, *The Future Relationship of State and Occupational Pensions* (London, 1968), p. 4.
103. Fawcett, 'Beveridge Straitjacket', p. 41.
104. Araki, 'Ideas and Welfare', p. 605.
105. Hannah, *Inventing Retirement*, p. 59.
106. Heclo, *Modern Social Politics*, p. 278.
107. LPA, Study Group on Security and Old Age, minutes of a joint meeting between the Social Insurance Committee of the TUC and the Home Policy Committee of the Labour Party, 12 March 1963.
108. Labour Party, *New Frontiers*, p. 9.
109. NA PRO PIN 47/141, 'Matters Relating To Labour Party Policy', 13 March 1964.
110. Ibid.
111. Crossman, *Pensions*, p. 21.
112. NA PRO CAB 134/3303, Official Committee on Social Security, 10 March 1967.
113. Crossman, *Pensions*, p. 21.
114. NA PRO CAB 134/3303, Official Committee on Social Security, 10 March 1967.
115. LPA, HART/11/3, 'Control of Occupational Pension Schemes', 14 July 1967.
116. Ibid.
117. NA PRO PREM 13/2394, Crossman to Wilson, 11 March 1968.
118. Crossman, *Diaries*, *vol 3*, p. 206, diary entry for 30 September 1968.

119. NA PRO PREM 13/2394, Crossman to Wilson, 11 March 1968.
120. Ibid.
121. Atkinson, 'Developing Relationship', pp. 220–1.
122. Heclo, *Modern Social Politics*, p. 276.
123. NA PRO CAB 134/3303, Official Committee on Social Security, 10 March 1967.
124. NA PRO PREM 13/2394, Crossman to Wilson, 11 March 1968.
125. Ibid.
126. PRO CAB 128/42, 43rd conclusions, 11 September 1969.
127. Heclo, *Modern Social Politics*, p. 276.
128. Crossman, *Diaries, vol 3*, p. 616, footnote to diary entry dated 13 August 1969.
129. Ibid, p. 616, diary entry dated 13 August 1969.
130. Ibid.
131. DHSS, *Terms for Partial Contracting-out*, p. 16.
132. Crossman, *Diaries, vol 3*, p. 663, diary entry dated 2 October 1969.
133. Ibid, p. 626, diary entry dated 4 September 1969.
134. NA PRO CAB 128/42, 43rd conclusions, 11 September 1969.
135. Crossman, *Diaries, vol 3*, p. 625, diary entry for 4 September 1969.
136. NA PRO CAB 128/42, 43rd conclusions, 11 September 1969.
137. Crossman, *vol 3*, p. 632, diary entry for 8 September 1969.
138. Ibid, p. 682, diary entry dated 13 October 1969.
139. *Public Service*, Journal of NALGO, March 1969.
140. Crossman, *House of Commons Debates*, 5th series, vol 794, col 60, 19 January 1970.
141. Ibid.
142. DHSS, *Better Pensions*, p. 15.
143. Ibid, p. iii.
144. Ibid, p. 14.
145. Department for Work and Pensions (hereafter DWP), *Simplicity, Security and Choice: Working and saving for retirement*, Cm. 5677 (London, 2002), p. 19.
146. Whiteside, 'Historical Perspectives', p. 21.
147. Heclo, *Modern Social Politics*, p. 274.
148. Crossman quoted in Morgan, *Backbench*, p. 580, diary entry for 29 March 1957.
149. Morgan, *Backbench*, p. 580, diary entry for 29 March 1957.
150. Heclo, *Modern Social Politics*, p. 266.
151. Crossman quoted in Morgan, *Backbench*, p. 985, diary entry for 5 March 1963.
152. Ibid.
153. Labour Party, *New Frontiers*, p. 14.
154. NA PRO PIN 47/141, Matters Relating to the Labour Party, March 1964.
155. Ibid.
156. NA PRO T 227/2216, Working Group on Pensions, 6 October 1964.
157. Ibid.
158. NA PRO CAB 134/3303, The Earnings-Related Pension Scheme, First Report of the Official Committee on Social Security, 10 March 1967.
159. Whiteside, 'Historical Perspectives', p. 29.
160. LPA, HART/11/3, Earnings Related Pensions, 1 May 1967.

194 RICHARD CROSSMAN AND THE WELFARE STATE

161. Crossman, *Diaries, vol 3*, p. 153, diary entry for 23 July 1968.
162. Ibid, pp. 153–4, diary entry for 23 July 1968.
163. Ibid, p. 176, diary entry for 26 August 1968.
164. Ibid.
165. Footnote by Morgan in Crossman, *Diaries, vol 3*, p. 176, diary entry for 26 August 1968.
166. Crossman, *Diaries, vol 3*, p. 439, diary entry for 15 April 1969.
167. Crossman, *Paying For The Social Services*, p. 13.
168. NA PRO PREM 13/3483, Powers of Investment under the National Superannuation and Social Insurance Bill, 16 January 1970.
169. Ibid.
170. Whiteside, 'Historical Perspectives', p. 31.
171. Labour Party, *54th Annual Conference*, p. 202.
172. Harold Wilson, *Final Term: The Labour Government 1974–1976* (London, 1979), p. 146.
173. Wilson quoted in Richard Minns, *Pension Funds and British Capitalism* (London, 1980), p. 8.
174. DHSS, *Strategy for Pensions*, Cmnd. 4755 (London, 1971).
175. Ellis, *Pensions in Britain*, p. 41.
176. Pensions Commission, *The Second Report*, ch 10.
177. Pemberton, 'Politics and Pensions', p. 49.
178. DWP, *Personal accounts: a new way to save*, Cm 6975 (London, 2006), p. 7.
179. Peter Butler quoted in Noel Whiteside, 'Occupational Pensions and the Search for Security', *Britain's Pension Crisis*, p. 134.
180. Seldon, 'Ideas', pp. 265–6.
181. Crossman, *Pensions*, p. 20.
182. Hannah, *Inventing Retirement*, p. 56.
183. Whiteside, 'Historical Perspectives', p. 21.
184. Heclo, *Modern Social Politics*, p. 275.
185. Crossman, *Diaries, vol 3*, p. 276, diary entry for 29 November 1968.
186. Ibid, p. 462, diary entry dated 28 April 1969.
187. Ibid, p. 482, diary entry dated 8 May 1969.
188. NA PRO CAB 128/42, 43rd conclusions, 11 September 1969.
189. LPA, HART/11/3, 'Contracting-out under the new pension scheme', 25 July 1967.
190. Bridgen, 'Remedy For All Ills', p. 12.
191. Crossman, *Pensions*, p. 21.
192. Crossman, *Diaries, vol 3*, p. 168, diary entry for 1 August 1968.
193. Richard Crossman, 'Mr Herbert Lewin – Creating Labour pensions plan', *The Times*, 3 December 1970.
194. Crossman, *Pensions*, p. 26.
195. Bridgen, 'Remedy For All Ills', p. 14.
196. Crossman, 'Lewin'.
197. LPA, HART/11/3, Lewin to Hart, 'Redistributive effect of the earnings-related pension proposals', 14 August 1967.
198. Crossman, *Diaries, vol 2*, p. 135, diary entry for 23 November 1966.
199. Timmins, *Five Giants*, pp. 276–7; future minister Frank Field was also heavily involved in this dispute as CPAG's director, having succeeded Tony Lynes in that post.

200. Timmins, *Five Giants*, p. 277.

201. Crossman, *Diaries, vol 3*, p. 921, diary entry for 14 May 1970.

202. Townsend, 'Obituary: Professor Brian Abel-Smith'.

203. Kingdon, *Agendas*, p. 56.

CONCLUSION – CROSSMAN'S LEGACY

1. Crossman, *Diaries, vol 3*, p. 931, diary entry for 29 May 1970.

2. Ibid.

3. DHSS, *The Reform of Social Security*, Cmnd. 9517, (London, 1985).

4. Carl Emmerson, 'Pension Reform in the United Kingdom: Increasing the Role of Private Provision?', *Pension Security in the 21st Century*, pp. 173–4.

5. Ibid.

6. Personal correspondence, letter from Baroness Castle, 21 April 1999.

7. Barbara Castle, Bryan Davies, Hilary Land, Peter Townsend, Tony Lynes, and Ken Macintyre, *Fair Shares for Pensioners: Our Evidence to the Pensions Review Body* (London, 1998), p. 16.

8. Kingdon, *Agendas*, p. 141.

9. Townsend, 'Obituary: Baroness Castle of Blackburn', *The Guardian*, 7 May 2002.

10. Pensions Commission, *The Second Report*, p. ix.

11. DWP, *Personal accounts*, p. 5.

12. Crossman, *Diaries, vol 3*, p. 904, diary entry for 28 April 1970.

13. Pemberton, 'Politics and Pensions', pp. 39–42.

14. Howard, *Crossman Diaries*, p. 9.

15. Fred Hoyle and Chandra Wickramasinghe, *Astronomical Origins of Life: Steps towards panspermia* (Dordrecht, 2000).

16. For more information about the links between biological evolution, the journey of ideas, and public policy see, for example, Peter John, 'Ideas and interests; agenda and implementation: an evolutionary explanation of policy change in British local government finance', *The British Journal of Politics and International Relations*, 1999, vol 1 no 1, pp. 39–62; Peter Kerr, 'Saved from extinction: evolutionary theorising, politics and the state', *The British Journal of Politics and International Relations*, 2002, vol 4 no 2, pp. 330–58.

BIBLIOGRAPHY

Abel-Smith, B., *The Reform of Social Security*, Fabian Research Series no 161 (London, 1953).

Abel-Smith, B. and Townsend, P., *New Pensions for the Old*, Fabian Research Series no 171 (London, 1955).

Abel-Smith, B. and Townsend, P., *The Poor and The Poorest*, LSE Occasional Papers on Social Administration no 17 (London, 1965).

Araki, H., 'Ideas and Welfare: The Conservative Transformation of the British Pension Regime', *Journal of Social Policy*, 2000, vol 29 no 4, pp. 599–621.

Atkinson, J., 'The Developing Relationship Between the State Pension Scheme and Occupational Pension Schemes', *Social and Economic Administration*, 1977, vol 11 no 3, pp. 216–225.

Banting, K., *Poverty, Politics and Policy* (London: 1979).

Baumgartner, F. and Jones, B., *Agenda and Instability in American Politics* (Chicago, 1993).

Benn, T., *Years of Hope: Diaries, Papers and Letters 1940–62* (London: 1995).

Bevan, A., *In Place of Fear* (London, 1952).

Beveridge, W., *Social Insurance and Allied Services*, Cmd. 6404 (London, 1942).

Beveridge, W., *House of Lords Debates*, 5th series, vol 182, col 676, 20 May 1953.

Bochel, C. and Bochel, H., *The UK Social Policy Process* (Basingstoke, 2004);

Boyd-Carpenter, J., *Way of Life: the memoirs of John Boyd-Carpenter* (London, 1980).

Bridgen, P., 'Remedy For All Ills: Earnings-Relation and the Politics of Pensions 1950s/1960s', an unpublished paper given at the conference 'Relative decline and relative poverty: signposts to the sixties?' at the University of Bristol, 13 May 1999.

Bridgen, P., 'The One Nation Idea and State Welfare', *Contemporary British History*, 2000, vol 14 no 3, pp. 83–104.

Bridgen, P. and Lowe, R., *Welfare Policy Under the Conservatives* (London, 1998).

Butler, D. and Rose, R., *The British General Election of 1959* (London, 1960).

Castle, B., *The Castle Diaries 1964–70* (London, 1984).

Castle, B., Davies, B., Land, H., Townsend, P., Lynes, T., and Macintyre, K., *Fair Shares for Pensioners: Our Evidence to the Pensions Review Body* (London, 1998).

Chavallier, G., *Clochemerle* (London, 2004, first published 1934).

Cobb, R. and Elder, C., *Participation in American Politics: The Dynamics of Agenda-building* (Boston, 1972).

Cohen, M., March, J. and Olsen, J., 'A garbage can model of organisational choice', *Administrative Science Quarterly*, 1972, vol 17, pp. 1–25.

Cohen, M., March, J. and Olsen, J., 'People, Problems, Solutions and the Ambiguity of Relevance', *Ambiguity and Choice in Organizations*, second edition, J. March and J. Olsen (Oslo, 1979).

Cole, D. and Utting, J., *The Economic Circumstances of Old People*, Occasional Papers on Social Administration no 4 (London, 1962).

Cole, J., *As It Seemed To Me*, revised paperback edition (London, 1996).

Craig, F., *British General Election Manifestos 1900–1974* (Basingstoke, 1975).

Crossman, R., 'The Wykehamist', *New Statesman and Nation*, 18 September 1954, p. 328.

Crossman, R., 'The End of Beveridge', *New Statesman and Nation*, 11 December 1954, p. 772.

Crossman, R., *Paying For The Social Services*, Fabian Tract 399 (London, 1969).

Crossman, R., 'Towards a Philosophy of Socialism', *New Fabian Essays*, ed. R. Crossman (London, 1970, first published 1952).

Crossman, R., *House of Commons Debates*, 5th series, vol 794, col 60, 19 January 1970.

Crossman, R., *House of Commons Debates*, 5th series, vol 794, col 61, 19 January 1970.

Crossman, R., 'Mr Herbert Lewin – Creating Labour's pensions plan', *The Times*, 3 December 1970.

Crossman, R., *The Politics of Pensions*, Eleanor Rathbone Memorial Lectures no 19 (Liverpool, 1972).

Crossman, R., *The Diaries of a Cabinet Minister, vol 1: Minister of Housing 1964–66* (London, 1975).

Crossman, R., *The Diaries of a Cabinet Minister, vol 2: Lord President of Council and Leader of the House of Commons 1966–68* (London, 1976).

Crossman, R., *The Diaries of a Cabinet Minister, vol 3: Secretary of State for Social Services 1968–70* (London, 1976).

Dalyell, T., *Dick Crossman: A Portrait* (London, 1989).

Deacon, A. and Bradshaw, J., *Reserved for the Poor: The Means Test in British Social Policy* (Oxford, 1983).

Department of Health and Social Security (DHSS), *National Superannuation and Social Insurance*, Cmnd. 3883 (London, 1969).

Department of Health and Social Security (DHSS), *National Superannuation: Terms for Partial Contracting-out of the National Superannuation Scheme*, Cmnd. 4195 (London, 1969).

Department of Health and Social Security (DHSS), *Strategy for Pensions*, Cmnd. 4755 (London, 1971).

Department of Social Security (DSS), *A New Contract for Welfare: Partnership in Pensions*, Cm. 4179 (London, 1998).

Department for Work and Pensions (DWP), *Simplicity, Security and Choice: Working and saving for retirement*, Cm. 5677 (London, 2002).

Department for Work and Pensions (DWP), *Personal Accounts: A new way to save*, Cm. 6975 (London, 2006).

Dolowitz, D. and Marsh, D., 'Who learns what from whom: a review of the policy transfer literature', *Political Studies*, vol 44 no 2, pp. 343–357.

Donnison, D., 'The Academic Contribution to Social Reform', *Social Policy and Administration*, 2000, vol 34 no 1, pp. 26–43.

Dorey, P., *Policy Making in Britain* (London, 2005).

Ellis, B., *Pensions in Britain 1955–1975* (London, 1989).

Emmerson, C., 'Pension Reform in the United Kingdom: Increasing the Role of Private Provision?', *Pension Security in the 21st Century*, ed. G. Clark and N. Whiteside (Oxford, 2003).

Fawcett, H., 'The Privatisation of Welfare: The Impact of Parties on the Private/Public Mix in Pension Provision', *West European Politics*, 1995, vol 18 no 4, pp. 150–169.

Fawcett, H., 'The Beveridge Straitjacket: Policy Formation and the Problem of Poverty in Old Age', *Contemporary British History*, 1996, vol 10 no 1, pp. 20–42.

Glennerster, H., *British Social Policy Since 1945* (Oxford, 1995).

Gordon Walker, P., *Political Diaries*, ed. R. Pearce (London, 1991).

Harris, J., *William Beveridge: A Biography*, second edition (Oxford, 1997).

Hannah, L., *Inventing Retirement: The development of occupational pensions in Britain* (Cambridge, 1986).

Healey, D., *The Time Of My Life* (London, 1989).

Heclo, H., *Modern Social Politics in Britain and Sweden* (New Haven and London, 1974).

Hennessy, P., *The Prime Minister: The Office and its Holders since 1945* (London, 2000), p. 288.

Houghton, D., *Paying for the Social Services* (London, 1967).

Howard, A. (ed.), *The Crossman Diaries* (London, 1979).

Howard, A., *Crossman: The Pursuit of Power* (London, 1990),

Hoyle, F. and Wickramasinghe, C., *Astronomical Origins of Life: Steps towards panspermia* (Dordrecht, 2000).

Hickson, K., 'Review: *Labour Forces* by Kevin Jefferys (ed.)', *Political Studies Review*, 2003, vol 1 no 3, p. 389.

Jefferys, K. (ed.), *Labour Forces: From Ernest Bevan to Gordon Brown* (London, 2002).

John, P., 'Ideas and interests; agenda and implementation: an evolutionary explanation of policy change in British local government finance', *The British Journal of Politics and International Relations*, 1999, vol 1 no 1, pp. 39–62.

Jones, J., *Union Man* (London, 1986).

Jordan, G. and Richardson, J., 'The British Policy Style or the Logic of Negotiation', *Policy Styles in Western Europe*, ed. J. Richardson (London, 1982).

Kerr, P., 'Saved from extinction: evolutionary theorising, politics and the state', *The British Journal of Politics and International Relations*, 2002, vol 4 no 2, pp. 330–358.

Kincaid, J., *Poverty and Equality in Britain*, revised edition (Harmondsworth, 1975).

Krasner, S., 'Approaches to the State', *Comparative Politics*, 1984, vol 16 no 2, pp. 218–30.

King, D. and Wickham-Jones, M., 'Bridging the Atlantic: The Democratic (Party) Origins of Welfare to Work', *New Labour, New Welfare State? The Third Way in British Social Policy*, ed. M. Powell (Bristol, 1999).

Kingdon, J., *Agendas, Alternatives and Public Policies*, second edition (New York, 1995).

Labour Party, *Report of the 54th Annual Conference* (London, 1955).

Labour Party, *National Superannuation: Labour's Policy for Security in Old Age* (London, 1957).

Labour Party, *Report of the 56th Annual Conference* (London, 1957).

Labour Party, *Report of the 59th Annual Conference* (London, 1960).

Labour Party, *Signposts for the Sixties* (London, 1961).

Labour Party, *New Frontiers for Social Security* (London, 1963).

Laybourn, K., *A Century of Labour: A History of the Labour Party 1900–2000* (Stroud, 2000).

Le Grand, J., 'A Religion of Doing Good – Obituary: Brian Abel-Smith', *The Guardian*, 9 April 1996.

Lowe, R., 'A Prophet Dishonoured in his Own Country? The Rejection of Beveridge in Britain, 1945–1970', *Beveridge and Social Security*, ed. J. Hills, J. Ditch and H. Glennerster (Oxford, 1994).

Lynes, T., *Pension Rights and Wrongs: A Critique of the Conservative Scheme*, Fabian Tract 348 (London, 1963).

Lynes, T., *Labour's Pension Plan*, Fabian Tract 396 (London, 1969).

Martineau, L., *Politics and Power: Barbara Castle* (London, 2000).

Macleod, I. and Powell, E., *The Social Services: Needs and Means* (London, 1952).

Macnicol, J., *The Politics of Retirement in Britain, 1878–1948* (Cambridge, 1998).

McBeth, M., 'Traditional theories of welfare', *Introducing Social Policy*, revised edition, ed. C. Alcock, S. Payne, and M. Sullivan (Harlow, 2004).

Mendelson, E. (ed.), *W.H. Auden: Selected Poems* (London, 1979).

Ministry of Pensions and National Insurance (MPNI), *Provision for Old Age*, Cmnd. 538 (London, 1958).

Minns, R., *Pension Funds and British Capitalism* (London, 1980).

Morgan, J. (ed.), *The Backbench Diaries of Richard Crossman* (London: 1981)

Myles, J. and Pierson, P., 'The Comparative Political Economy of Pension Reform', *The New Politics of the Welfare State*, ed. P. Pierson (Oxford, 2001).

National Association of Pension Funds (NAPF), *The Future Relationship of State and Occupational Pensions* (London, 1968).

O'Hara, G. and Parr, H., 'Conclusions: Harold Wilson's 1964–70 Governments and the Heritage of "New" Labour', *The Wilson Governments 1964–1970 Reconsidered*, ed. G. O'Hara and H. Parr (Oxon, 2006).

O'Higgins, M., 'Public/Private Interaction and Pension Provision', *Public/ Private Interplay in Social Protection: A Comparative Study*, ed. M. Rein and L. Rainwater (Armonk, NY, 1986).

Page, R., 'A Guide to the Literature', *The Student's Companion to Social Policy*, ed. P. Alcock, A. Erskine, and M. May (Oxford, 1998).

Pearce, E., 'Denis Healey', *Labour Forces*, ed. Kevin Jefferys (London, 2002).

Pemberton, H., 'Politics and Pensions in Post-war Britain', *Britain's Pension Crisis: History and Policy*, ed. H. Pemberton, P. Thane and N. Whiteside (Oxford, 2006).

Pensions Commission, *A New Pension Settlement for the Twenty-First Century: The Second Report of the Pensions Commission* (London, 2005).

Pierson, P., *Dismantling the Welfare State: Reagan, Thatcher, and the Politics of Retrenchment* (Cambridge, 1994).

Pimlott, B., *Harold Wilson* (London, 1992).

Powell, M. and Stewart, J., 'Themed Section on History and Policy: Introduction', *Social Policy and Society*, 2005, vol 4 no 3, pp. 293–294.

Public Service, Journal of NALGO, March 1969.

Rawnsley, A., *Servants of the People*, revised edition (London, 2001).

Reisman, D., *Richard Titmuss: Welfare and Society* (London, 1977).

Report of the Committee on the Economic and Financial Problems of Old Age, Cmd. 9333 (London, 1954).

Riddell, P., 'Slimline team of 12 is recipe for confusion', *The Times*, 11 November 2003.

Roth, A., 'Obituary – A Politician of Quiet Integrity: Peggy Herbison', *The Guardian*, 31 December 1996.

Rose, R. and Davies, P., *Inheritance in Public Policy: Change Without Choice in Britain* (New Haven, 1994).

Seenan, G., 'Blair answers Booth on pensions', *The Guardian*, 2 September 2000.

Seldon, A., 'Ideas are not Enough', *The Ideas That Shaped Post-War Britain*, ed. D. Marquand and A. Seldon (London, 1996).

Shragge, E., *Pensions Policy in Britain* (London, 1984).

Sullivan, M., *The Development of the British Welfare State* (Hemel Hempstead, 1996).

Thane, P., *Foundations of the Welfare State*, second edition (London, 1996).

Thane, P., 'Labour and Welfare', *Labour's First Century*, ed. D. Tanner, P. Thane and N. Tiratsoo (Cambridge, 2000).

Thornton, S., 'Richard Crossman, the Civil Service, and the Case of the Disappearing Pension', *Public Policy and Administration*, 2005, vol 20 no 2, pp. 67–80.

Thornton, S., 'A Case of Confusion and Incoherence: Social Security under Wilson, 1964–70', *The Wilson Governments 1964–1970 Reconsidered*, ed. G. O'Hara and H. Parr (Oxon, 2006).

Thornton, S., 'Towards public–private partnership: Labour and pensions policy', *The Labour Governments 1964–1970*, ed. P. Dorey (London, 2006).

Thorpe, A., *History of the Labour Party* (Basingstoke, 1997).

Timmins, N., *The Five Giants*, revised edition (London, 2001).

Titmuss, R. *Problems of Social Policy* (London, 1950).

Titmuss, R., 'The Age of Pensions: Superannuation and Social Policy', *The Times*, 30 December 1953.

Titmuss, R., *Essays on the Welfare State* (London, 1958).

Titmuss, R., *The Gift Relationship* (London, 1970).

Theakston, K., 'Ministers and Civil Servants', *United Kingdom Governance*, ed. R. Pyper and L. Robins (Basingstoke, 2000).

Theakston, K., 'Richard Crossman: The Diaries of a Cabinet Minister', *Public Policy and Administration*, 2003, vol 18 no 4, pp. 20–40.

Thompson, P., 'Reflections on becoming a researcher: Peter Townsend interviewed by Paul Thompson', *Social Research Methodology*, 2004, vol 7 no 1, pp. 85–95.

Townsend, P., 'Obituary: Professor Brian Abel-Smith', *The Independent*, 9 April 1996.

Townsend, P., 'Obituary: Baroness Castle of Blackburn', *The Guardian*, 7 May 2002.

Walker, A. 'The third way for pensions (by way of Thatcherism and avoiding today's pensioners)', *Critical Social Policy*, 1999, vol 19 no 4, pp. 511–527.

Webb, A., 'The Abolition of National Assistance: Policy Changes in the Administration of Assistance Benefits', *Change, Choice and Conflict in Social Policy*, P. Hall, H. Land, R. Parker, and A. Webb (London, 1975).

Whiteside, N., 'Historical Perspectives and the Politics of Pension Reform', *Pension Security in the 21ˢᵗ Century*, ed. G. Clark and N. Whiteside (Oxford, 2003).

Whiteside, N., 'Occupational Pensions and the Search for Security', *Britain's Pension Crisis: History and Policy*, ed. H. Pemberton, P. Thane and N. Whiteside (Oxford, 2006).

Wilson, H., *The Labour Government 1964–1970: A Personal Record* (London, 1971).

Wilson, H., *Final Term: The Labour Government 1974–1976* (London, 1979).

Young, H., *The Crossman Affair* (London, 1976).